Jay J.R. Zajas, PhD, CM, CPC
Olive D. Church, PhD

Applying Telecommunications and Technology from a Global Business Perspective

"**I**n their book, Drs. Zajas and Church present an excellent introduction and overview of tele-communications in the modern technological world. Of special significance is an emphasis on the historical development of new forms of communication, the ways in which these innovations have impacted how people live and function, and an examination of emerging trends. This book should serve well not only those who must depend upon such forms of communication to operate businesses, but all who rely on such technology on a daily basis as they carry out the normal routines of life in modern society. Consequently, it is important to all of us.

The book is written in textbook form. Its major strengths lie in the number of thought-provoking questions that are raised, the focus on case studies, and the individual and group projects that are directed toward assisting the reader in comprehending the concepts. It is well written and supported."

Stephen M. Pusey, PhD
Vice President for Academic
Affairs, Trevecca Nazarene
University, Nashville, TN

"**A**pplying *Telecommunications and Technology from a Global Business Perspective* provides an excellent, applicable overview of how to apply telecommunications, technologies, and telemarketing principles to business. The book provides a good level of depth, without being too technical or getting lost in the details. The authors also do an admirable job of providing up-to-date material on a field that is changing very rapidly."

Ed Crowley, MBA
Manager, Product Marketing,
VTEL Corp., Austin, TX

"**A**pplying *Telecommunications and Technology from a Global Business Perspective* is a book every business leader should read. As a senior executive, many books I have read only serve as a reference guide in providing some little detail or fact. After reading Zajas and Church's book, it has not only met my expectations as a reference book, it has become a corporate guide used in implementing the strategic long-term initiatives of our firm. The book is highly readable, practicable, comprehensive, and most important, it has multifunctional qualities. For example, the book includes case studies that provide

The Haworth Press, Inc.

Applying Telecommunications and Technology from a Global Business Perspective

HAWORTH Marketing Resources
Innovations in Practice & Professional Services
William J. Winston, Senior Editor

New, Recent, and Forthcoming Titles:

Church and Ministry Strategic Planning: From Concept to Success by R. Henry Migliore, Robert E. Stevens, and David L. Loudon

Business in Mexico: Managerial Behavior, Protocol, and Etiquette by Candace Bancroft McKinniss and Arthur A. Natella

Managed Service Restructuring in Health Care: A Strategic Approach in a Competitive Environment by Robert L. Goldman and Sanjib K. Mukherjee

A Marketing Approach to Physician Recruitment by James Hacker, Don C. Dodson, and M. Thane Forthman

Marketing for CPAs, Accountants, and Tax Professionals edited by William J. Winston

Strategic Planning for Not-for-Profit Organizations by R. Henry Migliore, Robert E. Stevens, and David L. Loudon

Marketing Planning in a Total Quality Environment by Robert E. Linneman and John L. Stanton, Jr.

Managing Sales Professionals: The Reality of Profitability by Joseph P. Vaccaro

Squeezing a New Service into a Crowded Market by Dennis J. Cahill

Publicity for Mental Health Clinicians: Using TV, Radio, and Print Media to Enhance Your Public Image by Douglas H. Ruben

Managing a Public Relations Firm for Growth and Profit by A. C. Croft

Utilizing the Strategic Marketing Organization: The Modernization of the Marketing Mindset by Joseph P. Stanco

Internal Marketing: Your Company's Next Stage of Growth by Dennis J. Cahill

The Clinician's Guide to Managed Behavioral Care by Norman Winegar

Marketing Health Care into the Twenty-First Century: The Changing Dynamic by Alan K. Vitberg

Fundamentals of Strategic Planning for Health-Care Organizations edited by Stan Williamson, Robert Stevens, David Loudon, and R. Henry Migliore

Risky Business: Managing Violence in the Workplace by Lynne Falkin McClure

Predicting Successful Hospital Mergers and Acquisitions: A Financial and Marketing Analytical Tool by David P. Angrisani and Robert L. Goldman

Marketing Research That Pays Off: Case Histories of Marketing Research Leading to Success in the Marketplace edited by Larry Percy

How Consumers Pick a Hotel: Strategic Segmentation and Target Marketing by Dennis Cahill

Applying Telecommunications and Technology from a Global Business Perspective by Jay Zajas and Olive Church

Strategic Planning for Private Higher Education by Carle M. Hunt, Kenneth W. Oosting, Robert Stevens, David Loudon, and R. Henry Migliore

Applying Telecommunications and Technology from a Global Business Perspective

Jay J. R. Zajas, PhD, CM, CPC
Olive D. Church, PhD

The Haworth Press
New York • London

The Haworth Press, Inc., 10 Alice Street, Binghamton, NY 13904-1580

Cover design by Marylouise E. Doyle.

Library of Congress Cataloging-in-Publication Data

Zajas, Jay J. R.
    Applying telecommunications and technology from a global business perspective / Jay J. R. Zajas, Olive D. Church.
       p. cm.
    Includes bibliographical references.
    ISBN 0-7890-0115-2 (alk. paper)
    1. Business–Communication systems. 2. Telephone in business. 3. Telemarketing. I. Church, Olive D. II. Title.
HF5541.T4Z35 1997
658.8'4–dc21
                                               96-48936
                                               CIP

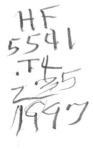
This book is dedicated to our life-long partners—Jann and Stan, and to the good Lord, from whom all blessings come.

ABOUT THE AUTHORS

Jay J. R. Zajas, PhD, CM, CPC is Chairman of The Corporate Management Group, Senior Professor of Management and Business at Trevecca Nazarene University, a Certified Professional Manager, BBB Mediator, Arbitrator, and Certified Personnel Counsellor. He received the Who's Who Award for Outstanding Business Executives in America in 1995 and the Marquis Who's Who in America and Who's Who in the World after more than 20 years of service as a professor, marketing director, college dean and director, high school principal, corporate trainer, city administrator, and senior management advisor. Author of eight books, including *The Marketing of Executives & Career Development Success* and *The Total Career & Life Portfolio,* and more than 40 scholarly articles and keynote presentations, he specializes in mediation, marketing research, executive development, and strategic management. His articles appear in such publications as *The International Journal of Management, Executive Development,* the *Journal of Customer Service in Marketing & Management, Health Marketing Quarterly, Business Perspectives,* the *Journal of Product & Brand Management,* and many others. He has received several "Excellence in Teaching Awards" and in 1995 received the "Master Teacher's Award for Leadership Excellence" as a school principal.

Olive D. Church, PhD, is Senior Professor of Business, Marketing, and Economic Education at the University of Wyoming in Laramie. She has taught business for 30 years at the secondary school, community college, and university levels. The author of *Human Relations in the Electronic Office, Business in an Information Economy,* and *Electronic Office Procedures,* Dr. Church has written or co-written more than 20 textbooks as well as numerous articles and reports on office systems, keyboarding, communications, human relations, basic business, and entrepreneurship. She offers training in these areas to companies and organizations coast to coast. Currently a management consultant for the Office Dynamic Company, Dr. Church has served as Executive Director of the Wyoming Council on Economics Education, President of the Wyoming Business Education Association, and President of the National Association of Classroom Educators in Business Education.

CONTENTS

Foreword   **xiii**
          Charles Royce Patton

Preface   **xv**

Overview   **1**

   Recent Research   1
   Objectives   2

Introduction   **3**

   Regulations and the Telecommunications Law of 1996   5
   Summarizing the Anticipated Impact of the 1996 Act   13
   Regulation as an External Business Force   14
   Technology as an External Business Force   16
   Competition as an External Business Force   19

SECTION I: DEFINING AND USING
   TELECOMMUNICATIONS   **25**

Chapter 1. Telecommunications Around the World
   and in the Office   **27**

   Facsimile   28
   Electronic Mail   29
   Computer Networks   29
   Data Searches Using Commercial Databases
     and Interactive TV   36
   Teleconferencing   38
   Multimedia   41

Chapter 2. Using the Telephone   **43**

   Telephone Functions   43
   Placing Long-Distance Calls   44
   Voice Mail   45

Keeping Telephone Records   45
The Five Cs of Effective Telephone Manners   46
Listening and Providing Feedback   46

Chapter 3. Emerging Trends   **49**

Things Are Getting Smaller!   49
Wireless or Cellular Items   50
Digital Superhighway: Marriage of Cable TV
    and Telephones   50
Telecommuting for Others and for Self   51
Some People Are Staying Home and Traveling Less   52
Some People Are Traveling More   53
Newspaper Printing via Telecommunications   53
Transportation and Communication Systems   53

What Do You Think? Review and Opinions   **55**

From Cave to Satellite   **57**

Activities for Section I   **61**

Bibliography for Section I   **85**

**SECTION II: THE COMMUNICATIONS
    IN TELECOMMUNICATIONS**   **89**

Chapter 4. Communications   **91**

Why Do People Communicate?   91
How Do People Communicate?   93

Chapter 5. Understanding Ourselves   **99**

Maslow's Hierarchy of Human Needs   99
Other Types of Human Motivators   103
Time and Space   104
Dual-Brain Theory   106
Learning Through Whole-Brain Thinking   109
Genders, Cultures, and Generations   112

Chapter 6. Workplace Applications   **119**

Human Relations   119
Public Relations   121
Telecommunications and Promotion   122

What Do You Think? Review and Opinions   **123**

From Cave to Satellite   **125**

Activities for Section II   **131**

Bibliography for Section II   **155**

SECTION III: BUSINESS APPLICATIONS AND OPPORTUNITIES   **159**

Chapter 7. Standard Industrial Classifications   **161**

Goods (Tangible Products)   163
Services (Intangible Offerings)   174

Chapter 8. Basic Economic Concepts   **181**

Business and Entrepreneurship   182

What Do You Think? Review and Opinions   **187**

From Cave to Satellite   **189**

Activities for Section III   **195**

Bibliography for Section III   **221**

SECTION IV: DEFINING AND USING TELEMARKETING   **225**

Chapter 9. Defining Telemarketing   **227**

The Use of 800 and 888 Numbers   227
The Use of 900 Numbers   229
Handling Outbound Calls   230
Coordinating Print and Broadcast Advertising
  with Telemarketing   234

Handling Inbound Calls   235
Legal Issues and Telemarketing Scams   237
Telemarketing Occupations   239
Telemarketing Operator Competencies   240

Chapter 10. Essential Marketing Concepts   **243**

Human Needs   243
The Marketing Mix   245
The Store Mix   248
Human Demographics   249
The Life Cycle of a Product   250
Market Niche and Market Share   251
Competition   252
Risks of Going into Telemarketing (or Any Other)
    Businesses   253

**Chapter 11. Innovations and Technology from Around
the World**   **255**

A Multiuse Telephone   255
Photo Machines in Malls   256
On-line, on Cable, or in Print   256
Global Economic and Media Activities   257
New Jobs Emerging, Old Jobs Disappearing   261

What Do You Think? Review and Opinions   **263**

From Cave to Satellite   **265**

Activities for Section IV   **271**

Bibliography for Section IV   **287**

**SECTION V: RECORDS SYSTEMS
AND TELECOMMUNICATIONS**   **291**

Chapter 12. Records and Telecommunications   **293**

Telecommunications and Records   295
Telemarketing and Records   297
Data Collections and Databases   299

Chapter 13. Some Rules of the Game   **303**

Alphabetic Filing   303
Numeric Filing   306

**Chapter 14. Records Management Supports
the Need for Information**   **311**

Records in Support of the Needs of Organizations   311
Records in Support of Personal Needs   313
Records and the Law   314
Human and Public Relations in Managing Records   317
Virtual Reality   318
Careers and Competencies   319

What Do You Think? Review and Opinions   **325**

From Cave to Satellite   **327**

Activities for Section V   **333**

Bibliography for Section V   **347**

Glossary   **351**

Index   **369**

Foreword

As a Professor Emeritus, reflecting on the many changes that have taken place, both in my business career spanning thirty years, and then in my academic career for the past twenty years, I can say that the word "telecommunications" did not even exist when I had my first summer job as a clerk in a midwestern city. The most exciting contacts with the outside world were a separate long-distance line, which no one dared use for local calls, and a wall button for Postal Telegraph, a competitor of Western Union, which summoned a young man to pick up your telegram.

Two decades ago, my life in academia included no personal computer on my or any other desk in the Business Administration Department, and when the first fax machine came, it was hard to believe that a perfect copy of a proposed paper could be received by my longtime co-author in Turku, Finland in minutes. Even today, in 1997, e-mail and the Internet are still new to most people on my campus. On some days I look at my IBM Selectric and think of all the syllabi and publications spawned on it, versus today's occasional use only to address a menial envelope!

Resistance is common in academia, and perhaps in business too, when new telecommunications devices are introduced. We got along perfectly well without them. One strategy to overcome resistance is simply to place a P.C. on someone's desk, or put a new fax machine in an office, and then use the "sink or swim" technique. There is always anxiety about change, and users may be cautious at first, but soon all are wondering how they existed without the new device.

A book about future shock captured the imaginations of many about two decades ago. Many of the same principles still exist; it seems to be human nature to fear the unknown, which is often associated with the future. The field of telecommunications is expanding so rapidly that businesspeople, educators, and the general public are often confused about which new development in this field should command their undivided attention. Most of us can remember some step in the past that we had to take which has now been superseded by newer, faster communications equipment. This book will help explain what is happening and hopefully prepare the reader for future developments in the fields of telecommunications, technology, and global business.

Charles Royce Patton
Professor Emeritus
School of Business and Management
The University of Texas
Brownsville

Preface

During the time it takes to read this preface, a dozen or more innovations in telecommunications will have been developed. That's how fast the industry is booming. That's what usually happens when a new industry is born.

Billions of dollars will be made in designing and selling products for business and consumer markets and in stock investments. But billions of dollars will also be lost as dreams are dashed on the shoals of unrealized goals. These predictions are founded in historical facts. From the birth of fuels, transportation, and computers, for example, the history of technology has followed basically the same pattern.

Telephone, computer, and television systems are merging to provide a variety of business and personal services. Transmitted over wires and fiber optics, through the air and space via satellites are voices, data, graphics, and images. People interact from their computer stations over wide-area networks because they need to send or retrieve information fast or because they just want to chat. They use interactive television to get information and to select from a wide range of menu options exactly what they want when they want it—from shopping and banking to playing games, choosing movies, music, sports, horoscopes, etc.

The things that link telecommunications, telemarketing, and record functions are the telephone, the computer, and video capabilities plus the human relations competencies that people use when communicating. People buy and sell over the telephone. Using telecommunication and computer systems, they track and record data that must be saved in a systematic manner so it can be retrieved.

This book focuses on the business perspective, which includes addressing the profit motive. Telemarketing topics are based on principles that have their foundation in marketing, economics, entrepreneurship, law, psychology, and sociology. Related fields include history, geography, science, and the fine arts. Knowledge of concepts from these disciplines also contributes to finding and succeeding in a career where telecommunications are used.

Readers will learn how telecommunication promotes the interaction and interdependency of companies and countries in a multicultural world that has helped to develop the global marketplace. They will develop telecommunication competencies to use in support of business and in support of your own information needs. Most careers require knowledge of telecommunications. Also needed in the job market are competencies in communications, human relations, business, marketing, and economics.

A feature that appears in each of the book's five sections is called "From Cave to Satellite." These special discussions provide historical glimpses that trace earlier inventions, many of which have led to our present-day sophisticated technological developments. Geographic, cultural, and philosophic topics contribute to viewing the world as a global economic village, as a place where competencies from many disciplines interact and are interdependent.

Overview

RECENT RESEARCH

From a series of state, national, and international studies culminating in the report "Business Education Is Alive and Thriving!" (funded by Delta Pi Epsilon national research society), there is evidence to indicate that telecommunications and international business are of keen interest to business educators. NBEA and AVA national conference programs and articles published in four professional journals since 1990 all contain many discussions and articles on these topics.

Furthermore, research findings show that business educators seek materials that integrate telecommunications and international business concepts with meaningful applications.

This textbook simulation is unique, however, in that telecommunication is also integrated with telemarketing and records topics. Companies use telemarketing in a variety of ways to advertise and sell their products (goods and services). Records of every business contact and transaction must be kept and managed to support the needs of business. These three functions of business are happening throughout the world.

Educational Pedagogy

Current themes coming out of state departments of education, teacher education programs, and current educational pedagogy include competency-based or outcomes-based education and cooperative learning. From the first system comes the term *portfolio*, a permanent collection of key concepts demonstrated in various ways; e.g., reports, clippings, annotated bibliographies, and checklists that demonstrate both performance and the acquisition of knowledge.

Another trend, cooperative learning, has students working together on team projects, as they will do on the job. This cooperative effort produces both an individual and a group grade per project.

Technology Enhancements

Working in the modern business world, one may be exposed to a variety of documents, checklists, data lists, shell documents, forms, and scripts that office workers use in responding to customer queries and complaints, menu-scripts for telemarketing and switchboard operators, and databases for records clerks, accountants, and secretaries.

It is helpful for businesspeople to learn good habits when communicating with callers and customers. Receptionists and others are shown how to reply to these callers in the communications section and telemarketing representatives in the telemarketing section. Responses can be conducted by dictating using a tape recorder or a dictating machine, or live in one-on-one scenarios.

Special Print Feature

A special feature in each section, titled "From Cave to Satellite," traces the development of technology and integrates brief glimpses of history, U.S. and world geography, art as media, and so on. These are designed to promote analytical thinking.

OBJECTIVES

1. Discuss the purpose of telecommunications and its impact on people and businesses.
2. Locate and tour sites where telcommunication is used and interview users.
3. Access a computer document and manipulate data.
4. Commence the collection of data for your portfolio.
5. With a cooperative learning group, discuss cases, design a major group project, and evaluate section objectives.

Introduction

Welcome to the world of free enterprise, global business, telecommunications, and modern technology!

With the accelerating pace of change in the fields of telecommunications, technology, and international business, it is important that business leaders and organizations have a way to obtain current information. One way is through participating in state-of-the-art seminars on technology, computers, the Internet, and telecommunications. For those persons who have the time and money to complete such seminars, this is one way to stay informed. Another way is by reading informative, professional journals and magazines that periodically provide some of the latest changes in technology and telecommunications to their readers. These periodicals (*Forbes, Fortune, the Harvard Business Review, Computer Monthly, On-Line*, and others) are generally published monthly (or weekly as is the case with *Barron's* or *Business Week*). Some, for example, *The Wall Street Journal* or *USA Today*, are published daily. Another way to keep informed is by reading current textbooks or professional reference books in the desired subject of specialization. This is often an excellent way to get a complete survey in telecommunications, technology, or a related field.

This book is written with the purpose of providing the reader with an overview of key innovations, trends, and developments in the field of telecommunications, telemarketing, and technology as they apply to business from a global perspective. Many readers will find it helpful as a professional reference book. Others will use it in a seminar or class to advance their knowledge, skills, and/or understanding in any of the topics covered herein. Some will find it useful for developing a strategic technology or telecommunications plan for their business. And many others will find this book to be invaluable in the way it integrates telecommunications with technology, telemarketing, business applications, and records management systems.

Regardless of your reasons for reading this book, it offers numerous benefits and topics that can be applied to improve your understanding of the impact of telecommunications and technology on global business. Because of its applications and relevance in the modern business arena, the book has much to offer both the professional businessperson and the academic student. Some of the benefits and topics that one may find to be useful are listed below, together with the chapter number where the information herein is presented. Refer to the table of contents for additional information on subtitles and details of the various chapters and topical areas of this book.

This book should prove to be especially useful to those persons who are interested in advancing or updating their knowledge and understanding of the following topics:

- The impact of the Telecommunications Law of 1996 on consumers and business and the changes or developments the law will initiate. (Refer to the introductory section following this outline of topics.)
- Trends and changes in telecommunications around the world (Chapter 1).
- Proper use of the telephone and the Five C's of effective telephone manners (Chapter 2).
- Emerging trends and developments in telecommunications today (Chapter 3).
- The importance and role of communications in telecommunications and business today (Chapter 4).
- Examining various models and theories of human behavior so as to better understand ourselves (Chapter 5).
- Applying human relations, telecommunications, promotion, and public relations in the workplace (Chapter 6).
- Categorizing goods and services with the use of standard industrial classifications (SICs) (Chapter 7).
- Reviewing economic, business, and entrepreneurship principles in one's study of global business, telecommunications, and technology (Chapter 8).
- Defining telemarketing issues, functions, occupations, services, and scams (Chapter 9).

- The use of marketing concepts and the marketing mix in business, telemarketing, and consumer issues. Some innovations and trends from around the world (Chapters 10 and 11).
- The roles and rules of record systems in telecommunications (Chapters 12 and 13).
- Supporting the need for records management and information in modern business (Chapter 14).

REGULATION AND THE TELECOMMUNICATIONS LAW OF 1996

The first major communications law in the United States was adopted in 1934, largely to regulate the advent of radio (invented by Guglielmo Marconi) and the ever-expanding telephone market (and to balance the monopoly held by AT&T). Despite the emergence of the information age, complete with satellite television and communication systems, e-mail, high speed telephone modems, fax, cable, pagers, teleconferencing, computerized and electronic on-line communications, it took more than 60 years for Congress to significantly overhaul the 1934 legislation. This replacement came with a landmark regulatory reform bill known as the Telecommunications Act of 1996, passed by the Republican-controlled 104th Congress.

The new act is intended to reduce layers of bureaucratic federal regulations (the Act cuts the Federal Communications Commission's (FCC's) bureaucracy by at least 15 percent), eliminate thousands of pages of antiquated FCC regulations, rules, and administrative rulings, usher in the information age, create jobs, promote economic growth, give consumers better choices and more competitive rates, and increase competition in all areas of the communications and electronic information markets. It may be a bit premature to estimate the Act's expected, overwhelming impact on creating jobs, promoting economic growth, and reducing consumer rates for telecommunication services, etc., but it is certain the Act will do a great deal to advance the future of the telecommunications industry in the United States. With its likely impact on the U.S. economy, it should also help to promote competition abroad, in Europe, South and Central America, and the Far East, because of its deregulatory effects.

In addition to creating new jobs and promoting economic growth in the telecommunications market, the Telecommunications Law of 1996 may serve to lower prices in some offerings, while providing consumers with more choices and better access to new services (such as e-mail, Internet user services, expanded satellite and cable television, telemedicine in rural areas, distance learning for job training and career development purposes, etc.). Some of the major changes and expected benefits that the Act will introduce, or effectuate, are summarized in the following pages, as highlighted below.

"V-Chip" Authorization for TV Installation

Tough measures are included in the new Act to prevent or minimize children's viewing of violent and/or obscene programs on television. The new V-Chip provisions require television manufacturers to install such chips on all new sets to give parents greater control over the violence their children may be exposed to on television.

Provisions to Protect Children from Cyber-Porn

Tough criminal and civil measures have been included in the new Act to cut down or eliminate the dissemination to minors of obscene or otherwise pornographic materials via the Internet. Title V of the Act aims at preventing the transmission of obscenity or violence by means of a telecommunications device, and it provides for severe penalties in the form of fines or imprisonment of up to two years, or both. The actual language was borrowed from Section 502 of the Communications Act of 1934 that prohibited obscene or harassing use of telecommunications facilities. The new Act continues such measures and adds the following prohibition:

> *Whoever—(1) in interstate or foreign communications knowingly—*
>
> *(A) uses an interactive computer service to send to a specific person or persons under 18 years of age (generally known as a minor), or*

(B) uses any interactive computer service to display in a manner available to a person under 18 years of age, any comment, request, suggestion, proposal, image, or other communication that, in context, depicts or describes, in terms patently offensive as measured by contemporary community standards, sexual or excretory activities or organs, regardless of whether the user of such service placed the call or initiated the communication; or

Whoever—(2) knowingly permits any telecommunications facility under such person's control to be used for any activity prohibited by paragraph (1) with the intent that it be used for such activity, shall be fined under title 18, United States Code (USC), or imprisoned not more than two years, or both.

Opens Up the Telephone Markets to Competition

The new Act authorizes the Regional Bell operational companies (RBOCs) to enter the long-distance telephone market that is presently dominated by AT&T, Sprint, MCI (and other regional companies such as GTE). This means that customers who so desire may eventually be able to have the same carrier company for both their local and long-distance calling.

Measures such as this are also designed to promote competition and encourage decentralization within telephone and telecommunications companies. An interesting article by Edmund L. Andrews in *The New York Times*, titled "Justice Department Vows Scrutiny of Bell Deal" (April 29, 1996), indicates that the Justice Department plans to advocate and apply tough new rules to promote vigorous competition in the telephone markets. Because of two powerful mergers, namely a 22.1 billion-dollar deal proposed by Nynex Corporation and the Bell Atlantic Corporation, the Justice Department will do everything in its scope to carefully apply the deregulatory measures of the new Act. Future mergers will be scrutinized under the terms of traditional anti-trust laws and the sweeping reforms of the new Telecommunications Law of 1996. (Note: In 1996 alone there were proposed mergers being considered among four of the seven regional Bell companies, known affectionately as "the Baby Bells.")

Other firms are using the new Act as an invitation to enter the long-distance telephone market. For example, Ameritech Corporation began a strategy to enter the long-distance telephone market when the firm agreed to allow MFS Communications Company to sell local telephone services in the Bell's five-state region. This should open up competition between local and long-distance telephone providers as well. This is the result of the deregulatory provision in the Telecommunications Act of 1996 that permits long distance carriers to move into each "other's market only after they prove that local phone competition exists in their own territory." (*The Wall Street Journal*, "MFS to enter Ameritech turf via local calls," by Gautam Naik, Eastern edition, May 23, 1996.) Also, the new Act has prompted the FCC to revise and adopt new rules to foster competition in the local phone market and to ensure that businesses and consumers can switch local telephone companies without having to change their phone numbers. (*The Wall Street Journal*, "New FCC rules ensure phone numbers will transfer when switching carriers," by Bryan Gruley and Scott Ritter, Eastern edition, June 28, 1996.)

Deregulates Cable TV Markets and Facilities Competition Therein

Just as the new Act allows for increased competition in the local and long-distance telephone markets, it also deregulates the cable TV market and relaxes ownership restrictions on radio and television stations. This should promote economic growth in these sectors, while also promising the possibility of more choices, better services, and more competitive rates for consumers. However, it is difficult to estimate the overall impact of such deregulation.

The new Act reduces restriction on cable TV rates, yet this worries many cable TV company executives. In 1995, Cox Enterprises' firm acquired Times Mirror's cable company to form the fifth largest cable firm in the United States, with approximately 3.2 million subscribers. Soon thereafter, Cox Enterprises sold a 25 percent share of its newly enlarged firm to the public. The acquisition nearly doubled Cox's revenues and expanded the number of its subscribers by nearly 70 percent. With annual cable television revenues in excess of 25 billion dollars, the growth possibilities and competition fury worries such cable company executives as Cox Enterprises' CEO Jim Robbins. Cable companies have to offer more services, and soon may have to compete with a variety of other telecommunications firms that are eyeing the cable TV market. Satellite television technology is emerging, which opens the market to entry competitors. Cable operators are gearing up to offer high-speed data transmission services to send information 300 times quicker than most current telephone modems. Moreover, because the U.S. telephone market is about four times the size of cable television, some cable companies (Cox Enterprises, for instance) are preparing to offer local telephone service in select markets throughout the United States. (For additional information see the article, "Pass the Sominex," by Pablo Galarza, *Financial World*, May 20, 1996.) Wireless cable operators are also prepared to compete with current telephone and TV companies. Under the terms of the new Act, cable operators are allowed to enter the telephone markets, and telephone companies will be able to enter the cable television market. In addition to deregulating rates for the customers of small cable TV systems (about 20 percent of the 61 million U.S. cable subscribers), the new Act will deregulate rates for all other cable customers by March 31, 1999, or sooner, if a cable operator competes against a telephone company for cable customers.

Relaxes Ownership Restrictions on Radio and TV Stations

In addition to allowing any telecommunications company to offer a host of telephone, television, and Internet services (see April 22, 1996 edition of *Financial World*), the Telecommunications Act of 1996 will relax ownership restrictions on radio and television stations. The Act relaxes prohibitions against owning more than one TV station in a market, allows for possible dual ownership of radio and TV stations within a market, and permits a single entity to buy or own shares in more than one television network. However, local television ownership rules will remain under the auspices of the FCC.

In June 1996, resulting from liberties under the new Act, it was announced that Westinghouse Electric would acquire the Infinity Broadcasting Company in a 3.7 billion-dollar deal made possible by the Telecommunications Law of 1996, which lifted the limits of TV and radio station ownership. A merger of Westinghouse (that already owns the CBS radio and television networks), and Infinity Broadcasting, the United States' largest independent broadcasting company, would result in the creation of a radio giant (with about 83 stations) that would be one of the largest ever in the world. It would also include radio celebrities such as Howard Stern, Don Imus, and Charles Osgood. (Merger announced in the Late Edition of *The New York Times*, [East Coast edition], Business Digest Summary, June 21, 1996. See *Times* article titled "Two Radio Giants to Merge, Forming Biggest Network," by Geraldine Fabrikant, [East Coast edition], June 21, 1996.)

Some critics of the new deregulation argue that the large firms will swallow up the smaller stations and independents. The power of the largest networks also raises concerns among some regulators that the program diversity of radio is threatened. There is some merit to such arguments, given the greater financial resources of the bigger stations and networks. To offer some protection, radio markets will continue to be defined by FCC rules that require the measurement of an AM or FM station's signal strength. Unlike television markets, radio markets are defined on an individual basis. Under the new Act and current FCC rules, a broadcaster may own one station out of every five or six in a given market (or about 8 stations in a market of 45 to 48 commercial radio stations). Under no circumstances may one person or entity own more than half the stations in one market. (For additional information, refer to the article in *Broadcasting & Cable*, "Mapping Out New Ownership Rules," by Elizabeth Rathbun, Volume 126, Issue 8, February 19, 1996, or the article in *Nation's Business*, "New Horizons in Communications," by Tim McCollum, Volume 84, Issue 8, August 1996, U.S. Chamber of Commerce, Washington DC.)

Promotes Competition in All Telecommunications Markets

As noted in the above summaries, a primary outcome of the 1996 Act will be to promote competition in all telecommunications markets, including but not limited to the following: local and long-distance telephone, wireless, cable and satellite television, cellular and digital pagers, the Internet, and other electronic media. By opening up these telecommunications markets to free-market competition, it is expected that new jobs and career opportunities will be created to take the place of those positions that are made obsolete by changes in demographics, global economics, and technology. Local phone companies will be able to offer long-distance service and vice versa. Cable operators will be able to offer telephone service and the phone companies (local and long-distance carriers) will be able to enter the cable television market. Ideally, such competition will help to provide consumers and business users access to a broad new spectrum of telecommunication services with greater conveniences, and possibly at lower, or more competitive prices. Increased competition within the United States helps to foster greater competition abroad as well. The new U.S. Act has contributed to new telecommunications laws elsewhere in New Zealand, Australia, and even Taiwan. Recently, a new telecommunications law opened parts of Taiwan's market to private and foreign investment for the first time and has contributed to Taiwan's bid to join the World Trade Organization. (See the article in *The Wall Street Journal*, "World Wire: Taiwan Telecommunications Legislation," by editorial staff, [Eastern edition], January 18, 1996, p. A-11.)

Eliminates Burdensome Federal Regulations

A major benefit of the Telecommunications Act of 1996 is the direction it provides for eliminating layers of burdensome FCC rules, regulations, and other bureaucratic requirements. Cited as the most deregulatory bill in U.S. Congressional History (see "Congress Overhauls Telecommunications Law at: *http://www.house.gov/packard/telecom.htm*), the Act breaks up the final telecommunications monopolies and helps to unleash competition in every sector of telecommunications. It serves to reduce the FCC's bureaucracy by at least 15 percent, while eliminating thousands of pages of antiquated FCC rules, regulations, and administrative rulings. By eliminating outdated, bureaucratic rules and regulations, the Act empowers American businesspersons and entrepreneurs to introduce dynamic, innovative, and expanded products and services to the free market. It is hoped that the 1996 Act will usher in a new era in America, where telecommunication innovations and technological product development will be put to the test in the free market, instead of in Washington DC and the U.S. federal courts. As other countries see how the new Act serves to eliminate costly, time-consuming, and restrictive rules or regulations, it is expected that they will consider adopting similar measures to advance the telecommunication markets within their borders. In any event, because of the interrelationship of the global economy, many international firms (AT&T, Sprint, and others) will take advantage of the new law to initiate progressive growth strategies. (For additional information on the deregulatory impact of the 1996 Act on the Federal Communications Commission, refer to the *ABA Journal* article, "Era of Change for the FCC," by Henry J. Reske, Volume 82, Issue 2, June 1996, American Bar Association, Chicago, IL.)

Consolidation and Expansion of the Electronic Information Age

It is expected that the 1996 Act will usher America into the Electronic Information Age by leading to technological innovations and revolutionary changes that have not been seen since the advent of the railroad. Thanks in part to the misguided regulations of the Japanese government on the Japanese telecommunications industry (who imposed an analog standard on their industry), America is the world leader in the areas of electronic communication and high-resolution television. The 1996 Act will further enhance the market opportunities in telecommunications and will empower American broadcasters, electronics manufacturers, and consumers to exploit this advantage.

Numerous advances in the telecommunications and technology fields are helping to make the United States a global leader, such as indicated above. One of the most significant benefits of the 1996 Act for U.S. consumers and small businesses will be the availability of telecommunication service packages that will combine local, long-distance, or wireless calling with paging, voice mail, e-mail, and/or Internet access, for example, from one provider at a discounted price on one invoice. Despite the fact that the FCC has yet to issue definitive guidelines to structure multiservice telecommunications competition, firms such as AT&T, Sprint, MCI, Excel, and several of the regional Baby Bells have begun to package multiple telecommunication services, many of which are aimed at small businesses. The latest in telecommunications networking technology,

ISDN (integrated services digital network) will give consumer and business customers the equivalent of two phone lines by enabling them to access or receive data and voice calls simultaneously. ISDN, just now coming into widespread usage, could eventually replace analog phone modems.

Another new telecommunications innovation, known as personal communications services (or PCS), combines voice and messaging capabilities to allow communication over a digital network via the use of small, lightweight, hand-held telephones or handsets. A key advantage that PCS has over cellular systems is that it uses a digital technology, whereas most cellular communications use analog. With analog communications, signals are transmitted (as with local and cellular calls) by sound. PCS phones use digital technology to convert sounds relayed by telephone into computer data (a series of ones and zeros). Such data is transmitted by phone over the network and is converted back to sounds at the point of destination. The result is a much clearer signal (many cellular phones are known to break up in valleys or at unclear reception points). Moreover, unlike analog systems, the PCS networks can carry data. Thus, users are able to access voice, data, and other screen-displayed messages on their handsets. By using satellite networks and the Internet, companies have greatly enhanced their communication capabilities. Video-conferencing, messaging, and data communications services have helped to expand the effectiveness of telecommunications for both consumers and businesses. The list of such innovations and technological product advancements continues to expand daily and it serves to further illustrate the acceleration of society into the newly emerging Electronic Information Age.

SUMMARIZING THE ANTICIPATED IMPACT OF THE 1996 ACT

The Telecommunications Act of 1996 is a complex, lengthy, but long-awaited piece of legislation. Because of its scope, magnitude, and deregulatory focus, it is likely to have a worldwide impact on technology, telecommunications, and the economy. As highlighted above, the 1996 Act is expected to initiate many changes and advancements in the telecommunications field. The long-term effects of the 1996 Act cannot be fully predicted at this time due to the rippling process that it has set in motion in the world telecommunications markets. For quick referral, the anticipated outcomes, benefits, and/or impact of the Act are outlined below.

- Requires V-Chip installation for all new televisions manufactured for the United States
- Provides strict provisions to protect children (minors) from cyber-porn
- Intensifies competition in the local and long-distance telephone markets
- Deregulates cable TV markets and facilitates competition therein
- Relaxes ownership restrictions on radio and television stations
- Promotes competition in all major telecommunications markets
- Eliminates or reduces burdensome federal (FCC) regulations
- Consolidates numerous telecommunication services and moves America into the new Electronic Information Age

REGULATION AS AN EXTERNAL BUSINESS FORCE

Most regulation is imposed by government. Some is self-imposed by a business itself. Much regulation is not wanted or appreciated by many businesses. However, sometimes the best regulation is self-imposed, when a firm takes the initiative to go above and beyond legal duties to serve their customers, employees, and stakeholders. A good example of a firm that practices this is Ben & Jerry's Ice Cream, which is known for its outstanding social conscience and self-imposed business ethics. Many of the most ethically run businesses in the world practice self-imposed ethics and regulations that exceed the legal duty mandated by government regulators or inspectors.

The predominance of business, social, and technological regulation is frequently perceived as an external, restrictive force on free enterprise. From the perspective of many businesses, most regulation is seen as complex, restrictive, debilitating, burdensome, and costly to comply with. In many countries of the world, there is an adversarial relationship between business and government, or between a business entity and its regulators. Since most regulation is imposed by government, it is often seen as another cost that is added to the production or service process.

Typically, the more socialistic (or liberal) the politics of a nation, the greater its emphasis and enforcement on governmental, social, business, and technological regulations. Conversely, the more free-market-based (or conservative) the politics of a nation, the lesser its emphasis and enforcement on governmental, social, business, and technological regulations. Historically, these generalizations appear to be true. But with most generalizations, exceptions do exist. The important thing to remember about regulation is that political freedom promotes economic freedom and vice versa. It will be interesting to see whether Hong Kong will be allowed to maintain the economic and political liberties under the government of China that it had enjoyed for many decades under the rule of Great Britain. It will also be fascinating to see how united Germany (East and West) develops economically, especially in former Communist-ruled East Germany (and East Berlin), with its newfound liberties of political unification.

Included in the force of regulation is divine or natural law, man-made (or legislative) law, and custom. Whenever a business fails to comply with the scope and spirit of a natural law, eventually negative consequences will result. Just as a firm cannot avoid negative feedback by continuously disregarding the requests of its customers, one cannot violate natural laws (such as defying gravity) without suffering the consequences. First in order of significance and authority are the laws of nature, then the laws of society, and last, the informal social laws, known as norms and customs. Businesses and managers around the world would be wise to learn, honor, and obey these laws if they seek prosperity, goodwill, and success in their daily lives. The degree to which these laws impact a firm depends on the nature of the industry, the regulatory standards therein, and the concomitant responsibility between the firm and its third parties (customers, competitors, creditors, stakeholders, and the like).

In summary, regulation restricts or governs business in several ways. First, it limits what a business or market can or cannot do. Second, it sets the threshold standards of performance within many industries. Third, when structured optimally, regulation can promote economic and competitive growth, such as is anticipated with the U.S. Telecommunications Law of 1996. Unfortunately, when regulations are overly bureaucratic or restrictive, they may inhibit growth, independence, and compliance. Some contend that this is one reason why much of the economic growth and new patent innovations have originated in countries of the world that favor a free-market economy (such as the United States, South Korea, and Japan). To assess the impact that regulation has on a firm's telecommunications and business operations, one does well to contemplate and respond to the following questions:

1. Which regulations most impact our business and how we operate?
2. Do we violate any divine or natural laws in our business?
3. How well do we honor God, our nation's laws, and our VIP's (very important persons such as our customers, creditors, etc.) in the daily decisions, policies, and actions we take?
4. What new regulations will impact our firm's telecommunications systems in the next one to five years?
5. How will we proactively predict, prepare, and manage these new regulations?
6. How will these new regulations change the way we do business?
7. In what ways do we meet the external regulations imposed on us by government, regulatory agencies, and/or watchdog groups?
8. How do we exceed these external regulations by the standards, ethics, and/or requirements we impose on ourselves?

TECHNOLOGY AS AN EXTERNAL BUSINESS FORCE

Technology is a significant external force on contemporary global business. It is an external force in that it shapes and influences a business even if a business chooses not to participate in its development. Technology includes the systems, methods, and processes utilized by a firm to transform resources into outputs. It may represent a mechanical device (time-saving equipment such as home appliances or plant production automation), or electronic technology (such as a computer network, the Internet, or a personal communications service telephone handset device). It may even take the form of mental skills (such as applied creativity and functional intelligence) or physical resources (such as plant buildings, facilities, fuel, or commodities). When such resources are combined in a highly creative and productive manner (such as with the creation of fusion, solar, or nuclear energy) *synergy* can result. Synergy occurs when two or more things (market and service agencies such as a bank, post office, hair salon, or photo lab) are combined to create a multiservice organization (such as a modern supermart). An advanced and competitive global business market results in expanded technology (and often business synergy) within a firm.

Many business historians believe technology has had a formative impact on telecommunications. The advent of the telegraph, telephone, television, personal computer, Internet, or analog and digital electronic devices (cellular phones, PCS, ISDNs, etc.) have had a tremendous role in the evolution of telecommunications and are all the by-products of human technology. As Professor Charles Royce Patton notes in the foreword, just a few decades ago the word telecommunications did not even exist. At that time telecommunications for most firms consisted of long-distance lines reserved for the select few, and a wall button for Postal Telegraph, Western Union, or a competitor telegraph company, whichever company had closest physical access. For many decades, AT&T was the monopoly long-distance provider, with very few competitors even in the local telephone markets. The areas listed below are components in "the wheel of telecommunications" that have been largely shaped, or birthed, by technology in recent years.

1. Telephone, pagers, and other voice messaging devices.
2. Multimedia and teleconferencing innovations
3. Telemarketing services and programs (inbound and outbound)
4. Television (cable, wireless, network, and satellite TV)
5. Radio, police scanners, and high-frequency devices
6. Internet, e-mail, and personal computer networks
7. Computer software programs and innovations
8. Records and information systems management
9. Analog and digital communication devices
10. Other telecommunications innovations or trends

These components are grouped together by the authors to create a "wheel of modern telecommunications." Refer to the Zajas/Church R.T.C. Model of Telecommunications (Figure I-1) for an illustration of the three external forces that impact the wheel of modern tele-communications. The model is offered to the reader to provide an outline of the key components of telecommunications in modern business. Each of the components are the result of technology in various business applications.

When one considers the relationship between telecommunications and technology, a few thoughts come to mind. Does technology drive telecommunications, or vice versa? What price does

FIGURE I.1. The Zajas/Church "R.T.C. Model" of Telecommunications: Three External Forces that Impact "The Wheel of Modern Telecommunications"

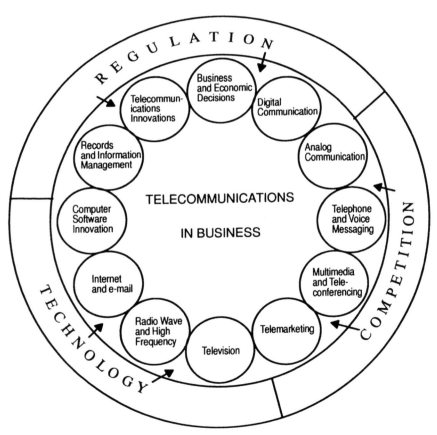

technology bring to modern business? Is it one that all businesses can afford to pay? Like the double-edged sword of the noble knights from medieval times, technology has two sharp sides: friend and foe. For those business firms caught up in the cycle of change, technology offers many benefits and time-saving devices (often at a high price). But for those organizations unable to pay the price for the latest, cutting-edge technology, outmoded equipment or systems are often the alternative. In many industries, this can translate to lost or dissatisfied customers.

In summary, technology and telecommunications are closely related. Technology is a tremendous external force in the world of business, and a major driving force for change. If channeled properly, it can be used to promote efficiency, communications, and improved productivity. When assessing a firm's technology, there are many helpful questions to contemplate. The following questions will be helpful to a firm interested in assessing the level, usefulness, or efficiency of its present technology:

1. How do we (and our competitors) define and use technology?
2. What is the condition, value, and quality of our technology?
3. Is our current technology state of the art?
4. What technology is most needed to improve our business?
5. How many alternative suppliers exist for this technology?
6. Is it better to lease or purchase our new technology?
7. How can our resources be synergized to enhance our technology?
8. How can we most economically improve our technology?

COMPETITION AS AN EXTERNAL BUSINESS FORCE

In addition to regulation and technology, there is a third major external force that shapes businesses in the modern global marketplace: competition. (A fourth external force is the environment, such as the weather, nature, or what is commonly referred to as an "act of God.")

Together, the three external forces discussed herein represent the letters of the acronym in "The RTC Model of Telecommunications." (Refer to the illustration provided on the preceding page.) The "R" stands for regulation, the "T" stands for technology, and the "C" stands for competition. Developed by the authors, The RTC Model is one way of conceptualizing how the uncontrollable, external forces of business shape the components of telecommunications in today's fast-paced, electronic information age. By applying the components of the model to their industry and customers, and by responding thoroughly to the questions provided herein under the areas of regulation, technology, and competition, business executives and owners can develop a systems perspective in their enterprises. They can also utilize these questions and components for developing their own strategic business, telecommunications, or technology plans.

This concluding section (of the book's introduction) deals with the role that competition has as an external force in impacting a business entity. No matter what their business may be, nearly every business entity now has, or will have, competitors. Other companies or enterprises that serve similar customers, or that purchase, exchange, trade, manufacture, market, sell, or otherwise deal in similar products or services are viewed as competitors. A firm's competition can be local, regional, national, international, or viewed by sector, industry, or product line. Typically, a firm's competition can change based on the stage of the product life cycle in which a firm finds itself (the four stages of the PLC are: introduction, growth, maturity, and decline). Depending on one's perspective, competition can be seen as a healthy force that helps to motivate an enterprise, or a nuisance to which one must respond, struggle, or keep pace with.

The following diagram illustrates "The Competition Continuum" that divides the reactive firm from the proactive firm:

The Competition Continuum Diagram

Reactive Firms -------------------------------------- *Proactive Firms*

Believe and/or Act as if . . .	Believe and/or Act as if . . .
Competition is an unwelcome evil . . .	Competition is a means to improve . . .
There's not much we can do . . .	There's always a way to work it out . . .
That's the way we've always done it . . .	We'll work smart to find better ways . . .
Our way is the right (or only) way . . .	Win/win solutions are always best . . .
This is really not possible . . .	Almost all things are possible . . .
We must go by our policy . . .	People come before policy . . .

Where Is Your Firm on the Competition Continuum?

The two most extreme types of firms are found on the opposing ends of The Competition Continuum. On the right side is the Proactive Firm, which sets the standards and trends for its competitors. This is typically the firm that is customer oriented, strategic and development minded, and operationally lean and efficient. On the left side is the Reactive Firm, which follows the lead of its competitors, seldom takes risks or bold initiatives, and is often tradition and product oriented, not customer or market responsive. This is typically the firm that resists change, prefers the predictable, and spends very little time and effort on research and development, employee training, operational auditing, and new product innovation and development. Generally, the more proactive a firm's management team is, the more receptive they will be to the planning and conducting of a quality, operational audit. Moreover, this type of firm is most responsive to the latest developments in technology and telecommunications.

Competition is like a generator that gives greater energy to maintain the power of a better idea, program, or development. The greater the competition, the more dynamic the market or business. When assessing a firm's competition, there are many helpful questions to consider. Some of these questions are listed below to assist the reader in assessing the nature and competitiveness of business.

1. What is our current market share for each product or service we offer?
2. How does this compare with one, two, or three years ago?
3. Who are our major competitors, and what are their main strengths?
4. How do our strengths and resources compare with theirs?
5. What are their most vulnerable weaknesses or limitations?
6. What do they do better than we? What do we do better than they?
7. What are the greatest opportunities and threats in our market?
8. Competitively, how well prepared are we to deal with these?
9. What are we doing today to improve our competitiveness?
10. How can we gain a "king of the mountain niche" in the market?

[For additional information on competition and the marketing forces that shape businesses today, refer to Chapters 8 and 10. To gain additional information on the impact technology has on business and telecommunications, refer to Chapters 1, 3, and/or 11.]

This concludes our discussion of "the RTC Model of Telecommunications" and the external forces that impact businesses in the global market. For a discussion of telecommunications around the world refer to the following chapter.

REFERENCES AND FURTHER READINGS

Andrews, Edmund J., "Justice Department Vows Scrutiny of Bell's Deals." *The New York Times*, (East Coast edition), April 29, 1996.

Business Digest, "Merger of Westinghouse and Infinity Broadcasting." *The New York Times*, (East Coast edition), June 21, 1996.

Church, Olive D., "Crushed by the Job Crash? Analyze, Energize!" *Executive Development Journal*, (Guest Editor/Jay J.R. Zajas), Volume 8(3), MCB University Press, 1995.

"Congress Overhauls Telecommunications Law." (HTTP://www.house.gov/packard/telecom.htm.) April 1996, Internet, World Wide Web.

Crowley, Ed, and Jay J.R. Zajas, "Evidence Supporting the Importance of Brands in the Marketing of Computer Products." *Journal of Professional Services Marketing*, Volume 14(2), The Haworth Press, 1996, pp. 120-137.

Fabrikant, Geraldine, "Two Radio Giants to Merge, Forming Biggest Network," *The New York Times*, (East Coast edition), June 21, 1996.

Galarza, Pablo, "Pass the Sominex." *Financial World*, May 20, 1996 (New York, NY); see also April 22, 1996 issue of *Financial World*.

Gruley, Bryan, and Scott Ritter, "New FCC Rules Ensure Phone Numbers Will Transfer When Switching Carriers." *The Wall Street Journal*, (Eastern edition), June 28, 1996.

McCollum, Tim, "New Horizons in Communications." *Nation's Business*, Volume 84, Issue 8, August 1996 (U.S. Chamber of Commerce, Washington, DC).

Naik, Gautam, "MFS to Enter Ameritech Turf Via Local Calls." *The Wall Street Journal*, (Eastern edition), May 23, 1996.

Rathbun, Elizabeth, "Mapping Out New Ownership Rules." *Broadcasting & Cable*, Volume 126(8), February 19, 1996.

Reske, Henry J., "Era of Change for the FCC." *ABA Journal*, Volume 82(4), June 1996 (American Bar Association, Chicago, IL).

"World Wire: Taiwan Telecommunications Legislation." (Editorial Staff) *The Wall Street Journal*, (Eastern edition), January 18, 1996, p. A-11.

Zajas, Jann R. Michener, and Jay J.R. Zajas, *Effective Planning for the Success-Oriented Manager*, (The Corporate Management Group, 1996).

Zajas, Jay J.R., *Excellence: A Way of Life.* (An unpublished Doctoral Report Submitted to the New College of Technological Studies, The University of Wyoming, 1983).

Zajas, Jay J.R., "Strategy Formulation: How Customer Responsive Is Your Firm?" *Executive Development Journal*, Volume 6, Issue (5), MCB University Press, 1993, pp. 18-21.

Zajas, Jay J.R., *How to Strategically Plan and Prepare for Business Success.* (The Corporate Management Group, 1992).

Zajas, Jay J.R., "A Group Process Assessment for Interpersonal Growth, Communications and Managerial Development." *The International Journal of Management*, Volume 11(3), September 1994, pp. 772-777.

Zajas, Jay J.R., "Obstacles to Real Strategic Marketing In Health Care: An Experiential Framework." *The Journal of Hospital Marketing*, Volume 8(2), The Haworth Press, 1994, pp. 18-31.

Zajas, Jay J.R., and Ed Crowley, "Brand Emergence in the Marketing of Computers and High Technology Products." *The Journal of Product & Brand Management*, Volume 4(1), MCB University Press, 1995, pp. 56-64.

Zajas, Jay J.R., and Cynthia Zavodny, "Marketing Services Through Cross-Selling and Quality Customer Service." *The Journal of Customer Service in Marketing and Management*, Volume 1(4), The Haworth Press, 1995, pp. 68-77.

Zajas, Jay J.R., and Lawrence P. Zotz, Jr., "Integrating Customer Satisfaction into the Strategic Plan." *The Journal of Customer Service in Marketing and Management*, Volume 1(3), The Haworth Press, 1995, pp. 50-66.

SECTION I:
DEFINING AND USING
TELECOMMUNICATIONS

The prefix "tele" refers to many technological innovations, from telephone to television systems—the two most common devices. The computer is part of this tripartite of systems that collectively is bringing about all sorts of technological and societal changes. Some innovations can serve to isolate while others bring people closer together.

This section describes basic and related systems, including voice mail, facsimile, electronic mail, computer networks, teleconferencing, commercial databanks to aid with electronic research, and the trend to work from the home either as telecommuters or entrepreneurs. Examples of how people use telecommunications come from around the world. The growth of telecommunication technology is linked with both the print media and with transportation systems.

Photo 1.1. AT&T Control Center

The AT&T Worldwide Intelligent Network is one of the most advanced in the world. State-of-the-art computer software technology speeds the flow of voice, data, and image transmission over 2.3 billion circuit miles worldwide, handling more than 150 million calls a day. The center has a screen video wall that is two stories high and 60 feet across, which continuously monitors AT&T customer requirements, 24 hours a day, 365 days a year. Courtesy of AT&T Archives.

Chapter 1

Telecommunications Around the World and in the Office

In an airplane traveling across the North American continent, a young businesswoman picks up an airphone from the back of the seat in front of her, inserts her telephone calling card (a credit card), and is soon speaking to her contact. In a motel parking lot outside of Amsterdam, a well-dressed businessman speaks into a cellular phone to direct shipments of goods around the globe.

A dispatcher clerk sitting in an office in Canada keeps in contact with trucks over a triprovincial area via citizen's band (CB) radio. A widow, living 30 miles from town on an isolated Australian ranch, yells into her CB that she is hurt and is heard.

Two dozen teachers, all members of an international business teacher organization, "get together" by audioconference to conduct three hours worth of business. No travel time is involved but the chairperson's responsibilities include arranging the session with a company that makes such conferences possible.

In the middle of the night, Brazil time, South American stockholders call the Tokyo stock market to place buy or sell orders. An agent in London uses telephone, e-mail, and fax to make travel, lodging, and rental car reservations for a group of Chinese tourists who will travel in Europe.

Trainers at DuPont's New Jersey center provide sales representatives all over the world with updates on major new product developments by outlining details on electronic blackboards connected to computers and TV monitors. News items are regularly distributed via the bulletin board program on computer networks.

From her office in mid-America, Kimberly sends and receives fax messages to her boss who is on safari in Africa. Kim says, "Since businesspeople who go on safari must keep up with their business, the first things the safari company sets up at every camp site are the telephone system and the fax machines."

Television brings to living rooms everything from live concerts and ball games to a front-row seat inside Congress. Viewers are seemingly "right there," whether in the middle of a war or a courtroom battle. Such things are possible with telecommunications.

The modern office has telephones, computers with modems, and copiers. When these are linked over telephone lines or via space satellites and microwave dishes, they make up a telecommunication system. Today's sophisticated telecommunication systems would not be possible without the communication satellites that continually circle the earth to pick up and transmit messages.

FACSIMILE

Linked by telephone lines, *facsimile machines* transmit and receive hard copy (paper) documents. Senders and receivers do not communicate with each other except by the written word and graphics.

Dedicated lines that separate the functions of telephone or voice transmissions from fax transmissions are the norm. However, both systems can be combined over a single line.

A *fax attendant* integrates voice mail and fax communications. One outgoing feature allows a document to be faxed simultaneously to several people at various locations; another feature stores frequently used mailing lists to save time by skipping the entry process. One feature alerts recipients of incoming fax arrivals via voice messenging; another feature stores messages in a voice mailbox, and transmits the information to other fax machines at distant sites.

The fax attendant also has a *fax response* system. Callers who request information can get it 24 hours a day, providing the data requested is standardized and thus able to be stored in the system. Callers hear a recorded menu of options, which leads them via touch tone entry to the number of the choice preferred.

ELECTRONIC MAIL

Electronic mail (e-mail) is the term used to describe the transmittal of messages from one computer to one or more others over telephone lines. Sender and receiver(s) can "talk" back and forth by entering messages and providing keyed feedback. When the recipient is not present, the message is stored until accessed by the receiver at a later time–a procedure similar to using a telephone answering machine. Printers are used to make hard copies when written information must be obtained and stored for later use or for legal reasons. Compatible telecommunication software is needed at both the sending and the receiving ends. Telex and TWX are both recognized mediums of electronic mail transmission.

E-mail is organized into drawers and folders. This structure allows the organization of messages into related groups. Initially, there is one drawer containing several folders. Two of the most frequently used folders are inbox and mail. The *Inbox* "folder" holds new messages. After being read, new messages are moved to the mail folder unless they are marked for deletion immediately. The *Mail* folder holds old mail. New messages are automatically moved here after being read.

To get into the system and establish the right to use it, one must enter some key data, such as name, social security number, and possibly address and telephone number. The system will ask for a password. The user should choose a word that is easy to remember but that is unfamiliar to others. Thereafter, whenever e-mail is accessed, the password allows the user to reach his or her own drawer(s) and folders and no others.

COMPUTER NETWORKS

There are local area networks (LAN) and wide area networks (WAN). Both operate on the basic principles of e-mail as described above. To function interactively, systems must be compatible. Compatibility comes in the form of computer software, telecommunication software, and peripherals such as printers and modems.

Local area networks (LAN) link computers to each other and also to printers. Software application programs are loaded into LAN, which saves having to install programs at every terminal. Also, fewer printers are needed. With LAN, people can use e-mail.

Often, on college campuses, all the offices and terminals need access to a student's registration and grade transcript records. In other cases, a local area network can enhance the interaction that takes place between an instructor and the students of a class, provided they have access to the LAN. The instructor gives assignments and instructions via computer and students compose and enter assignments. The instructor retrieves these assignments, reviews them, and assigns a grade. No personal interaction other than by e-mail and/or telephone is necessary until either party requests a personal conference.

To print documents prepared in a LAN system, a printer utility tool helps to route files to the appropriate printer. The operating program captures all data entered and saved and routes it to a queue. The system assigns a queue name to remote printers and their computer host stations. When a document is ready to be printed, it is saved and then sent into the system by the same process as from a stand-alone station to its own printer. Queue data go to the printer in a first-come, first-served order. Data stays in the queue until printed or cleared by a host user.

Wide area networks (WAN) provide contacts and interaction between computers throughout a given system, whether company-wide, division wide, country wide, or world wide. Using Centrex, Telecopier, or Telex (TWX) systems, telephones and teleprinters are linked to other branches within the same company. With an interface unit, Telex terminal and computer, Telex subscribers can send messages to locations outside the Telex system (Western Union, the company that developed Telex, was bought by American Telephone & Telegraph [AT&T], and is now known as EasyLink Services).

Worldwide, Telex has direct-dial access from teleprinter to teleprinter. An unattended terminal automatically receives messages. Exact copies appear at both sending and receiving terminals.

Transmission size, baud, and protocol. Data transmission size is limited by the medium carrying the transmissions, as well as by the protocol used for the transmission. The transmission capacity of a medium is known as its *bandwidth*. Think of water flowing through a pipe, with the diameter of the pipe represented by bandwidth. One way to increase the rate of water flowing through a pipe is to increase the diameter of the pipe. Increasing the bandwidth of a communications line is analogous to increasing the diameter of the pipe. See Figure 1.1 as illustrative of the bandwidths of different data sources.

With telecommunications, *protocol* refers to the set of rules used for communicating between devices on a network. *Baud* means the speed of the communications channel. The authors know of a businessperson who spent 12 hours one day online, cruising through the four major databases to which he subscribed. When he was ready to download (from CompuServe into his own computer and available to print locally), he switched baud rates. Before requesting the lengthy graphics file, he terminated his slow-speed connection to CompuServe and logged back on at the fastest rate. After deciding to retrieve a large file, he opted for the higher-speed rate to hurry things along.

Applications of e-mail and networking in business include accounting and legal records, sales and order records, shipping and receiving materials and inventory control records, payroll and personnel records, production information, and documentation between a firm and its major customers. Time is the essential factor. "Time is money" in business. The ability to get information fast in order to make swift and accurate business decisions is essential.

FIGURE 1.1. Bandwiths of Different Data Sources

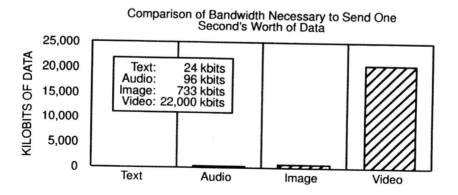

Comparison of Bandwidth Necessary to Send One Second's Worth of Data

Text:	24 kbits
Audio:	96 kbits
Image:	733 kbits
Video:	22,000 kbits

Photo 1.2. AT&T Public Phone 2000

A businessman using Public Phone 2000, his fingers on the keyboard and information on the screen. This phone can function as a portable office, which enables travelers to plug in their laptop computers or portable fax machines. Courtesy of AT&T Archives.

Personal networking is so popular that a whole new set of jargon has emerged. The following is a sample of the vocabulary, some of which is also used in business:

chat line–a group of people discussing a given topic

cyberspace–the world of WAN e-mail chitchatting with a forum or discussion group on a specific topic, from sports, entertainment, rock stars, soap operas, travel, and hobbies to a multitude of scientific, cultural, business, economic, or political topics

cyberpunks–persons who regularly participate in WAN e-mail cyberspace forum chitchatting

electronic lounge–a group of people discussing a given topic; see also chat line and cyberspace

FAQ–frequently asked question, such as from a new cyberpunk (see also newbie) or, in business, from a customer; answers are stored for automatic retrieval whether by networking, voice mail, face-to-face (F2F), fax, or telephone

flaming a newbie–teasing a newcomer (new cyberpunk) to a specific chat line forum group using the WAN network or cyberspace

F2F–face-to-face communications

techno-nerd–another term for cyberpunk

timed out–when a text file that has been downloaded from a company's or library's database or from another cyberpunk/techno-nerd's files and requested to be stored automatically deletes itself; in other words, a disaster of lost data!

Bulletin board networks may be either LAN or distance. They allow member subscribers access to news that is regularly updated, often more than once a day. Members of a given profession or activity get access to detailed information that would be of little use or interest to outsiders. For example, medical doctors need medical news and lawyers need legal news. Researchers often access specific, narrow, and detailed topics. By the early 1990s, nearly 14 million people in the United States alone were using bulletin boards.

With the AGNET bulletin board, farmers and ranchers in the north-midwestern plains states get agricultural information that is updated every day. Pilots and boat or ship captains get weather data described in their own jargon. (*Jargon* is the specialized vocabulary and abbreviations familiar to people in a particular profession, trade, or field.)

Stockholders using XPRESS can personalize their stockmarket portfolio and get 15-minute updates from the New York Stock Exchange. The XPRESS program uses computer and television, which is generally linked by a specialized modem. From the TV set (which must be connected to cable, not to antenna or microwave dish), the linkage goes to the local cable TV company and then on to the cable headquarters. From there, the system uplinks to satellite.

National and international networks. The *Internet* is a loose connection of over 50,000 networks around the world and is supported in part by the United States Federal Government. The Internet is an ad hoc group of private and public networks that share a common computer code and backbone network.

The Internet is a cooperative "network of networks." Everything that moves over networks connected by Internet codes travels at a fraction of the cost of traditional carriers. Access is typically inexpensive because institutions pay a flat fee and there is no charge per message; there is often a minimal hourly rate. However, e-mail and other services are now provided at highly competitive rates. Some access providers charge little or no fee to users and instead earn their revenue by billing sponsor companies who advertise on their network.

E-mail and networking developed rapidly in the United States for several reasons: telephone tag (time wasted trying to reach people by phone), the several time zones one must work around in the United States, the federal subsidy for the Internet, and the apparent curiosity of Americans. E-mail/networking is actually "delayed network communications." (See Figure 1.2, a chart that addresses the significance of both time and distance in the communications process.) People choose the medium for communication, usually based on time and distance. The matrix in Figure 1.2 illustrates these choices. In the lower left corner, people meet face to face, now. The upper left-hand corner shows that when we want to speak with someone at a remote distance, we can use telephone, television, or teleconference. When neither F2F or present time are available, data can be stored by a message in a voice mailbox or words in a letter, as noted in the upper right-hand corner of the matrix.

Photo 1.3. AT&T Public Phone 2000

The AT&T Public Phone 2000 features an optional built-in keyboard for travelers to access their electronic mail or dial-up home or office databases. Courtesy of AT&T Archives.

FIGURE 1.2. Time and Distance Effects on Communication

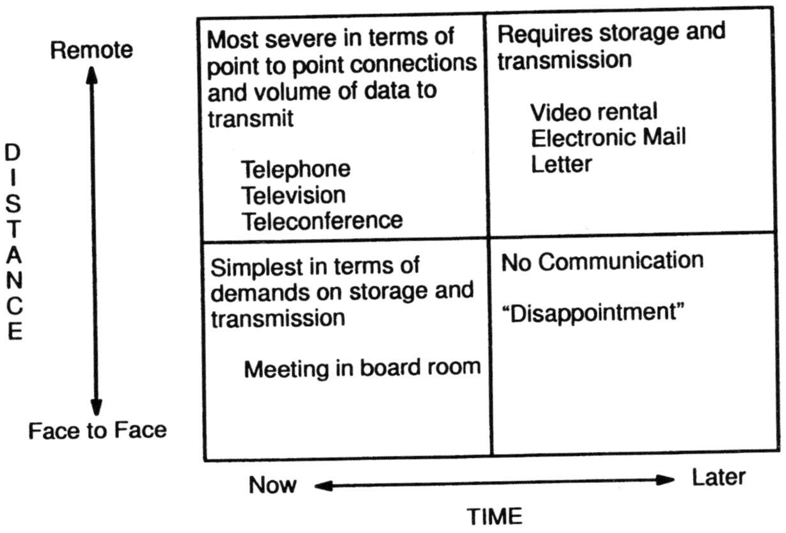

	Now ← TIME → Later	
Remote (DISTANCE)	Most severe in terms of point to point connections and volume of data to transmit Telephone Television Teleconference	Requires storage and transmission Video rental Electronic Mail Letter
Face to Face	Simplest in terms of demands on storage and transmission Meeting in board room	No Communication "Disappointment"

By comparison, Japan, Great Britain, and most European nations lagged far behind the United States. When the United States had over 3,000 databases, the European Community (EC) had fewer than 2,000 and Japan's databases were not linked so they could not be accessed from a single network like the Internet. Via the Internet, both businesses and individuals can access data on a wide range of topics and network with others as well.

DATA SEARCHES USING COMMERCIAL DATABASES AND INTERACTIVE TV

A *commercial database* is an on-line library containing thousands of records, documents, articles, references, and so on. Requesting specific information from interactive TV is another means of collecting data.

Commercial databases. One on-line company that specializes in particular industries is Meade, which has, among other libraries, databases for law (Lexus) and medicine (Nexus). Other commercial databases include America Online, CompuServe, GEnie, Prodigy, and ERIC (Educational Research Information Center). Some descriptions of these database services include the following:

- America Online–owned in part by the Tribune Company, advertises that it is family-oriented. It is popular among its almost one million subscribers who are mostly computer hobbyists who want to link up with chat line forum networks.
- CompuServe–owned by H & R Block, has Internet connections and is popular among computer hobbyists who use its chat forums. By the late 1990s, it had nearly two million personal subscribers (more than the others listed here), and was also the oldest.
- GEnie–owned by General Electric's Information Service unit, was the youngest among the most popular databases of the mid-1990s with about a half-million personal subscribers; it caters to the corporate market.
- Prodigy–owned jointly by IBM and Sears, Roebuck & Co. Its monthly subscription cost in the 1990s was $14.95 with an additional hourly user rate of $3.60 to $4.80 and at that time, it had about a million subscribers. It is perceived as a conservative database with "netiquette" (network etiquette) rules.
- ERIC–used by educators, is owned and offered by the Educational Research Information Center, and is usually available through school and university libraries.

Customers pay a subscription to a commercial data bank, just as they would to subscribe to newspapers and magazines. For this subscription fee, customers receive the telecommunication software and a password. Thereafter, they are charged a monthly rate. Most subscribers now use a local telephone or 1-800 number to avoid long-distance charges while online.

Commercial vendors provide their customers/users with manuals and 800 numbers as a means of training, assistance, and support. It does not take the competence of a librarian to gather data in this manner but it does take patience and some practice.

Another means of gathering data, especially for individuals, is simply to go to a university or large public library and ask a librarian to conduct a search. The fee for such a service will depend on the amount and type of data one wants to access and how many, if any, hard copy printouts are requested. One can expect to pay a higher per-item fee (e.g., $.75) for a financial abstract, compared to about $.25 for other types of abstracts.

Financial abstracts are often more expensive than general consumer information because the vendor assumes that the information will help users make money. (Since it usually "costs money to make money," financial consumers are more likely to pay the higher subscription or single-search fees.)

It is important to have a list of subjects or *descriptors*, because the librarian or data search clerk will need subtopics in addition to one or more major subjects. For example, the topic of accounting might yield tens of thousands of articles published worldwide over the past decade. Narrowing the search to payroll accounting in the construction industry for the last two years in Canada only could yield no more than a few articles. You need not request an entire article, either. An *abstract* contains highlights of the article with a complete bibliographical reference.

Interactive television. Information that has generally been available through the print media, including in hundreds of different specialized hobby magazines and trade journals, can be accessed with interactive TV. Personalized data searches, like those described from the on-line databases, are among the emerging innovations. Real-time interactivity and a menu of options come from the merging of cable television, telephone, and computer systems. Names given to these new systems include Super Digital Highway and High-Tech Highway. (Note the comparisons between telecommunication and transportation systems.)

TELECONFERENCING

The ability to get together without traveling makes the variety of teleconferencing options of keen interest in business and to people who need to save both time and money. Under this communications category are audioconference, teleconference, closed-circuit TV, dedicated and ad hoc videoconferencing, and compressed video.

Photo 1.4. Teleconference in Session

In use with teleconferencing—in addition to the technology—are verbal language, nonverbal language, and paralanguage.

Audioconference works on the concept of the two-way radio, with sending and receiving parties able to speak and hear. The conference may be conducted between two or more sites, with one or several speakers and listeners at each end.

Teleconference works like audioconferencing, with the addition of cameras and sight. Since people see one another, messages conveyed by body language are added to the communication formula.

Closed-circuit TV is a one-way transmission of sight and usually but not always sound. With telephone or computer network interaction, however, feedback can be added to the formula.

An example of one-way TV use without sound is a security system. Video cameras are aimed at key locations, such as exit doors, cash registers, and valuable merchandise. Security personnel investigate in person only when suspicious activity is noted. One

Photo 1.5. Close-up of Presentation Equipment

Presenters who use teleconference equipment can use a variety of presentation media, from handwriting and print copying, computer graphics, music enhancements, TV and video films, to materials for the overhead projector, such as those used with the overhead pad shown here.

person can monitor a dozen or more separate sites. An example of one-way transmission with both sight and sound is a class offered to selected audiences such as a group of company managers or technicians. At the Hewlett-Packard plant in Fort Collins, Colorado, employees may use company time to take a management class offered by Stanford University in California over closed-circuit TV.

Compressed videoconferencing is closely related to the closed-circuit TV system, except that it is less expensive. The quality is lower, also, since by "compressing" the image, any movement appears in slow motion. College classes and company training sessions are often offered through this system because of the cost savings. Like the more expensive direct-TV version, compressed video sends and receives both sound and sight.

Technicians need specialized knowledge about how to set up and operate the equipment, software, telecommunications systems, and so on. However, every person who sends must have some competence. Switches direct which camera to transmit and to focus on any one of several receiving stations in addition to the senders. Senders also use peripheral equipment, such as a type of overhead projector and a graphics pad on which to write and transmit written messages, pictures, diagrams, and so on.

Desktop publishing videoconferencing. With the merger of TV, cable, telephone services, and computers, people hold conferences that use all these technologies simultaneously. Desktop publishing software provides the interfacing and communicating of graphic and three-dimensional color materials as well as voice, sound, and sight.

MULTIMEDIA

Generally, *multimedia* refers to using a variety of media on which to produce special projects, whether for school assignments or in research, marketing, production design, and so on. The media need not include telephone lines, but it does usually include some type of interaction between computers, televisions, VCRs, videos, and perhaps some music enhancers–stereophonic players, pianos and other instruments. (See also desktop publishing videoconference.)

The operator composes hard copy at the terminal and inserts graphics, hard copy print or pictures, or graphics and pictures taken from TV or video. Linked together at the station are the computer, screen, keyboard and monitor, plus TV and VCR or compact disc player. Another line (cable or series of electrical cords) might connect the computer with an electronic music keyboard (all types of instruments are programmable from this device), stereo player, organ, piano, voice recording equipment, or other instruments.

Marketers, product designers, inventors, and students can all benefit from gaining competence with multimedia systems. Students and educators as well as advertising agents and other professional presenters can use the system to prepare projects.

Chapter 2

Using the Telephone

Subscribers can have a lot of telephone options if they are willing and able to pay for them. It doesn't matter whether the system is simple or complex, though, human relations competencies are also important. (See Section II.)

TELEPHONE FUNCTIONS

Call forwarding allows people to leave their telephones and still get their calls. Incoming calls are automatically transferred to the designated alternate line. Call waiting tells a person while he or she is talking to someone that another party is trying to get through. A buzz or beep alerts the person to the second incoming call. A *conference call* permits three or more people to connect into the system for the purpose of holding audio conferences by phone. *Hold* allows a person to have one caller wait while he or she accesses another incoming call, such as with call waiting. Give the first party an option, though. People dislike being put on "hold" and may resist. If they prefer, they can be called back or asked to call back later.

Answering Machines and Answering Services

Individuals use answering machines in their homes. So do owners of some small businesses. Often these people must be out of the firm frequently and they cannot afford to hire office employees to take messages.

The answering service allows callers to talk to a person instead of a machine, although these people do not work as employees for the contracting firm. They are subcontractors, and the firms whose phones they answer are their clients. When a telephone goes unanswered in a client's office past a programmed number of rings, the service operator picks up the telephone. On the computer screen in front of the operator, the client's data are retrieved so that the operator can respond intelligently to queries and questions from these callers. Automated voice mail software programs are now available on a wide-scale basis. These programs offer callers a variety of options to hear prerecorded messages before being put through to a desired party or to their voice mail system. In many businesses, these systems have replaced the traditional answering service system.

Some specific reference materials help the operator find often-used information quickly. These references should be kept within reach for fast and easy access: local telephone book(s), company directory, ZIP Code directory, dictionary, wordfinder manual, office manual, and any procedures and policy or product manuals developed by the company.

PLACING LONG-DISTANCE CALLS

There are numerous ways that long-distance calls can be placed by businesspersons. Office workers are sometimes expected to perform this task for their managers and supervisors. Direct Distance Dialing (DDD) and station-to-station calling are the least expensive methods, but person-to-person calls are sometimes better. If the person called is not available, then no charge is made to the caller's firm. Operator-assisted calls are charged as station-to-station, not person-to-person calls.

Frequently, long-distance access codes are assigned to authorized parties in a company. The caller typically keys in his or her access code (or personal identification number) either immediately before *or* after dialing the long-distance telephone number. This access code, or PIN, is then recorded by the company's long-distance compiler program, for later reference by the company. This is one way for the companies to track their long-distance usage, time, and costs. It also helps to decrease the number of long-distance calls by unauthorized persons in a firm.

Toll-free long-distance calls are 800 and 888 numbers; 900 numbers are not toll-free. Callers using 800 or 888 numbers pay no charge; the called party pays by establishing a block-rate fee with the telephone company.

Collect calls should not be placed unless the called party has approved. Employees should know their company's policy so they will understand when they may accept collect calls and under what conditions such calls should be refused. Selected company personnel, such as sales representatives ("reps") and executives, are usually authorized to carry their firms' telephone credit card. Some calls from the owners' family members as well as calls about emergency situations may also be authorized.

VOICE MAIL

Although similar to answering machines, voice mail has more options. At first one cannot tell the difference, since the called party's recorded voice greets the caller. Thereafter, the system differs, as noted from the following illustration.

Caller	*Automated voice in the mail box*
	"You have reached 555-1616. If you wish to leave a message, press 1. If you need help, press 0."
(Presses 1 on the telephone)	"You may talk as long as you like. If you are satisfied with your message, press 1. If you would like to hear your message so you can correct it, press 2. If you need help, press 0."
(Leaves a message)	
(Presses 1, 2, or 0, as desired)	

KEEPING TELEPHONE RECORDS

Large firms usually have automatic, computerized call recording systems. Records are kept and charges posted per phone and department, with monthly billing or account records made available. Telecommunication accounting personnel must account for every charge and know to whom or to which department to bill it.

Smaller firms also account for charges, but the procedure may be conducted manually. Each person who is authorized to place long-distance calls at the company's expense fills out a form, uses an approved access code, or keeps a journal record. These records include number and person or firm called, date and time, and purpose of the call. An office worker coordinates this information with the monthly bill data.

THE FIVE Cs OF EFFECTIVE TELEPHONE MANNERS

Smile with your eyes as well as with your mouth and this warmth will come through over the telephone as courtesy, interest, and kindness. The five Cs is a catchy way to remember telephone manners.

Courtesy means using good etiquette and compassion. Words like *please* and *thank you* make people feel good and assure them of your respect. Invite and give feedback. Do not interrupt unless necessary and then be gracious. For example, "Pardon me, Mr. Smith, but I'd like to answer each question one at a time before going on, if you don't mind."

Clear means speaking clearly, without mumbling or running words together, using grammar correctly and making correct word choices, and providing clear and accurate feedback.

Correct includes all of the above and also refers to clearly stating facts and figures accurately.

Concise means brief, with no extra dialogue. Respond courteously to the caller's digressions but quickly return to the point.

Complete means being thorough by covering the essential elements of the subject (or issue) being discussed.

LISTENING AND PROVIDING FEEDBACK

Many oral messages and instructions come to office workers both in person and over the telephone. Switchboard and secretarial personnel spend many hours every day in situations that require the use of verbal communication.

The listening competency includes concentration, thinking, interpreting, and providing the speaker with feedback. *Feedback* is the repeating of information but in your own words. Feedback is also in play when one asks questions to get the speaker to clarify points. Speakers help to ensure understanding when they correct the inaccurate or incomplete feedback they get. With feedback, there is a greater likelihood that people will understand one another.

Chapter 3

Emerging Trends

The ability to produce smaller computer chips influences the development and use of technology. Other emerging trends include wireless equipment, the marriage of telephone and cable TV, telecommuting, home-based electronic entrepreneurships, and the interest in staying home as a result of crime, overcrowding, and so on. The relationships between the print media and telecommunications and between communications and transportation are two other topics that have historical significance as well as future implications.

THINGS ARE GETTING SMALLER!

The basic telephone instrument must be large enough to reach from ear to mouth, but the internal mechanisms can be quite small. Although televisions are getting bigger, 42 or more inches, many other devices are getting smaller; for example, robots the size of a gnat. A paper-thin four-inch wafer can contain up to 200 chips and each chip can carry hundreds of micromachines.

In microland, silicon becomes powerful. It is as mechanically strong as some types of steel. Micromachines will make homes as well as the workplace "smart," from managing security and air-control systems to communicating potential disasters, such as alerting adults that a child is at risk of falling.

Other examples of smaller (and better) items are the pocket calculator, the micro-dictating machine, the laptop computer, miniature radios and TV sets, and amplifiers for all sorts of purposes. Auctioneers, politicians, and others who need to amplify their voices now use an electronic bullhorn. They speak (or sing) into a microphone that is connected to an electronic box that has its own bullhorn.

WIRELESS OR CELLULAR ITEMS

It is estimated that by the year 2000 at least half of the people in the United States will have wireless or cellular telephones that they can carry with them wherever they go. This type of phone will eliminate the need for pagers and beepers—the system whereby a pager hooked to one's belt or carried in the purse beeps, thus directing the owner to go to a phone and call in to headquarters.

Another idea associated with the cellular phone is to give people a single telephone number, such as the current social security number. Instead of numbering phones, this system would number people. Instead of "call forwarding" from phone to phone, the single number assigned to a person will reach that person, providing that he or she is currently carrying the cellular phone.

DIGITAL SUPERHIGHWAY:
MARRIAGE OF CABLE TV AND TELEPHONES

On August 24, 1993, a U.S. district judge in Alexandria, VA threw out a federal law that forbade telephone companies from entering the TV-programming business. This legal decision paved the way for innovations in the marriage of cable TV and telephone company services; in other words, a "digital highway." This digital revolution promises viewers hundreds of channels and dazzling interactive services.

Moreover, in February 1996, with the enactment of the 1996 Telecommunications Act by the 104th U.S. Congress, cable, local, and long-distance telephone companies will be able to enter the deregulated market and compete with each other by providing customers greater services, lower prices, and a host of new interactive services. Such services will include, but will not be limited to, telemedicine in rural areas; distance learning to improve training and development for companies and consumers; home shopping; on-line access; combined telephone, television, and Internet services; and single-line transmission of combined data, voice, and video images. This new technology and such telecommunication services will make activities such as interactive home shopping much more available to the general public.

However, despite such developments only a small percentage of people actually use such services. In Los Angeles, for example, interactive shopping has been available on television since 1989, yet less than 15 percent of TV viewers use the system.

TELECOMMUTING FOR OTHERS AND FOR SELF

Telecommuting is the system of working at home with a telecommunication station. Instead of traveling, people "commute" by telecommunication linkage in a variety of configurations. The station might include computer terminal, keyboard, monitor, built-in modem, and telecommunication software that connects the station to the LAN of an office. Wide area networking (WAN) allows the telecommuter to communicate via e-mail with numerous other locations as well as to access data from on-line databases.

Telecommuting for others means that the home worker is an employee of an established company. The pay, however, is usually based on the amount of work produced rather than on an hourly rate. This is because there is no supervisor present to monitor the hours worked but the amount of work completed can be verified.

In a half-dozen or more Asian countries, housewife data entry clerks work out of their homes to process data for U.S. firms. The raw data is sometimes transported to them in huge mail sacks. Operators enter and process the data, and complete procedures by transmitting processed information on-line to U.S. headquarters.

Home-based electronic entrepreneurship allows people to work for themselves out of their homes. One can be self-employed, the "boss," the firm's owner. All sorts of ideas have emerged from this basic premise, from people who provide word processing and desktop publishing services to their customers, to those who specialize in labels for mail order shippers, or prepare and submit income tax records electronically, or compose and publish monthly newsletters.

A couple in Maine became multimillionaires from their "cheapskate gazette" newsletter–telling consumers how to save money. Another newsletter, a high-priced financial paper, has been rated among the world's top ten and is published from a log cabin deep in Montana's northwest forest. Its publisher has his own uplink to a communications satellite. Although it is expensive to link up with one of these sophisticated space vehicles, thereafter it costs no more to call Singapore from Montana than it would to call across the street! The publisher has access via the Internet to databases, to very up-to-the-minute news from around the world, while simultaneously he is able to print, e-mail, fax, computer network, or even use the mail system to distribute his paper to subscribers.

SOME PEOPLE ARE STAYING HOME AND TRAVELING LESS

In response to such phenomena as the population explosion, the overcrowding of cities, the long commute from suburbs to workplaces, and the growth of crime and pollution, some trends are emerging. According to Yankelovich Partners, a research firm, more people are staying home for more activities. NordicTrack reports zooming sales of gym equipment for home use. Consumers can shop, bank, play games, and respond to political surveys using TV and telephone. Consumers also shop with mail-order catalogs, often calling in their orders on 800 numbers instead of using the mail.

The big three TV networks still select the most sensational footage for their news reports but they no longer dominate television. Prior to cable, 95 percent of the prime-time audience watched these networks. No longer. In the age of the sound bite, news stations like CNN and C-SPAN bring us in-depth discussions. With more and better coverage of news and cultural events, people can stay home for even more reasons. The print media must also find more ways to compete with the broadcast media.

At the workplace, people can "travel" or convene by teleconference. At work and at home consumers are discovering how they can telecommunicate. In fact, telephone contacts now far outweigh the use of mail. And e-mail is rapidly becoming a very popular medium of electronic communication.

People who stay at home to work often experience social isolation, even when a mate or other family members are present. The rapid increase in personal networking and wireless communication demonstrates people's need to communicate, to "reach out and touch someone."

SOME PEOPLE ARE TRAVELING MORE

With TV news putting people in the center of the action around the world, people are more curious about getting out and seeing things. Global business operations send people around the world to communicate in person as part of the total communication process. See communication and psychological theories in Section II to help understand why face-to-face communications continue to be important.

NEWSPAPER PRINTING
VIA TELECOMMUNICATIONS

How is it possible for people living in Laramie, Wyoming, to get their copy of the current day's *Wall Street Journal* at 6 a.m., while people living in New York City are picking it up off their newsstands at the same time if not later? National newspapers such as *The Wall Street Journal* and *USA Today* are published in the Eastern United States, but they are printed in key locations throughout the world.

The news goes via telecommunications or on-line to distant sites where key news from those regions is inserted before these newspapers are printed. The papers are then loaded onto trucks in the wee dark hours of the morning and transported to smaller cities. Presto! The same news, plus regional news, is made available to everybody all over the country and world simultaneously.

TRANSPORTATION
AND COMMUNICATION SYSTEMS

During the centuries before the telegraph was invented, people could only communicate by using some transportation system.

People and items first traveled by foot, then by animal (horse, mule, oxen) and water. Later came rails, roads, and airways. People, goods, and communication items such as letters and packages are still moving from place to place. Thus, we cannot address communication systems without also referring to transportation systems.

What Do You Think?
Review and Opinions

1. Discuss some technological changes that have occurred during your lifetime and the impact that these changes have made on (a) how you do your work–at home and on the job; (b) how you telecommunicate with others, locally and over distance; and (c) increasing your knowledge of a global society and economy.

2. Express your opinions (rational insights) and feelings (emotions) about some things that have *not* changed, despite the innovations in telecommunications; for example, in the management of work and productivity, human relationships, manners, and so on. Be specific and use examples from your own work and personal life.

3. Share examples of how you were eager to change (to new technologies, new procedures) in some cases and how you were late and reluctant to change in other situations. Through discussion, seek to identify the reasons for your eagerness versus your reluctance. With this knowledge, discuss how you could help co-workers adapt to technological and procedural changes in the workplace.

From Cave to Satellite

Early people recorded news and accounting tallies on cave walls as a means of keeping and communicating permanent records. These notations, using pictures and symbols, are called hieroglyphics. Tallies (////) of wheat (✻) would show the number of sheaves of wheat harvested in a given season. Tallies of animals would account for animal inventories.

Smoke signals were used to send coded news across distances no farther than one could see and decode these messages. Native Americans also used a "signaling glass" to reflect the sun and convey messages over distances. In the military (the signal corps), flags are still used to convey coded messages across the sea, from ship to ship and ship to land. In the Canary Islands, a second language is whistling, which can be heard for up to two miles. This communications method uses different sounds for each letter of the alphabet.

In frontier America, during the seventeenth and eighteenth centuries, mail was a key communication method. However, because the mail was carried by train, Pony Express, or stagecoach, it often took days or even weeks to go from the midwest to either coast (e.g., Boston or San Francisco). For example, the mail took about 26 days to travel from Independence, Missouri, to San Francisco by stagecoach. In the late 1800s, young Wild Bill Cody and other fellows in their late teens carried mail by Pony Express—at a cost of $5 per letter on very thin paper. Despite the fact that the delivery method lasted less than 2 years, the Pony Express could carry mail over the same distance in 3 days instead of 26 days.

Rural people were isolated, and even national and global news, such as news about national elections or of distant wars, often took weeks to reach them. Small-town people (then as now) usually knew one another. Walking and buggy or horseback riding were slow compared to today's high-speed vehicles. People were more observant, of each other as well as of their neighborhoods. Everybody knew everybody and social norms were more likely observed because "everybody would know" if one misbehaved. This "social pressure" encouraged people to engage in honest business transactions, in which agreements were often established on a mere "gentleman's handshake."

City dwellers too were place-bound. Without fast means of transportation, they were forced to live within walking distance of their workplaces, including smoke-belching factories. Their smelly, polluted neighborhoods were not nice places in which to live. Company owners and managers went to work in buggies, traveling to work from their nicer outlying neighborhoods, thus communicating to others their affluence and prestige.

Early humans had no true mechanical devices, only their own muscles. About 2,500 years ago, people learned to harness draft animals such as workhorses and oxen. Waterwheels harnessed energy from water flowing in rivers, followed by sails to propel boats. About a thousand years ago, windmills began harnessing wind energy.

Fire was discovered thousands of years ago but was used mostly for cooking and warmth. Eventually, energy based on fire used coal, gas made from coal, petroleum, natural gas, electricity, and nuclear power. Many of these energy sources, including animal muscle and wind, are based on the energy radiated by the sun. Much of today's energy is derived from alternative sources locked up in fossil fuels. Fuels, including electricity, are needed to run engines that make both transportation and communication systems possible. See the map of early America's road system and the charts of energy consumption worldwide.

People do not create or invent natural resources, such as fuels. They can discover them and create uses for them. Benjamin Franklin is credited with harnessing electricity and identifying possible uses.

From 1817 to 1871, Congress gave monetary grants to promote the building of canals and railroads. The Erie Canal ran 364 miles through New York state to Lake Erie and was the most extensive internal waterway. Its importance was eventually bypassed by the faster railroad. The first transcontinental railroad was completed in the late

1860s, linking the eastern half of the United States to the Great Plains, and the Great Plains to the coast of California.

The first road carriage powered by an engine was invented by Siegfried Marcus in 1864 and roused interest only in the police, who barred the noisy little contraption from the streets. The idea languished until the 1880s when Daimler and Benz, two other Germans working independently of each other, managed to harness an internal combustion engine to wheels.

By the mid-1890s, there were several hundred auto machines, which gained acceptance in France where there were smooth roads; hence the French influence on automotive vocabulary—carburetor, chauffeur, and garage, for example. In the United States, with its vast plains, mountains, and remote horizons waiting to be gathered together, the innovation should have impressed bankers and manufacturers, but leery investors stayed away.

It was left to pioneering young Americans to test, refine, and advance the early "automobiles." Because of poor, slow communications, they knew nothing of one another. Yet in Detroit alone, Henry Ford, Ramson Olds, and the redheaded Dodge brothers were busy inventing different versions of the auto.

We've come a long way from the stagecoach to the trains, to the automobile, to the airplane, and to the sophisticated transportation systems of the twentieth century. From transportation systems to modern satellites, modern society enjoys many benefits and rewards. Today's satellites provide communication, meteorological (weather), space, and spying information. Yet not everything works. The satellite designed to observe and report on Mars disappeared!

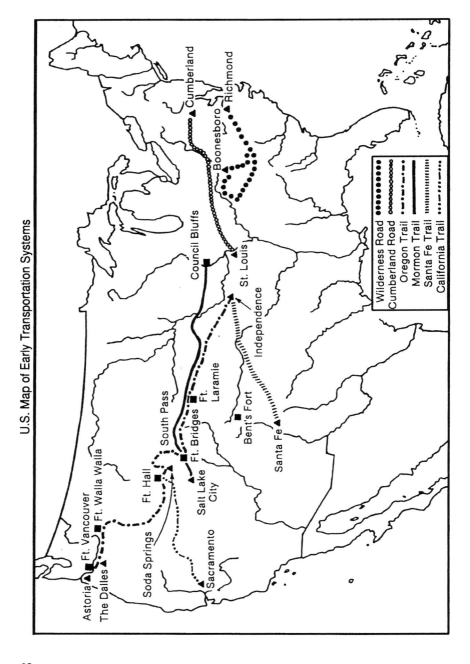

U.S. Map of Early Transportation Systems

Cumberland
Richmond
Boonesboro
Council Bluffs
St. Louis
Independence
Ft. Laramie
South Pass
Ft. Bridges
Bent's Fort
Santa Fe
Salt Lake City
Ft. Hall
Soda Springs
Sacramento
Astoria
The Dalles
Ft. Vancouver
Ft. Walla Walla

Wilderness Road
Cumberland Road
Oregon Trail
Mormon Trail
Santa Fe Trail
California Trail

Activities for Section I

ACTIVITY I-1: COOPERATIVE LEARNING– TOURS AND INTERVIEWS

Name: _____ Date: _____

Directions for Tours and Hands-On Experiences

1. Form a small group of four to five people. Designate one person as the supervisor, one as the recorder, and one as a memo processor.

2. Share knowledge of sites where someone is likely to provide the group with a demonstration of one or more telecommunication devices or systems, for example: electronic mail (e-mail), local area network (LAN), distance learning or compressed video transmission, closed-circuit TV, the production of/use of multimedia, the conducting of electronic data searches, or a variety of telephone options. The following are possibilities:

- campus or business facilities for LAN or e-mail
- campus, city, or county library for data search
- campus, business office or copy center for fax

The preferred choice is the campus, so check with the business offices, library, counseling, and other staff offices as well as with computer lab and telecommunication teaching facilities. The supervisors of the small groups meet with each other to coordinate arrangements so that a variety of class tours are arranged. Coordinate dates with tour site personnel and verify that tours can be scheduled during class time.

3. Get permission to *use* the tour facilities as well as to observe demonstrations. Hands-on experiences are invaluable in learning. With campus systems, particularly in teaching labs, it should be possible to

get one or more appointments for each small group and partnership within groups. (See the next two activities in this section—Activities I-2 and I-3—for the type of assignments to be conducted on site.)

Directions for Interviews

1. Arrange to interview one or more users at each tour site. Within each group, students may form partnerships so that two or three persons question each interviewee.

2. Develop your own list of questions, using the blanks below. The following ideas may be used in developing the interview questionnaire: (a) problems experienced in training on a new system (e.g., feelings of excitement versus inadequacy); (b) type of company—its goods, services, and variety of customers; (c) types of transmissions made and the most typical or frequent; (d) tips for new trainees soon to enter the job market; and (e) what the interviewee likes and dislikes (or find is most challenging or rewarding) about his or her job.

_____

_____

_____

_____

_____

_____

_____

_____

3. You will return to this activity later. Note that group members should continue to complete the other activities in this unit and that you will return to this activity only after all scheduled tours have been completed. CLOSURE WILL BE ENCOURAGED LATER when the groups meet to share their interview results and discuss what they learned during each tour. Be sure to allow each group equal time (10 minutes or so) to talk about their experience in conducting the interviews.

ACTIVITY I-2: REDESIGN A FAX FORM AND LETTERHEAD

Name: _____ Date: _____

Background

You conduct all office duties for a self-employed inventor, Dr. Julie Emilyne, who has incorporated her company. The company currently uses a fax transmittal form that is a full-size sheet of stationery paper–8½″ × 11″. Fax messages are taken to a service company who charges per page for each fax transmittal. Thus, it is important to reduce the number of pages every time you send a fax. Presently, you average from 50 to 100 separate transmittals per week at a cost of $1 per page. These messages are sometimes memos but are also drawings of inventions and small one-page changes to drawings.

You had an idea about how to save the firm money, which you shared with your boss, the inventor. She suggested that you put your idea into practice by redesigning forms.

Directions

1. Refer to the fax transmittal form that the company now uses. Notice that it appears on the company's letterhead. This form uses a full page of paper, size 8½″ × 11″.

2. Design a fax transmittal form, size 3″ × 3″. Ensure that the most pertinent data from the original form appear on this new form. Play around with the design by manipulating data right at the computer. When you are satisfied, print the form. Be sure to save this fax form on the computer, since you will be using it later. This document is named FAXFORM.

3. Notice with the current company letterhead design, that there is no place to attach the new fax transmittal form without covering part of the letterhead information. Thus you have decided to redesign the letterhead so that all of the data appears on either the left or the right side. The new fax form can then be attached to the opposite side and data from both forms will appear at the receiving end.

800/555-XXXX   FAX — 888/555-XXXX

TO: _____

FROM: _____

DATE: _____

Number of pages (including this page)_____

— — — — — — — — — — — — MESSAGE — — — — — — — — — — — — — —

_____

_____

_____

_____

_____

_____

_____

_____

_____

_____

4. Redesign the company letterhead at the computer. When you are satisfied not only with its appearance but also that the new fax form will fit over the letterhead page, print the letterhead.

5. In the blanks below, explain how your new designs will save the company money every time the new fax form is used:

_____

_____

_____

_____

_____

_____

6. At what point will the business want to buy its own fax machine?

_____

_____

_____

ACTIVITY I-3: TRANSMIT A MEMO BY FAX

Name: _____ Date: _____

Directions

1. Arrange to use one of the tour sites from Activity I-1.

2. Access MEMOHEAD from your disk. This is a shell document for the headings on a memo. If you prefer to compose your own headings each time you prepare a memo, refer to the format below:

TO: Name of recipient

FROM: Your name (aligned with the above)

DATE: Current date (aligned with the above)

SUBJECT: THE SUBJECT IS TYPED IN ALL CAPS

3. Compose a memo to a member of your group. The memo may address any topic. Talk about yourself if you like and ask the person questions about him/herself.

4. Access FAXFORM off your disk. This is the $3'' \times 3''$ form that you created in Activity I-2.

5. Copy the form so that you will have a form to work with while leaving the original form blank and unused on the disk.

6. Fill out the data on the fax transmittal form.

7. Arrange to exchange (real) transmittals with the person to whom you addressed your memo. If your school has two or more fax machines, this exchange can be made on campus.

8. Transmit and receive memos with fax forms attached.

9. Record any problems that arose in the transmittal and tell how you solved them. Describe your reaction to this means of communicating. Hold materials for later discussion.

_____

_____

_____

_____

ACTIVITY I-4: RESPOND TO THE FAX MEMO BY USING E-MAIL

Name: _____ Date: _____

Directions

1. Arrange to use the tour site or a campus facility that has electronic mail (e-mail).

2. The same two people who wrote to each other and transmitted their memos by fax continue to communicate, this time by e-mail.

3. Access MEMOHEAD on the disk or create your own memo headings. Answer the memo that you received.

4. Record below the problems you encountered, if any, and describe how you solved them. Describe your feelings.

_____

_____

_____

_____

_____

5. *Optional.* If your instructor has access to e-mail, use the system to transmit this activity via telecommunications instead of hard copy printout.

6. *Optional.* Access one or more bulletin boards, if any are available to your instructor, the school, or a lab site that you have arranged to use. Describe details of how you conducted the procedure and some current information that you retrieved.

_____

_____

_____

_____

_____

ACTIVITY I-5: LISTEN, PRACTICE ORALLY, AND PROVIDE FEEDBACK

Name: _____ Date: _____

Background

Oral communications are so important over the telephone that a person who does not use language well can make or break a sale, lose the goodwill of a firm's clients, and be an embarrassment to co-workers. Listen to people who speak well so you can emulate them. National TV newscasters provide good role models.

The ability to provide accurate feedback over the telephone and in face-to-face situations helps to facilitate communications. You provide feedback when you repeat or rephrase what you have already said or you answer a caller's questions.

Directions for Listening to TV Newscasters

1. Listen to several current or past network news shows and select a speaker that you admire. Some well-known news anchors of recent years include Peter Jennings (ABC), Dan Rather (CBS), and Tom Brokaw (NBC). Speak aloud, right along with them or directly afterwards.

2. If you have access to a VCR or tape recorder, record a short segment and listen repeatedly, mimicking oral language (words and word choices) and paralanguage (accents or lack of regional accents). Stop the tape after each sentence and repeat it.

3. Notice that the news anchors avoid repeated use of slang, such as: "Okay?" "Know what I mean?" "Ya know," and "Hey, man." They also avoid these errors: "He *don't*. . ." and "They *was*. . ." ("He don't" means "He do not do it.") Instead, notice that they say "He (or she) *doesn't*. . ." (does not) and "They *were*. . ."

4. Use the blank lines that follow to record the errors that you sometimes make, in comparison to the correct choices that you hear on TV. Under the heading, "Type of Error," use these descriptors: word choice, grammar, miscellaneous. In the last column, record the correct choice. Practice these, perhaps hundreds of times, until your verbal choice of words is correct.

5. Save this page for your own practice.

Error	*Type of Error*	*Correct Choice*

Directions for Providing Feedback

1. Meet with a partner. Each of you silently and individually write directions for how to get from campus to your home or to some other site that you often visit. Use proper English.

2. In rotation, partners read their directions to each other.

3. When you are the listener, ask questions so your partner will provide you with feedback. Or you may provide feedback by repeating or rephrasing the directions that you heard. When you use the latter technique, the first speaker must also listen carefully and then rephrase the original directions.

4. Use the blanks below for writing your set of directions:

_____

_____

_____

_____

_____

_____

ACTIVITY I-6: COOPERATIVE LEARNING–
REACH CLOSURE ON TOURS AND INTERVIEWS

Name: _____   Date: _____

Directions

1. Following the last tour that is scheduled to take place during this first unit, reconvene in your small groups. The supervisor leads discussion and directs the recorder to take notes and, later, directs the composer to prepare a memo from the group to the instructor.

2. From the recorder's notes, the composer prepares a memo. Access MEMOHEAD from your disk or create your own memo headings.

3. The supervisor proofreads the memo with the subject LEARNING OUTCOMES FROM TOURS and makes recommendations for revisions, if any. The supervisor then makes photocopies of the memo, distributing the original to the instructor and one copy to each member of the group.

4. Use the blanks below to coordinate individual/group learning outcomes with the unit objectives. These notes are from the TOURS AND INTERVIEWS only:

Objective   *Learning Outcome*

_____   _____

_____   _____

_____   _____

_____   _____

_____   _____

_____   _____

_____   _____

_____   _____

_____   _____

ACTIVITY I-7: COOPERATIVE LEARNING–GROUP MAJOR TERM PROJECT

This is an international project on telecommunications, telemarketing, and records systems (TTR). Form groups of three or four people each. Select a leader to manage the completion of tasks as selected by group members. At least one task per member should be completed by the close of each unit.

Each group selects one country from one continent. During the group presentations at the close of Section V, you will glean vital information about TTR and related business practices on a global basis. Before beginning, *read all Cave to Satellite sections.*

Country Selection

The total country/continent selections should represent distribution throughout the world: western Europe, Asia, South or Central America, Africa or the Middle East, and a country close to the United States such as Canada or Mexico. Some countries that appear often in economic news (both broadcast and print media) include England, France, and Germany in Europe; China, Hong Kong, Japan, Korea, Taiwan and Vietnam in Asia; Iran, Iraq, Israel, Kuwait, Libya, Saudi Arabia, South Africa, and others in the Middle East and Africa; and Argentina, Brazil, and Colombia in South and Central America; and the "down under" countries–Australia and New Zealand.

Suggested Topics

Choose from the following tasks and develop your own group ideas. The following topics are suggested to stimulate the imagination. These topics should focus on the selected country:

- The language(s) that predominate (e.g., in France it would be French but also English and German).
- The procedures for and the cost of mailing a first-class letter from the United States *to and from* the selected country.
- The procedures for and the cost of calling long-distance and talking for ten minutes *to and from* the selected country.

- The travel arrangements and typical cost of a round-trip flight ticket *to and from* someone in the selected country.
- The currency used and the rate of exchange with American dollars.
- The price of selected items as posted by the country's currency and in relation to U.S. currency; e.g., one McDonald's Big Mac, a Coke, a pair of jeans, a gallon of gas, a word processor's or secretary's annual salary, a one-month's rental on an apartment, home, or typical living quarters.
- The use of the metric system and the number of kilometers from the capitol city to three or more other cities or famous landmarks within the selected country. (The only countries in the world that do *not* use the metric system are Burma, Libya, and the United States.)
- Keep track of differences in road or traffic laws (e.g., which side of the road is the driving rule—right or left?).
- The predominant political system (e.g., democracy, communism, dictatorship). Notations about how the government functions and the impact of this type of government on business operations and the rights of citizen consumers.
- The operation and common practices of the country's judicial system (e.g., how are criminals tried and punished?).
- Some goods that the country is famous for (e.g., in France, one might suggest wines and fashions). How goods are manufactured and products (both goods and services) are distributed and marketed. The use of telemarketing in marketing these products worldwide.
- The stock market, if any, and in which city it is located. How its services are marketed (and telemarketed) throughout the world to attract global investors.
- Some well-known products and firms that are located in the country or have their headquarters there (e.g., Bayer, which makes aspirin and other pharmaceuticals, is headquartered in Germany; Fiat, the auto manufacturer, is an Italian firm; and Sony, which produces electronics, is Japanese.
- Examples of records systems and how they are managed— filing rules, manual versus computerized databases, or both.

- Social and business customs, especially those that business people should use or avoid because of their significance to the country's people and their culture. For example, in some countries, bribing is an acceptable business practice. Discuss some of the different social and business practices that were evident. Include nonverbal communications and gestures under this topic. (Consider these needs as related to people who travel on business versus tourists who travel to vacation sites both in the United States and abroad.)

Potential Sources

There are many sources and resources to use in collecting data about the above topics or any others, including human and broadcast media sources. The following are suggested:

- Your own knowledge and background—which should be confirmed by other sources. Don't neglect the impressions of group members. Some will have traveled abroad. Some will know or have met people from other countries. Many will have been affected by the marketing and telemarketing of news (both positive and negative) of the country, its people and products, government, customs, etc.
- Foreign students on campus from the chosen country or continent. A campus multicultural or foreign student department may help you locate individual students with whom to conduct interviews.
- Instructors of foreign languages and world culture courses on your campus or a nearby university. Someone may have traveled to your selected country or can advise you about the types of print resources that are available and where to go to get them.
- Business people in your community whose origins are from your selected country or continent—notice last names and ethnic characteristics. If approached courteously, they are often willing and able to describe business practices and products and provide valuable insights that may not be available from any other sources.

- Travel agencies, where colorful brochures that market the country and continent (with many pertinent details that travelers need) are available, as well as an agent who might answer some of the questions on your group-developed task list.
- Libraries contain all manner of print media, from encyclopedia and publications about foreign countries, to books, magazines, and newspapers that publish articles *and* advertise products. (Check ads in magazines and newspapers.)
- Television, as an educational and learning tool. This telecommunications medium provides much more than mere entertainment. Check TV listings every week for the duration of the project, looking especially for "news magazines" (*60 Minutes, Nightline, Prime Time Live, 48 Hours, 20/20, Dateline,* etc.), travelogues, and business news shows.

Note, for instance, that in a recent tally of one week's TV shows, there were 33 different business/finance shows alone! Some of these run for 30 minutes while others as long as two hours. ESPN (a popular sports channel) aired a daily business show from 4:30 to 6:30 a.m. PBS offered hour-long shows on marketing, economics, and other business topics on Saturday mornings.

Even fiction (literature) can be used as source material. A well-researched or fact-based fiction show (movie, special), especially if filmed on location, provides much more than the story plot alone. Watch for famous landmarks that tell you in what city or country the story is filmed. Notice architecture, fashions, foods, social and business customs, language choice, nonverbal language clues, and business practices. Note any uses of telecommunications, telemarketing, and records systems. Imagine how these are used, if they are not clearly portrayed on the show.

Project Presentation

Group leaders facilitate the planning of the presentation, which may be given in a half-hour or hour-long time period. A panel discussion is one method of presentation, or members can speak in sequence.

Wear business dress and practice using oral language that is preferred in business. Avoid slang, including the overuse of "okay," "okay?" "stuff," "stuff like that," and "know what I mean?"

Develop some materials to enhance the presentation. These visuals include any one or more of the following:

- Transparencies to use on an overhead projector. Use large, dark print, and don't crowd too much onto each master. You may use desktop publishing, bold and underlined print, and variations in font type and size. Ordinary-sized print, if enlarged on a copy machine, will suffice.
- Handouts, typed or desktop published, for people to keep.
- Brochures, pamphlets, and other materials to pass around, when one or just a few copies are available and you or the group would like to retain them. Photographs, postcards, etc., that one or more group members have collected also fit into this category.
- Posters or bulletin boards may be used, but the artwork and print copy should be large enough for everyone to see.
- A skit or series of short how-not-to and how-to scenes could be played before the audience or could be produced earlier and video-recorded, then presented at the time of the presentation with TV and VCR (telecommunications).
- A slide series might help to demonstrate the presentation. Slide film in a camera, used to take local shots including ones of foreign students or businesses and their owners, enhances the presentation. You may also film with a videocamera and present findings with a VCR.

Another method of preparing a slide show is to use pictures from travel or other brochures, ads marketed in magazines, and print copy prepared on desktop publishing to use as the slide's title shot and headings for subtopics. Do not mount small pictures. The school's resource center will likely have the capability of turning your pictures and print copy sheets into slides. A tripod holding a camera pointing down is mounted at the top. Each slide item is placed on a platform below the tripod that holds the camera. For small pictures, the platform is raised; for full-sized 8½″ × 11″ pages, the platform is lowered. The result of any size rendering is a full-sized slide.

Also needed are a slide projector and a slide carousel. The script for the slide show may be written and prerecorded or a group member may speak spontaneously in describing the shots.

(Note: Someone in your group may already be competent with multimedia. If so, arrange to learn from this person; do not allow this person to prepare the whole project for the rest of you.)

Evaluation

The leader evaluates the contributions and performance of group members. The audience rates the group presentation. The instructor evaluates both the presentation and the individual portfolios of each student.

INDIVIDUAL ASSIGNMENT NOTES

As agreed upon by consensus, each group member should come away from this session with one or more specific task assignments. Record these below and the date on which your group expects you to have completed each task. If you will be working with a LAN (Local Area Network), discuss with your group members relevant comments they have made in their individual notes.

Task   *Due date*

_____

_____

_____

_____

_____

_____

_____

_____

_____

_____

_____

_____

ACTIVITY I-8: COOPERATIVE LEARNING: CASE STUDIES AND LEARNING OUTCOMES FOR SECTION

Name: _____ Date: _____

Directions for the Case Studies

1. Keep the same leadership personnel—supervisor, recorder, and processor. Read the following cases before meeting with your group and add notations that represent your individual opinions.

2. Under the supervisor's leadership, the group discusses the cases for the purpose of reaching a consensus. The supervisor directs the recorder in taking notes and summarizing ideas as the group reaches agreement.

3. The processor accesses MEMOHEAD from the disk and composes a memo—addressed to the instructor from the group—based on the recorder's summary of conclusions.

4. The supervisor proofreads the memo and makes recommendations, if any, for changes. The supervisor photocopies the final memo copy and submits the original to the instructor and a copy to each group member for inclusion in the individual portfolios.

Case Study 1: Welcome to the Twenty-First Century

J. D. Douglas uses telecommunications more than any other technical method to process communications. He has a laptop computer with modem, telecommunications software, and several other programs including word processors and spreadsheets loaded into the system. He can plug his computer into any phone anywhere in the world—in a telephone booth, on a plane, or in his car or hotel—to connect to anyone he wants to reach who also has a phone.

His personal and company cars have telephones and his wife, Georgia, has a car phone. The Douglas home in Seattle has 13 telephones, one in every room, plus telephones in the garage and on the deck within reach of the hot tub. Their beach condo has three more telephones. All of these telephones have *a complete variety of options*. So when you call J. D. or Georgia, you are almost always able to reach them. Except that you will have no idea where in the world they might physically be located at the moment! Call forwarding will reroute your call to Georgia or J. D. at home, at work, at the condo, in Hawaii or London—anywhere they might be!

Voice messaging allows J. D. to call his secretary's call box, leave messages and retrieve the messages she has left for him. Unlike an answering machine, there is no time limit; if necessary, J. D. can talk for ten or more minutes. However, in most cases, J. D. gets on and off the telephone in minutes.

An hour or so later—whether in the home of friends, in his hotel room, or popping out of a cab to jump into a phone booth—J. D. will redial the voice message system. By then, his secretary will have completed a number of the tasks he delegated to her and have left more messages and news for him. She will also relay tasks for him to do as they emerge in their Seattle office or as his boss has directed him. With these types of frequent and direct as well as indirect telecommunication systems, it seems that J. D. has not even left his office.

Carrying the laptop computer with him allows J. D. to work on data that are already stored, no matter where he is. Thus, whether using a variety of telephone options or communicating via e-mail and electronic data searches, his work goes where he goes.

When J. D. plugs the computer into a telephone, any telephone, anywhere, he is able to access data that are stored in the computer system in the home office. This is WAN (wide area network) rather than a LAN (local area network). His secretary can print from his computer, using the printer in her office. She and J. D. can communicate hard data by e-mail.

J. D. and his secretary also use some data search programs that allow them to access very current international news and bulletin board updates as J. D. travels around the world. His secretary sometimes uses a commercial data bank and downloads some research data into the system. Thus, J. D. can access or retrieve data, as well as input his own.

J. D. even has a cellular phone in his golf bag. When his beeper goes off, he turns on the phone and checks in, saving the time it formerly took to go to the club house to phone. Businesspeople have always done business on the golf course and in other social business settings. Recently a sales rep who wanted to do business with J. D.'s company joined J. D. at the club to play a round. However, the sales rep was due to fly out of town and, on the sixteenth hole, asked J. D. to cut the game short to drive him to the airport. "Heck no!" J. D. replied, still concentrating on his game. He then reached into his golf bag, took out the phone, and handed it to the sales rep, saying, "Please call a cab. I'm playing too great to quit right now!"

1. What trends are evident in this case? How is our way of life changing with the new telecommunication devices that many now enjoy?

2. How has the variety of telecommunication devices and systems changed the way people work and live? Bring to bear in your discussion some examples and ideas as gleaned from personal experiences, television, print, and human resources.

3. Use the blanks below to record ideas to be discussed with references to the previous two questions.

_____

_____

_____

_____

_____

_____

_____

_____

_____

_____

_____

_____

Case Study 2: Rocky Mountain Telecommunication Entrepreneurs

Economically, the 1990s produced a boom in the Rockies–from Montana in the north, through Idaho, Wyoming, Colorado, and Utah to New Mexico in the south. This sparsely populated region's ambiance seemed to combine the yearning for a simpler, rooted, front-porch way of life with the urban-bred, *high-tech* worldliness of computers and telecommunications.

When T.C. and his wife, Naomi, relocated from San Francisco to Utah, T.C. found he had more time to write. He submitted his journal pieces by fax and e-mail to his New York publisher. Bruce, who moved to the Rockies from Minneapolis, designs training systems for Toshiba and Syntex, among others. Distance is not an issue thanks to data communication, computers, and faxes. He says: "Our markets are farther west, anyhow, and when we need to get together in person, that's easy, too. The airport is only 45 minutes from here."

New arrivals like T.C., Naomi, and Bruce are called telecommuters or nicknamed "modem cowboys" or "lone eagles." Many people realize they can locate anywhere and live by their wits–provided they have the technology.

This boom didn't happen by accident. Promoters advertised the benefits of the region–clean air, plenty of space, willing workers, low crime rates, comparatively low taxes, and natural resources. Notoriously overreliant on natural resources since the silver rushes of the 1870s and 1880s, the region has recently diversified.

Some high-tech industries have located around Boise, Idaho. Wyoming has revived its coal fields with the world's most highly automated mining processes. Colorado financed an ambitious drive to make Denver an international hub with a new $3 billion airport. Utah absorbed unemployed miners into gleaming new aerospace, computer software, and financial services facilities. New Mexico used a $114 million tax incentive package to lure Intel into expanding its local semiconductor plant in Rio Rancho. In short time, Rio Rancho's population grew from 2,000 to 38,000. In Bozeman, Montana, gossip about Bob might mean Redford, and news of Ted and Jane probably refers to Ted Turner and Jane Fonda.

Like too many eagles in a wild life preserve, too many people within a specified space or territory produces a variety of physical and social problems. The infrastructure (a city's water, sewer, utilities, and road systems) becomes complex and overburdened and can blow out due to anything from natural disasters to sabotage. Fire fighting and police protection services are badly needed, but there is rarely enough money in the public coffers to pay for everything that all of the people need with a city's limited resources. Land (and thus buildings) is at a premium, so the cost of construction, mortgages, and rentals skyrockets. People produce things, meaning they manufacture goods. But they also produce garbage, waste, and pollution from their transportation, manufacturing, and infrastructure systems.

People crowded together within too small a space become irritable with each other. Too many people in a single area breeds strangeness. People no longer know their neighbors or the people beyond their immediate communities. Strangers do not readily worry about "what people will think or say" about their own behavior. People want what their neighbors have, and they feel needy and greedy. Soon they take what does not belong to them, or try to. Thus, crime proliferates. People fear for their lives and their belongings.

Many people have decided to escape the cities that produce the physical and social problems described here. From East and West coast cities, people are moving inland to rural areas. With the capabilities of telecommunication and transportation technologies, more people are able to live *and work* in more places.

Now people can live in rural areas and still hold sophisticated city or even global jobs. They can work with services, for others or for themselves. They can produce goods, run their own businesses, advertise and market their products around the world, and ship them to customers via modern transportation systems. Today, thanks to technology, people have more choices about both economic survival and personal lifestyles.

1. Discuss how telecommunication and transportation systems have made these income-generating options possible, for example, through working at home, whether in one's hometown, across the country, or around the world.

2. Discuss the motivations that sent early American settlers from the city to the country, from the East to the West, to leave their homes and emigrate elsewhere in search of economic survival opportunities. Draw comparisons with some of the relocation decisions that some people today are making. Share your feelings about relocating yourself–from city to country, from one state or region to another, from your nation to another. Use the spaces provided to make notes for discussion and/or analysis.

_____

_____

_____

_____

_____

_____

_____

_____

_____

_____

_____

_____

Directions for Addressing Learning Outcomes

1. Bring to the group session all of the notes and materials that you have completed or worked on during Section I.

2. The designated supervisor for this section leads discussion in reaching group consensus about whether the section objectives were met by everybody. Anyone who is not sure should get help from group members.

3. In addition to section objectives, individuals may have achieved some learning outcomes that were not anticipated. Some competencies may have improved. Individualize your notes by recording improved competencies below.

Objectives	Learning Outcomes

4. The group leader supervises the recorder in taking notes that represent group consensus on learning outcomes from the section. The processor accesses MEMOHEAD from the disk and composes a memo from the recorder's notes. The memo is addressed to the instructor and is from the group. The supervisor proofreads the memo and makes recommendations, if any, for revision.

5. The supervisor makes and distributes copies of the memo, with the original going to the instructor. *Attach the completed work of all members from all activities to this memo.* File or mount the copy of the memo in your PORTFOLIO.

6. The supervisor evaluates each group member and transmits these confidential forms to the instructor. (The supervisor collects from each individual the following evaluation form. Make a copy of this form from your book and submit it to him or her.)

SUPERVISOR'S EVALUATION–SECTION I

Person Evaluated: _____ Date: _____

Directions: Use the $+$, $\checkmark$, $-$ evaluation method; where $+$ = out-standing, $\checkmark$ = average/satisfactory, and $-$ = poor/unsatisfactory.

With this section, the group member was:

1. cooperative with co-workers   _____

2. responsive to assignments made by the group   _____

3. responsive to the supervisor's constructive ideas   _____

4. pleasant, cooperative, easy to work with   _____

5. dependable, attended class meetings   _____

6. dependable, attended out-of-class meetings   _____

7. responsible, produced work on time   _____

8. responsible, produced quality work   _____

9. reliable and willing to work   _____

10. positive team player who contributed greatly
to the group   _____

SUPPORTIVE COMMENTS:

Evaluator's signature (confidential):_____

Bibliography for Section I

Auctioneers at an estate sale, Walden, Colorado, September 18, 1993.

Bookey, Mike, "Technology in Instruction," talk presented at Casper, Wyoming, October 21, 1993.

Bonfante, Jordan, "Sky's the Limit," *Time*, September 6, 1993. (The Rockies—new home of telecommuters.)

Briskin, Jacqueline, *The Onyx.* NY: Dell, 1982. (Well-researched novel covering the history of the automobile.)

Burrell, Cassandra, "Judge Overturns Provision in 1984 Cable Television Law," *The Laramie Daily Boomerang*, August 25, 1993.

Carnevale, Mary Lu, "World Wide Web," *The Wall Street Journal*, November 15, 1993.

Carroll, Paul, *Big Blues: The Unmaking of IBM.* (Author interviewed by Bryant Gumbel on *The Today Show*, NBC, September 15, 1993.)

Church, Olive D., *Electronic Office Applications.* Albany, NY: Delmar Publishers, Inc., 1993.

_____, *Discovering America with Map Activities.* Portland, ME: J. Weston Walch, 1988.

Cubbler, Charlotte, John Olivo, and Len Scrogan, *Telecommunications Concepts and Applications.* Columbus, OH: South-Western Publishing Company, 1992.

"Denver International Airport–The Final Approach," PBS, September 30, 1993.

Duston, Diane, "Federal Regulators Clear the Way for Wireless Communications," *The Laramie Daily Boomerang*, September 24, 1993.

Graf, David, Olive Church, and Thomas Duff, *Business in an Information Economy.* NY: McGraw-Hill, 1990.

Georgano, Nick, "The Car Chronicles," *Modern Maturity*, August/September, 1993. (Cruising through a century with the horseless carriage.)

Henry Ford Museum, Pamphlet, Detroit, Michigan, November 1992. (Historical village and museum–autos and many miscellaneous items of early Americana.)

"How'd They Do That?" CBS, September 17, 1993. (Facilitative computer keyboard used to communicate by people with certain handicapping conditions.)

Iacocca, Lee, "Auto-biography of a Big Wheel," *Modern Maturity*, August/September 1993.

Illustrated Encyclopedic Dictionary, Volumes A-K and L-Z. Pleasantville, NY: Reader's Digest Association, 1996.

"Interactive TV," ABC News, September 29, 1993. (Peter Jennings interviewing Bill Gates, CEO of Microsoft computer software and John Malone, CEO of Time-Warner.)

Jeopardy, CBS, June 30, 1993. (Price of a letter sent by Pony Express.)

Keller, John J., "Net Assets," *The Wall Street Journal*, November 15, 1993.

Kiester, Edwin Jr., and Sally Valente Kiester, "Make TV Help Your Kids," *Reader's Digest*, October 1991. ("TV can be an invaluable learning tool if you know how to use it.")

Landler, Mark, and Bart Ziegler, "The Roadbed Has Been Laid for the Digital Superhighway," *Business Week*, September 6, 1993.

Leibson, Beth, "A Low-Tech Wonder," *Reader's Digest*, July 1992.

McNeil-Lehrer News Hour, "Big Bertha, Big Golf," PBS, August 17, 1993.

Miller, Michael W., "Contact High," *The Wall Street Journal*, November 15, 1993. (Computer networks have transformed campus life.)

Moore, Richard G., and Scott Wilkinson, "Communications Technology," *Hospitality Research Journal: The Futures Issue*, vol. 17, no. 1, 1993.

"Multimedia and Desktop Video Conferencing," CNBC (Consumer News and Business Channel), October 15, 1993.

Pope, Kyle, "To Whom It May Concern: Electronic Bulletin Boards," *The Wall Street Journal*, November 15, 1993.

Rather, Dan, "Postcard from Shanghai," *CBS Sunday Morning* (Charles Kuralt), CBS, September 12, 1993.

Reader's Digest, "Notes from All Over," September 1990. (Whistling used to communicate in the Canary Islands.)

Russell, C.M., *The Signal Glass*. Oil painting on canvas, 1918, displayed in the National Cowboy Hall of Fame, Oklahoma City.

Wheel of Fortune, CBS, August 23, 1993. (Prize given away on this game show—a picture phone priced at $800.)

Ponte, Lowell, "Dawn of the 'Tiny-Tech' Age," *Reader's Digest*, November 1990.

Schmid, Randy, "U.S., Europe Agree to Mutual Weather Satellite Protection," *The Laramie Daily Boomerang*, August 27, 1993.

Sesno, Frank, and Associates, "TV 2000," CNN, January 2, 1994.

Siegel, Lee, "Mars Observer's Day of Dashed Glory Brings Only Silence from Space," *The Laramie Daily Boomerang*, August 15, 1993.

Tours and interviews, During a visit to England (1991) and Western Europe (1992).

Wofsey, Michael, "Logging On," *The Wall Street Journal*, November 15, 1993. (A guide for the novice: "All it takes is a computer, a modem, and a simple communications program.")

Yankelovich Partners interview, PBS, July 5, 1993. (Discussion on automotive history, including the electric engine.)

Zajas, Jay J.R., *A Comparative Analysis of Interpersonal Communication, Motivation and Leadership Among Chief Executive Officers*. (A Doctoral Dissertation in Business Administration and Management, 1980.)

Zajas, Jay J.R., "Creating a Vision of Excellence as a CEO of a Quality Research University: An Interview with Dr. John M. Lilley." *Career Development International*, Volume 2(1). MCB University Press, 1997, pp. 59-63.

Zajas, Jay J.R., *How to Strategically Plan and Prepare for Business Success.* (The Corporate Management Group, 1997.)

Zajas, Jay J.R., and John M. Lilley, "A CEO's Perspective on Leadership, Values, Vision, and Change: Making the Paradigm Shift to Quality." *Career Development International*, Volume 2(2). MCB University Press, 1997.

SECTION II:
THE COMMUNICATIONS
IN TELECOMMUNICATIONS

One of the central characteristics of human beings is their ability to communicate with each other verbally (when a common language is shared), nonverbally, and symbolically. People must communicate, just as they must find various means to satisfy basic physiological, social, and psychological needs. As space satellites make instantaneous communications possible around the world, we must find ways of understanding each other and appreciating our multicultural differences as well as our human similarities.

Business is often conducted on the basis of the profit motive and with the desire to satisfy key customers' needs as well as to get along with others. Human relations and public relations are addressed when we communicate on behalf of our firm's business.

OBJECTIVES

1. Discuss the major themes in this section and reach a consensus on case studies and learning outcomes.
2. Interview senior citizens and foreigners about the way things were and how they are now in different locales around the globe.
3. Using a database format, enter interview data on your disk and compose a memo to report findings.
4. Participate in oral simulations to demonstrate effective communications, human relations and public relations.
5. Practice using right-brain strategies and whole-brain thinking to "make learning easier and better."
6. Use e-mail, fax, audioconference or compressed video conferences or meetings to continue developing the term project.

Photo 4.1. Purchasing Agent and Sales Rep

At the customer's place of business, the sales rep often calls on and visits with the purchasing agent—the person responsible for placing many sales orders. After getting to know each other in person, many subsequent sales contracts are made by telecommunication methods.

Chapter 4

Communications

Communications is at the heart of telecommunications: Understanding theories of human relations, behavior, and language helps us to communicate. Understanding ourselves and each other is a fundamental part of communications. Understanding who we are, what our purpose is in life, and why we behave as we do is a "by-product" of the communication process. Understanding business and our place in it helps to promote more effective business communications whether they be electronic or in person.

People communicate interpersonally when they use telecommunications as well as in face-to-face (F2F) situations. They communicate their needs, wants, attitudes, and fears. Communication occurs whenever information and/or meaning is exchanged from one person to another.

WHY DO PEOPLE COMMUNICATE?

People communicate for many reasons: to persuade, to inspire, to inform, to understand, and/or to relate to others. In short, people communicate to survive, and, in business, to buy and sell. Communication is as essential to health as food, water, sleep, elimination, breathing, and sex are elemental to human survival.

During the Vietnam War, American prisoners of war (POWs) were held captive for many years in tiny, freezing, roach-ridden cells. Despite their imposed isolation, they invariably found a way to communicate with one another. They used a 5 × 5 grid of 25 letters (C substitutes for K, thus omitting K); e.g.,

A	B	C	D	E	Row 2, letter 2 = G
F	G	H	I	J	Row 3, letter 3 = N
L	M	N	O	P	Row 2, letter 2 = G
Q	R	S	T	U	Row 2, letter 2 = B
V	W	X	Y	Z	MESSAGE: Goodnight, God Bless (GN, GB)

By knocking, with knuckles or pebbles, they communicated in shorthand: Knock 2, pause, knock 2 stands for G, see grid. The North Vietnamese denied the POWs healthy food, lodging, clothing, and every decent basic bodily need, yet they still found a way to communicate! People communicate their basic, social, spiritual, and psychological needs. To fulfill these needs, they teach and learn from others with whom they communicate. Captain Gerald L. Cof-

Photo 4.2. Business Meeting

People must communicate, whether face to face or by electronic means. When people communicate in person, they use nonverbal as well as verbal language. Graphics and other image data also assist businesspeople in presenting and using information.

fee (former POW) reported that the POWs taught each other everything from languages to math, science, literature, history, and so on. To think that such education took place even under the worst living conditions.

Any abbreviated communication system is designed for both speed and efficiency. Symbol shorthand systems allow users to take verbatim notes as they listen to speakers or those who originate messages. See also the description of Morse Code in the "Cave to Satellite" special feature in this section. Another code system is Braille–designed for people who are blind or severely sight-impaired. This code appears as raised symbols on paper so that blind persons can use their sense of touch to feel what they read. People can use a stylus or computer program to record these symbols for the blind. Sight-impaired people can take notes from listening and can communicate on paper or computer with other sight-impaired people. In such ways, modern technology has helped to improve our ability and/or means to communicate with one another.

HOW DO PEOPLE COMMUNICATE?

Oral communication uses nonverbal and facial language as well as words. Written communication uses words, symbols, and formats.

Nonverbal language accounts for about 60 percent of how messages are interpreted by the recipients. Vocal effect, or tone of voice, accounts for another 30 percent, which leaves about 10 percent of the interpretation left to the actual words one uses.

Nonverbal Language

Nonverbal language includes body postures, facial expressions, and gestures made with hands, face, or body. Think of "the five senses" as a quick reminder of the many factors involved in this most predominant of human communication methods. The five senses are sound, touch, smell, taste, and sight. (Recent research findings suggest that we have many more than the five senses with which we are familiar. However, addressing these five will suffice.)

We hear emotions (paralanguage) in the tone of voice. Sometimes the message conveyed in our tone of voice (delivery) is more

Photo 4.3. AT&T VideoPhone 2500

The AT&T VideoPhone 2500 was the world's first motion, full-color videophone that works over existing telephone lines. Customers can take it home, plug it in, and use it. Courtesy of AT&T Archives.

significant than the actual words themselves (content). We hear and translate the meaning of the actual words spoken. We touch objects to get a sense of familiarity—warmth versus cold, rough versus soft, etc. Touching each other can be good or bad, depending on the type of relationship that exists between toucher and touchee, and the desirability of the touch. Between friends and lovers, touching can be expressive and therapeutic; between boss and subordinate, touching may suggest the possibility of a sexual pass; and touching between strangers can be perceived as threatening.

People smell odors and taste flavors, which may evoke positive or negative reactions, depending on our prior experiences and also on each culture's impression of certain things as either good or bad. For example, in a strict religious community, the smell of perfume might be offensive because its use connotes the image of a prostitute. In a meat-and-potatoes community, one may do well to forget about exotic French sauces.

We see everything from gestures and body and facial expressions to clothing and grooming. Situation and place dictate the type of clothing we expect to see as well as the age, occupation, and socio-economic level of the people who make clothing selections. We not only judge others but also judge ourselves on the basis of clothing decisions. Choose the wrong type and style and one feels self-conscious, even stupid.

We see and hear people's behavior and often form first impressions. From these, people formulate generalizations. Research findings suggest that we formulate opinions about people within the first 17 seconds after meeting them! For example, the result of many observations suggests that Caucasians may be more demonstrative in public than Asians. Germans and Native Americans appear to be less publicly demonstrative than Italians and Latins.

Paralanguage (Vocal Effect)

Paralanguage concerns the tone and pitch of voice. Both positive and negative attitudes or emotions are conveyed through the voice. Use a nonverbal communication mode and it will often translate itself into the paralanguage. Smile with both mouth and eyes (facial expression), and the voice radiates warmth and friendliness. Stand up straight, stick out your chest and chin, step out quickly and smartly (body language), and your voice rings with authority and self-confidence. In other words, you can convince your subconscious to believe whatever you consciously choose. Soon, pretense translates subconscious messages into reality. You will not only sound confident, but soon you will also feel and be confident.

Conversely, if you allow yourself to sound nasty, you will soon feel and act nasty. Behave and sound like the schoolyard bully and people will accept your paralanguage messages and behavior as if they are the real you. In time, one can actually become what one thinks about most. This is why it is essential for good organizational and interpersonal health that we maintain positive thoughts and attitudes.

Electronic Communications

Communicating by telecommunication systems may or may not involve all three communication modes—oral, nonverbal, and para-language. Audioconferencing, for example, does not use nonverbal or body language because the communicators cannot see one another. However, since body language influences paralanguage, use positive nonverbal language over the telephone and during audioconferences even when people cannot see you.

Written communication uses words *and* sight, but not paralan-guage. Sight occurs when people see one's documents and formu-late opinions about the appearance and degree of accuracy of docu-ments, whether these are transmitted by hard copy (paper) or electronically (e-mail, facsimile, LAN, WAN, etc.).

Electronic Voice Communications

Businesses and individuals have been keyboarding for so long that it is difficult to imagine its obsolescence. Voice input to the computer is already a reality. (However, technology futurists predict that peo-ple will *continue to edit and manipulate data with keyboard input.*)

Dictating equipment has been on the market for decades and is used by many businesspeople. Typing teachers since the early 1900s have been encouraging people to compose at the keyboard. Yet 85 percent of writers pick up the pen before reaching for the microphone or the keyboard. Now they can use handwriting recog-nition computer software! Nevertheless, voice composition is faster than any other type of input. Oral dictation is therefore a worth-while competency to develop. This is why courses in shorthand, speed writing, dictation, composition, and oral communications are both practical and beneficial.

Photo 4.4.Two People Talking Face to Face

Face-to-face (F2F) conversations prevail in business despite the increasing use of telecommunications, including e-mail. Notice gestures, body posture, and facial expressions whenever people convene to exchange opinions.

Chapter 5

Understanding Ourselves

Humans have more similarities than they do differences, but the differences are interesting because they help to make us unique. Who wants to be lumped together like gravel pebbles in a huge dump truck?

One of the ways to increase an understanding of ourselves is to study human needs. All humans have needs, respond to time and space, and use one or both sides of the brain. However, cultural, gender, religious, and generational characteristics can help to describe some of the ways that humans differ. Human similarities and differences are conveyed to others via the three types of communications previously discussed.

MASLOW'S HIERARCHY OF HUMAN NEEDS

One of the most widely known theories of human needs is found in Abraham Maslow's Hierarchy of Human Needs (See Figure 5.1). Maslow theorized that people must satisfy their human needs on a daily and also on a life span basis. He held that humans are motivated to satisfy "unfulfilled needs." He spent about 20 years studying monkeys and another decade studying humans before formulating his theories. According to Maslow, most people are motivated first by their lower-level needs (basic physiological and safety needs). Because of the prepotency of human needs, Maslow asserted that the vast majority of people strive to fulfill lower-level needs before moving on to satisfy middle- or higher-level needs. He held that in general, only a small percentage of humans (2 percent or less) are truly self-actualized. However, those who are may be

FIGURE 5.1. Diagram of Maslow's Hierarchy of Human Needs

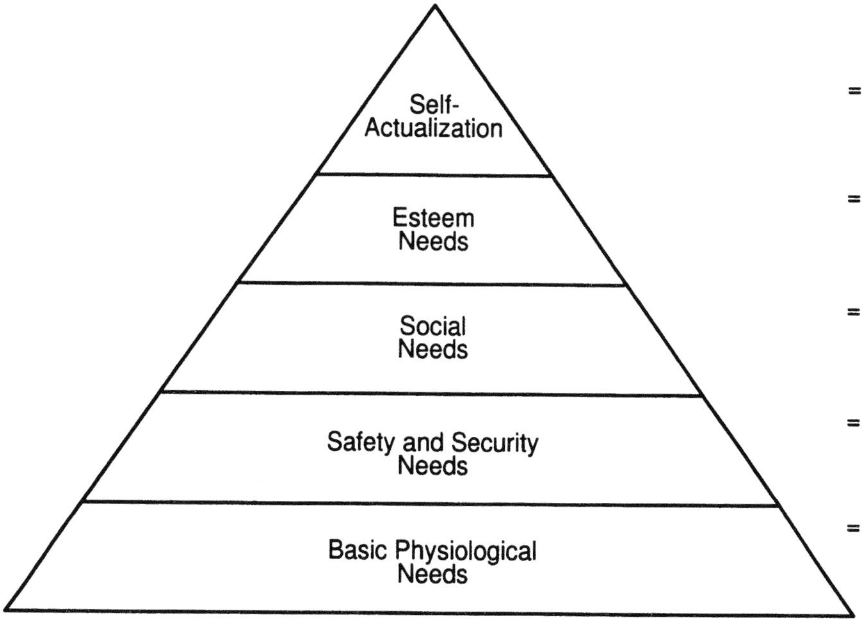

Self-Actualization = the quality or state of being all that one can be; to create, to love, to achieve at best

Esteem Needs = the need for self-respect or self-worth; to be approved and recognized by oneself and significant others

Social Needs = the need for contact and acceptance from others; to communicate, to belong, to touch, or to share

Safety and Security Needs = the need to be safe and protected, including economic and/or job security

Basic Physiological Needs = the need for "the basics," such as, food, water, clothing, shelter, and oxygen able to put off for some time the satisfaction of some lower-level needs. To comprehend how the needs hierarchy can be useful in sending and receiving accurate messages, his theories must be applied to hundreds of situations over time.

Physiological Needs

Physiological needs must be satisfied frequently, normally several times a day (such as the need for oxygen, shelter, and nourishment for the body). People cannot survive without food, water, elimination, clothing appropriate to the climate and season, oxygen, and some sort of shelter from the elements.

Although physiological needs are met mostly with tangible things such as food, tokens, and clothing, psychological and social needs are satisfied through intangible communication methods. These include the nonverbal pat on the back, hugs, smiles, and plenty of affirmation. Frowns, negative physical gestures, and physical violence produce opposite results, such as, fear, hate, resistance, withdrawal, and self-doubt.

Safety Needs

The need to be protected from harm, or to be safe from danger, is a basic human need. Humans need to feel safe. Thus, they seek security from the elements of nature (storms, weather extremes, perils, dangerous creatures, and acts of God). Economic and basic job security also are represented in the need for safety.

Social Needs

Humans also have a need for interaction or contact with other humans, which comes under the subtopic of social needs. Without positive verbal and nonverbal communication, including touch and smiles, some humans turn into strange creatures—amoral, abnormal people without conscience or caring, psychopathic or sociopathic personalities. Research on certain primates showed that when baby monkeys were deprived of touch and social contact with their mothers, they were, in later life, unable to relate socially with other primates. Social interaction, touching, and other nonverbal communication is essential for healthy human development.

Esteem Needs

Esteem is a measure of one's self-respect or self-worth. Self-respect is the result of having one's psychological needs met. These needs are normally satisfied through the approval and recognition of others, such as parents, other family members, neighbors, teachers and others in authority, bosses and preachers, and finally, peers and friends. Thus positive human relations in the workplace are of keen importance to the healthy mental survival of human beings. It is also essential for good organizational health.

People whose higher-level needs predominate often seek careers in which they will shine, through which they can get respect, applause, self-enjoyment, and even pleasure. Think of famous performers, professional athletes, authors, artists, and the like who have continued with their careers until death or at a very old age. When public accolades are of lesser importance to people, whether famous or not, they may retire as soon as they have made their fortunes (provided they have invested wisely so they will have an assured income for life).

Actualization Needs

Another level of human needs is self-actualization. People who feel comfortable with and accepting of themselves, and who are secure in their lifestyles and careers may seem to be functioning at this level, at least part of the time. When one gets so deeply involved in and intense over an issue or topic that all else is temporarily forgotten, sometimes even food and water, sleep and sex, one has become self-actualized.

Some researchers, inventors, professors, entrepreneurs, creators, and social nurturers (e.g., teachers, counselors, preachers, and volunteers) regularly exhibit this intensity of behaviors.

Humans' highest-level needs are seldom achieved by a large percentage of the population. Self-actualized persons are becoming all that they can be, by acts of self-sacrifice, love, service, invention, and/or exemplary accomplishments. Socrates, Aristotle, Plato, Lao-tzu, Cicero, Budda, Jesus Christ, Ben Franklin, William Shake-speare, Thomas Jefferson, Ghandi, Albert Einstein, Winston Chur-chill, Thomas Edison, Smith Wigglesworth, Mother Teresa, Margaret Thatcher, James Michener, Billy Graham, and millions of devoted mothers throughout history are viewed by many as being truly self-actualized leaders. There have been many others.

Age and experience do not necessarily make a difference in whether people are self-actualized. Since acceptance from others is of lesser importance to them, they are typified by lacking knowl-edge of the topics that interest people with dominant social needs—the latest fashions, sports scores, hit records, or movies. They might give little heed to how they look or whether they even appeal to others. We say, "they are all wrapped up in . . ." (whatever).

OTHER TYPES OF HUMAN MOTIVATORS

Sex and Marketing

Notice that while *sex* seems to be a physiological need, it is also a security, social, and psychological need. People often feel warm and secure (basic security need) when they see others looking at them as if they are physically attractive, which is called "sex appeal." With the sex that comes in a loving marital relationship, people feel accepted (social/love need). They may also feel ap-proved of (psychological need). Sex, according to psychologist Dr. Joyce Brothers, is "the language of intimacy"; in other words, a type of bodily expression or communication.

Perhaps sex prevails as a need at almost every human level to ensure that people will reproduce and perpetuate the species. From this perspective, it is not surprising that, as reported in *Advertising Age*, sexual themes, both overt and covert, are represented in 93 to 97 percent of ads and/or advertising campaigns.

Economic Needs

Economic needs are closely allied with the other human needs, since we must obtain the wherewithal (usually money or competencies) that can be exchanged for the goods and services that will meet our several other levels of human needs. Thus, people get jobs that pay salaries and wages–the wherewithal that is needed in order to survive and to help make life just a wee bit interesting.

People who do not want to work for others all their lives may consider several other options, including: (a) start one's own business; (b) invest wisely and retire early to live on the interest earned from those investments (or investments one's parents may have made); (c) take up criminal activity and work at illegal and immoral tasks instead of working at legal and moral tasks; (d) go on welfare; or (e) become a hermit (or leech or borrower).

Even self-actualized people must meet basic bodily needs. They might also need materials and tools with which to accomplish their research or entrepreneurial goals. Thus, they too have economic needs.

TIME AND SPACE

People communicate likes and dislikes and positive and negative messages on the basis of how they use both time and space. People can understand themselves better when they comprehend the significance of these two issues.

Time as a Communicator

Americans put a lot of emphasis on timeliness, whether in keeping appointments or meeting work deadlines. The English place even greater importance on punctuality, manners, and the like. Rank and prestige formerly allowed some leeway, but not necessarily in today's fast-paced climate. The boss (and many physicians) could keep people waiting up to a half hour or longer but underlings generally could not, not without harvesting some negative vibes and losing the company goodwill, if not actual sales.

In some American college classes, students are supposed to wait up to 30 minutes for a (full) professor, 15 minutes for an associate professor, 10 minutes for an assistant professor, and no more than 5 minutes for an instructor. Even today, people seem to expect to be kept waiting for medical doctors. The same sense of timeliness cannot be seen in all cultures. Native Americans and Hispanics may be more tolerant in their willingness to await the arrival of others.

Space as a Communicator

Space communicates in several ways. The larger the office, the more prestige the occupant is perceived as having. For example, having the corner office with windows in some companies is a symbol of power or status. Likewise, the larger the lot, home, work building, the higher the status of those who work and reside therein. The rich expect to have, and can pay for, a lot of space to surround their persons. Thus, they have large estates and houses that are far distant from the roads; passersby might not be able to see these homes at all. Where space (land) is at a premium, the wealthy use trees, creative landscaping, tall walls, or high, sturdy fences to conceal themselves from the public. The latter is typical in crowded countries and cities, e.g., Buckingham Palace in London and mansions of the wealthy in Mazatlan, Mexico.

The need for and use of space also communicates on a person-to-person level. In an elevator, on a crowded city street, and side-by-side in a teleconference, people must bunch up close together. Bad body and mouth odors are offensive. Pushing oneself and one's personal possessions into another person's territory may also offend.

Humans get their sense of space or territory from the bird and animal kingdom. A bird sings to claim the territory around its nest. A coyote urinates around its den to mark off personal territory. At work, one's desk is usually personal territory but at a meeting only a bit of air and table space can be claimed.

Four space zones mark off human relationships and thus affect communications, whether verbal, nonverbal, or paralanguage. They are listed as follows: (1) the intimate zone; (2) the personal zone; (3) the social zone; and (4) the public zone.

The *intimate zone* measures from zero to one-and-a-half feet and is reserved for lovers, family members, and close friends. For others to enter this space may imply a sexual pass or offensive behavior like that of the bully who needs to demonstrate power and control over another. It may also suggest an extreme interest in what another person is whispering. Exceptions, as noted above, are due to crowded conditions or situations in the workplace, such as attending a teleconference.

The *personal zone,* measuring from one-and-a-half to six feet, represents the socially acceptable area for conversation, work, and sitting by strangers in public places (e.g., restaurants). The *social zone*, from six to ten or more feet, exists by choice in uncrowded circumstances (e.g., sparsely occupied cafes, buses, subways, etc.).

The *public zone*, beyond ten feet, is represented by the distance between people attending a public meeting and those in charge (such as at church, civic or political meetings, and so on). Objects and height (e.g., a stage plus podium or pulpit) seem to extend distance under the public space category. Notice how often the front row remains empty in large sessions. If you prefer not to sit in the front row at large meetings, be sure to arrive early so as to be able to choose your seat. People wish to separate themselves from those "in authority"–the people who are in a position to give or withhold approval (Maslow's esteem/self-respect need level).

People who are physically demonstrative are likely to move close to others; they get into personal or even intimate space zones. People from cultures where space and distance are preferred need more personal space. The far end (five to six feet) of this zone is preferred in order to avoid discomfort.

Observing people to identify and analyze behavior patterns can lead to better understanding and thus to better communication patterns. Watch nonverbal communication and paralanguage for clues to reveal people's needs for and use of time and space. Even brain function theories can provide more clues to understanding human communication patterns.

DUAL-BRAIN THEORY

Modern neurological and medical research has shown that the brain has two hemispheres–left and right. The corpus callosum, a small bridge-like membrane, separates the two hemispheres. From over a century of brain research conducted by anthropologists, biologists, neurologists, neurological surgeons, and behavioral scientists, a number of theories have developed and been refined. It appears that most people utilize predominantly one side of their brain for about 90 to 180 minutes before crossing over to the other side. Within these time periods, the left-brain dominant person will prefer activities that utilize the left functions of their brain more so than the right side and vice versa. Whole-brain thinking makes good use of both sides equally, often simultaneously.

Left-Brain Hemisphere

The left side appears to work like a storage vault or computer. Here is where we store most facts and figures. This side of the brain is logical, orderly, mathematical, and/or *sequential*. Data are accessed in sequential fashion, such as going through the entire alphabet from A to Z when looking for Zeus or Zimmerman.

The left hemisphere produces adult, serious, businesslike behaviors. People who are left-brain dominant tend to be less attuned to jokes, childlike behaviors, or even music. While left-brain dominant, people can read, view TV for useable data, study, and engage in a variety of activities that contribute to learning and storing data.

One uses the left brain when conducting a data search for specific information; the individual knows what information is required and seeks that data and no other.

The findings from some anthropological studies suggest that the majority of white males are more likely to be left-brain dominant. Although they still cross over into the right side, they may reserve this side for off-work activities such as sports, sex, and other fun things.

Right-Brain Hemisphere

Because the right hemisphere is creative, it often asks "Why?" "Why not?" and "What if?" questions. The right hemisphere of the brain retrieves information in random order. It also stores data, but as visuals rather than as words or numbers. Thus when conference or seminar notes include diagrams, arrows, stars, etc., it is generally the right brain that stores the pictures. The left stores people's names, the right stores their faces. Meet 4,000 people and you'll have 8,000 or more pieces of information about them cycling around in the brain's storage cells.

From the right side comes creativity, visuals, music, sexual fantasies, and fun or childlike behaviors, as well as the *random* access of data. (The most primitive part of the brain also responds to emotions and sex.) Think about dreams and how much miscellaneous information gets commingled. Bits and pieces pop into play from last night's movie, last week's fight with a lover, a home from ten years ago, childhood scenes, *and* the answer to a puzzle you attempted to solve just before bedtime.

One way to make good use of the right brain is to give it a problem to solve just before bedtime or other rest or recreation period. While the conscious is busy with the present (or, in the case of sleep, in temporary hibernation), the right brain's subconscious goes right on working. Suddenly, the person's name that was elusive or the answer to that puzzle will pop up as clearly as if one had turned on a light—the cartoonist's version of "getting a bright idea."

A clear example of how the right brain retrieves data randomly while the left brain processes data sequentially occurred during an interview with a young woman in Corvallis, Oregon. She had said that she wanted to describe the auto accident that destroyed half of her right brain. She could not describe the accident until she had begun at the beginning, with her birth, and progressed in sequential order through her childhood, adolescence, courtship and matrimony, divorce and mid-adult work life. Interestingly, without the contributions of her right brain, she could not retrieve data randomly.

An example of using the right brain occurs when you use the TV to conduct searches for information. You don't know what you're looking for but your right brain's ability to randomly access and store data means that it will (with *practice*) take note of odds and ends. It's up to you to also use the left brain, or *whole-brain thinking* to remind yourself to take the physical actions that will retain the new data. Pick up pen and paper and record notes. Keep them readily available and use the dictionary and atlas, even the encyclopedia and other references, to verify accuracy and to add to the brief messages obtained from the TV show.

Ideas that come from the right brain's random access of left-brain stored data are often as elusive as dandelion fluff floating on the breeze. So capture them with note taking or a portable (or micro) cassette recorder.

Findings from anthropological studies suggest that the majority of blacks, Latins, Native Americans, and females of any and all races are likely to be right-brain dominants. Although they cross over to the left side, they may not stay there as long as they do on the right side and they also may rely more heavily on the contributions (including intuition and emotions) of the right brain.

Two more examples of left- and right-brain action are the way the typewriter works in comparison with a word processing program on computer. Typing involves starting from the beginning of a page and going to the end with no opportunity to insert or rearrange data. If something is left out, it is necessary to start typing all over again, right from the beginning, as with the girl who had the auto accident that deprived her of right-brain contributions. When using a word processing program at the computer, ideas may be inserted at random, in miscellaneous order. The finished product, however, should be as clear, coherent, and sequential as the left brain can make it.

Whole-Brain Thinking

From some anthropological studies, it appears that Asians, of all the world's peoples, are more likely to be whole-brain thinkers than anybody else. If this is in fact true, perhaps it is true because (a) their civilizations are older than others around the globe and thus they have had more centuries in which to perfect the use of the brain; or, perhaps, (b) because their society and social structure has been more homogenous and less cross-culturalized by other Anglo Saxon people. Nevertheless, in recent years, many Asians have made great strides forward to become world-class competitors in business, science, the arts, and politics.

LEARNING THROUGH WHOLE-BRAIN THINKING

Schools have typically leaned heavily toward left-brain learning. Textbooks and lectures usually list terms and then define them. To reinforce vocabulary studies, glossaries are provided at the back of textbooks. Tests require students to regurgitate facts and figures and many teachers prefer only clear-cut correct answers. Life does not typically work this way.

People learn more when they bring their whole brains into action. When they are made to *feel*, they engage emotions or the contributions of the right brain. (They "feel" emotions, as opposed to thinking thoughts). The *Reader's Digest* has long employed this strategy in capturing the reader's attention. A factual article about 10 million starving people in China does not start with the left-brain presentation of facts and figures but rather with the right-brain's visual imagery and emotional stimulators. The first two to four paragraphs of the article will feature one small, lonely, impoverished, sorrowful child with an injured body and hurt feelings who is in need of the reader's compassion and help.

> Notice the number of adjectives in the above statement; those that stimulate the imagination are of right-brain origin. How many textbooks use right-brain adjectives, adverbs, and verbs to get attention and allow one to learn with the imagination?

A Recipe for Remembering

Repetition is at the heart of learning and reinforces the storage of data in the brain so that it can be retrieved when needed, even years or decades later. But repetition does not mean storing data in the same way; rather, we must use many many "filing" techniques. To ensure that data is firmly and correctly stored, use all, not just one, of the following learning methods:

- Take notes manually, using outline format plus arrows and stars, bold and underlines. (Taking notes in outline form is logical and sequential, a left-brain skill. Taking physical action of manual writing is a right-brain function. Diagrams and visuals go into the right hemisphere.)
- When listening to lectures, organize what is being said into a logical and sequential order or outline (left brain). Since we can think at the rate of about 650 words a minute and speakers speak at the rate of only 200 to 250, use the gap between these two to insert personal experiences (right brain).

- Read from the print media, including library and news sources, references, business and government pamphlets, and the notes of team members (left brain). Use a highlighter to alert you visually to special items (right brain).
- View TV and movies and conduct human interviews to capture the stories and experiences of real people who *feel* (right brain) as well as *think* (left brain). This is a dual-brain activity, which will stimulate you to *feel*, to think, to care, and to learn.
- Enter notes and items from readings and highlighting into a computerized database, using a sequential—alphabetical or numerical—system (left brain). Add experiences from TV and human resource interviews and your own background to make each item memorable (right brain).
- Develop a portfolio that includes pictures and graphics (right brain), silly and dramatic stories (right brain), and facts and figures (left brain). Even if you never again refer to this scrapbook/portfolio, it appears that the right brain can "take a photograph" of any document that includes visuals. The right brain will be able to randomly select data later as needed.
- Discuss with a group the interpretation and use of the materials in your database and portfolio, including case studies (whole brain). Participate in role plays and simulations in order to integrate facts and feelings (whole brain).

A Recipe for Caring

When people feel for others and care about society, they may have reached self-actualization. When people really care, they really learn. It is important that we really care about others. If a person gets out of their own skin and life, they discover how much is interesting in the world around them and in the lives of others, both living and deceased.

In a segment of an *Andy Griffith Show* rerun, young Opie Taylor and friends decried the study of history. "It's boring and stupid," they told the teacher as an excuse for neglecting their reading assignment. Sheriff Andy Taylor gathered the boys around and, in storyteller fashion, made the lesson of Paul Revere sound as though it had happened yesterday, right in Mayberry. Andy then suggested that the boys form their own "Minute Man Club," and "be ready

Photo 5.1. Woman Using the Telephone

Maintaining positive human relations with co-workers and goodwill with outsiders is easier when we understand our human similarities as well as the differences that make us unique.

with the answers in a minute" in seeing who could learn the most, the best, and the fastest.

Andy captured their attention by making history come alive with imagery. The boys were also as keen on *competing* with others as they were about *cooperating* with each other.

GENDERS, CULTURES, AND GENERATIONS

There are differences (as well as similarities) between the genders—female and male—between and among cultures, and between and among generations. Certain traits and behaviors differentiate humans from primates, males from females, young from old, and people of different races and nationalities. If we couldn't tell the difference (differentiate) between and among people, we might as well all have been cloned from an android. It is often our differences that make us interesting because they are unique.

A majority is a mere 51 percent. When people say "typically" or "characteristically," they usually mean a simple majority.

Gender and Multicultural Differences

The Price is Right TV show demonstrates some distinct differences between female and male behaviors when contestants win. Females typically squeal and jump up and down, clap their hands and hug the host; these are right- not left-brain characteristics. When startled, females are also apt to scream or squeal.

Characteristically, white males and Asians (both male and female) appear to be less demonstrative, more serious, more left-brain dominant. They shake hands with the game show host rather than hugging him. Win or lose, they keep the display of emotions under control.

Males, typically, are larger in weight and frame size with bigger muscles; women, characteristically, are smaller and softer; moreover, their skin is often thinner. So should women take only white-collar jobs and professions and men stick to manual labor or blue-collar jobs? Both females and males have functioning brains and both have some manual dexterity skills. With the sophisticated technology that makes operating heavy machinery and equipment easy, maybe it doesn't matter who does what.

Marketers and telemarketers have a hard time keeping up with the changing times (refer to the case study in Activity II-9) and thus with making decisions about how to best pitch the advantages of their products. Women no longer take full responsibility for home management; both genders make home decisions. Men no longer take full responsibility for financial management; both genders are often knowledgeable (or not) and prepared (or disinterested) in making both short- and long-term financial decisions. In many societies, the traditional male and female roles are gradually disappearing.

However, in the workplaces of the industrialized nations, where traditional sex roles dominate, left-brain-originated procedures and behaviors are quite often the norm, not the exception. What would happen if other types of procedures and behaviors were the norm (a right-brain type of "What if?" question)?

Fun research on the topic of gender differences may be conducted by reading the comic strip, *Cathy*, by cartoonist Cathy Guisewite. She seems to have a good understanding of gender differences.

Technology and the Global Village

What changes, if any, are likely to occur in any and all societies as a result of efficient high-speed transportation and televised communications that make knowledge of other cultures possible? What gender, multicultural, and generational behavioral changes will be taking place in workplaces throughout the world as a result of technological innovations?

In the majority of world cultures (including in the male-managed "Homeboy" street gangs), men are considered superior to women. Men are the decision makers and women come second. Females do as they are told, in public at least, where they exhibit subservience. Males also dominate in Middle Eastern and Asian cultures where women are often relegated to secondary status.

When Hilary Clinton, American First Lady and attorney, visited Japan, some Japanese were disturbed. Others, particularly women, were challenged by Mrs. Clinton's achievements and the opportunities that America extends to its women via laws, social mores, and business practices. With TV, people all over the world watched Mrs. Clinton interact with women and men in Japan. When Margaret Thatcher served as the Prime Minister in England, all the world had ample opportunity to view her leadership and effectiveness as a great female politician.

A TV show of the 1970s, *All that Glitters*, switched male and female roles. The world wasn't ready for that yet. However, in addition to Margaret Thatcher's service as Prime Minister in Britain, there have been many women who have faithfully served their countries in civic, political, and official capacities (Sandra Day O'Connor, Jean Kilpatrick, Elizabeth Dole, Eleanor Roosevelt, and many others). How long do you think it will take before Americans elect a female president?

Technology changes frequently. If technology changes, why not social customs? Are we likely to adopt practices and procedures from one another? When AT&T commenced negotiations to purchase McCaw Cellular Communications (MCC), conservative AT&T executive Alex J. Mandl, who normally wears a suit and tie, showed up wearing jeans and a polo shirt. He did this to show his willingness to observe the more "informal corporate culture" of MCC. But it was the wrong time and place. Craig O. McCaw and his entourage filed into the room wearing gray suits! Maybe the accepted business dress code will someday be cut-off jeans and orange and green punk hairstyles or saris and turbans. To further assess how social customs do change over time, compare the average attire of public school students today with those teenagers who attended public school in the 1940s and 1950s. You'll see quite a difference.

Asians and Native Americans are characterized as having well-controlled emotions. Japanese are characterized as practicing courtesy at all times; they are extremely polite. Perhaps everybody should follow these examples. Why not bow or "high five" instead of shake hands? In Hollywood, it would appear from TV shows, men hug each other. In France, it is not uncommon to see "straight" men holding hands, hugging, or even kissing each other in public. In many other cultures, however, this would be taboo. Will we see changes in such gestures as these in business?

Technology has brought us closer together. We get a front-row seat to observe each other's cultures and practices. In addition to exploring the customs and people from foreign countries, courses in multicultural studies include understanding the many cultures within one's own country. Social customs differ because of race and nationality or ethnic background, geographical location, size of community (rural, small town, suburban and urban), occupation, genders and generations, amount of and type of education, and socioeconomic class.

Marketers must understand cultural differences in order to target their products to all these different types of people. Marketing and telemarketing campaigns must be pitched in a manner that will satisfy the needs of each group in each market niche. The underlying discipline of study is sociology—the study of people and how they act as a result of membership in all their different groups (see some group identifiers, in the previous paragraph).

Generational Differences

Sociologists have accurately described differences between and among the generations. They have also reported gender differences through our various passages or life cycles. People in their twenties are typically said to be occupied with finishing degrees, establishing their careers, marrying, and starting families. People in their thirties are often characterized as career achievers and parents of young children and teens, single and swinging, or single and nervously looking. People in their forties and fifties are often described as the movers and shakers. Their children are growing or grown and gone, their investments established, and they concentrate on managing affairs at work and in government–local, state, national, international. (Or they have failed dismally at some one or more things and are getting divorced and getting fired and starting over at everything!)

In recent decades, the teenage market was the most lucrative for discretionary products. Few adolescents pay for rent, utilities, food, and insurance. However, many teens work one, two, even three part-time jobs to get the money to pay for commercial entertainment and to buy all their stuff–*discretionary products*. During adolescence, adult hormones explode and sometimes run wild like a rampant river. These energies must have an outlet, such as through loud music, athletics, vigorous dancing, rambunctious parties, and so on.

People are living longer than they used to. Willard Scott, one-time weather man on NBC's *Today Show*, acknowledged the birthdays of people over 100 years old.

A 64-year-old grandmother enjoyed playing computer games and jumping on the trampoline with her grandchildren, who told her she was a lot more fun than their other grandmothers. The 64-year-old laughed and replied, "You're talking about your *great*-grandmothers; they're in their nineties!" It is as silly to lump everybody over retirement age together as it is to group infants with 35-year-olds. The "older citizen" of today represents a big market, as important as the teenage market, and one that marketers and telemarketers are exploiting in marketing their products. Old-timers have needs at all levels, even if they don't talk about them.

Seniors have many needs at the top two levels—self-actualization and esteem. Few of them appreciate the current American informality of calling people by their first names before getting permission. Last names only, please! In some countries (such as Great Britain), it is a common practice to use last names in one's business dealings. For more on the interaction of the young with the old, read "Dennis the Menace" cartoons, by Hank Ketcham, or see the movie by the same name with Walter Matthau.

Senior citizens, once known as "old-timers," like to talk about "how things were back in my day." Obviously, if they are still alive, then today is their day too. But by "my day," most people mean those formative years when they were children and teens. Then the world seemed stable and children—then as now—long to grow up and take their place in it. What they—and most of the rest of us—don't realize is that the world is always changing. The technology prevalent yesterday is no longer the norm today and will also be gone or have been revised before many more moons have passed. Change is a constant.

Chapter 6

Workplace Applications

Technology has revolutionized the way things are done in both the business and domestic workplaces, but technology itself has not changed people's needs. Technology may make work easier or more efficient but it alone does not improve communications and understanding between and among people. To enhance communications and understanding of people in the workplace, one does well to study human relations and public relations in business. Human relations and public relations address the human factor, leading to the study of the underlying psychological and sociological theories that make the comprehension of humans possible. (If your career path takes you into marketing or management, you will need this competency.)

HUMAN RELATIONS

Human relations deals with how people interact, communicate, and get along in the workplace, whether co-workers, workers and supervisors, or company people and outsiders. When people have difficulty communicating, conflicts can arise. Conflict resolution occurs as people mutually endeavor to understand themselves and others, acknowledge their differences as well as similarities, and pledge to work together to apply the five Cs of good communication: courtesy, clarity, completeness, correctness, and conciseness.

Two other C words—cooperation and competition—also enter the human relations formula. *Cooperation* comes from practice in working together and depending on one another. A CNN news show (July 1993) described a corporate personnel training program that sent people outdoors to take physical risks toward human sur-

Photo 6.1. Three-Member Conference

Finding ways to resolve conflicts, solve problems, make effective choices, and get along with and help others are some of life's challenges. In business today, team and committee members often work together cooperatively to solve problems and collaborate on possible solutions.

vival. Like basic training in the military, in the police, and in sports, wherever people are forced into cooperative endeavors to facilitate their very survival, they often develop trust. In developing the Internet, hundreds and thousands of people needed to cooperate with each other to establish networks, to forge electronic interrelationships, and to explore innovative ways to build alliances from Internet sites across the globe. The willingness to risk and to overcome adversity are often common bonds in such cooperative endeavors.

Competition is frequently derived from a need to survive. On the trails leading west and in the early settlements, settlers competed for land that was suitable for agricultural use and located close to roads, railways, and water. On the wagon trains heading west, people competed with each other for the best place in line (safety). Men often competed with each other for the attention of the women, and vice versa.

Today, cities compete to get industries to open businesses and to relocate to their area (see Case Study 2 in Section I) and to get awards for "best this" and "best that." Countries compete with each other to get more land, resources, and power among world nations and more and better arms to protect their own citizens. Everybody competes to get jobs, houses, mates, and opportunities for children. People compete to get promotions and raises in order to survive and protect themselves, their mates, and their children. Because of the most basic of economic principles, *scarcity*, people must invariably compete in order to survive.

Businesses compete to get customers, make sales, clear a profit in order to survive, create jobs, and pay wages to employees. Job applicants compete for jobs and employees compete for better jobs, higher wages, better offices, and so on. In their homes, people compete to "keep up with the Jones'," to buy more and better things and to get the latest technological devices to make life easier and to be "in the know," or "up on things."

It is hard to cooperate and be nice to people, when you must also compete and work diligently in order to survive and protect what is yours and your family's. Finding ways to resolve conflicts, solve problems, make effective choices, and to get along with and help others are some of life's challenges and are addressed in any comprehensive study of human relations.

PUBLIC RELATIONS

Public relations is the image that people project to outsiders about their company, country, home, family, personal reputation, and the like. They promote ideas, products, and themselves. People running for political office seek to garner votes. Preachers, teachers, philosophers, and authors seek to communicate their ideas and get others to agree with them.

Businesses promote products, quality service, and customer goodwill. *Goodwill* is the positive feeling that people have about a business, its services, and its products.

TELECOMMUNICATIONS AND PROMOTION

Sitting alone at the computer in the back room of a company or from the telecommuting workstation in your home may seem as far removed from your fellow passengers on planet earth as you can get. But it isn't. You reach people from your fingertips or across telephone lines. At the other end of your documents or voice are people with many of your same needs. The differences evident from group characteristics are few compared to human similarities. We have feelings, so do others. We hurt, so do they. We can care, so will they. Think people, people's needs, communication, and mutual understanding, and no matter the type of telecommunication devices used, you will do a better job for others and yourself as well as for your company.

What Do You Think?
Review and Opinions

1. Why is it important to understand communication principles as a part of telecommunications? For example, discuss the impact on telecommunications of nonverbal language and paralanguage. With audioconferencing or telephoning, where words and paralanguage (not sight) prevail, why should one observe nonverbal language?
2. Share personal, work, or school experiences to demonstrate the application of Maslow's human need levels. How do you use your own brain—left-, and right-, and whole-brain thinking? In what ways has your knowledge of human relationships helped you to get along with others at home or in the workplace?
3. Compare your beliefs and experiences with examples in the section about gender, generational, and/or cultural differences. Highlight and discuss findings. In what ways does it help for us to understand our similarities and differences?
4. Given that technology has seemingly brought the world's business markets and people closer together and given that technology and customs are always changing, how can you apply this section's concepts? In your response, use examples that apply in the workplace. For example, how can you help to improve human relations and public relations for your company? In what ways has modern technology improved your or your company's ability to communicate and conduct business?

From Cave to Satellite

Alexander Graham Bell (1847-1922) was born in Edinburgh, Scotland, and immigrated to Canada and then to New England. Inventor of the telephone in 1876, he founded the Bell Telephone Company in 1877. His telephone was the first electrical transmission of speech by an apparatus. Emma Nutt was the first telephone operator—employed in 1877.

For 75 years—from 1877 through the 1960s—young women aspired to follow in Emma's footsteps. A telephone operator's job was considered to be nearly as glamorous as flying the skies as stewardesses; they could communicate with people all over the world!

Direct dialing by each caller had not yet been invented. You picked up the phone and a live operator came on the line with "Number, please," and then she (females dominated this career field) made the connection for you. However, with the rapid increase in telephone traffic, an automated system was necessary. Otherwise, in the United States alone, millions of telephone operators would be needed to successfully handle all the calls placed in this country alone!

A more recent change in telephone operations replaced 3,000 operators with voice-recognition machines. This decision saved AT&T about $200 million annually in operator wages. Notice when you try to reach an operator that you are likely to get an automated voice directing you to "Press 1 for . . . , press 2 for . . . ," etc.

Bell also invented the audiometer, the first hearing aid. Today hearing-impaired people can get an amplifier attached to the listening end of the telephone instrument so they can hear. Some semi-deaf people who use this device prefer to talk to their friends *only* over the telephone.

Samuel Morse (1791-1872), an inventor and artist, invented telegraphy, a system of coded communication—dots and dashes or short and long sounds or signals—that traveled over telegraph lines.

The code represented words, letters, and numbers. The international (or continental) code has been adapted from the original, especially for use in radiotelegraphy. Marchese Marconi (1874-1937), a physicist, developed wireless telegraphy and received the first intercontinental telegraph message.

Telegraph lines were installed along the railroad rights of way (late 1800s), an example of the link between communications and transportation. Still another example is how rural businesspeople—farmers and ranchers—used the systems: they placed buy-and-sell orders for their crops and livestock by telegraph and then shipped by rail.

In the mid- to late-1800s, poor ole Charley Soles is credited, in part, with the invention of the typewriter, which at one point resembled a grand piano and at another a foot-treadle sewing machine! He was called "Poor ole Charley," because in the 50 years it took him to improve and market the typing machine, beginning in the 1860s, Soles lost his job, his wife, his home, his health, and finally, the patent to his machine to a large gun manufacturer. The reason that today's keyboard is so impractical is that Charles purposely mixed up the letters to "slow down the typing," since he could not seem to prevent the tangling of keys when typing fast. The machine was called a typing machine and the *people* who used them were originally called "typewriters."

Just as court reporters now take their own shorthand machines with them, the female "typewriters" in the early 1900s applied for office jobs armed with their own typing machines. Until then, men, not women, worked in offices as clerks, scribes, stenographers, bookkeepers, and secretaries. Women, the men presumed, would "want to dust, bring in flowers, and get rid of spittoons."

In the early 1970s, Steven Jobs, then about 21 years old, saw the commercial potential in Stephen Wozniak's easy-to-use small desktop computer that represented a marriage between the typewriter and the much larger computers of the period. The two friends raised $1,300 from the sale of Jobs' old Volkswagen and Wozniak's Hewlett-Packard scientific calculator and thereafter began their company on the dining room table and in the garage. With a quarter-million-dollar investment from A. C. Markkula (a former Intel marketing manager) who later helped to raise millions more, the

Apple Computer Company was born. Five years later, at the age of 26, Jobs' assets were valued at over $29 million dollars. With the emergence of such technology, the age of personal computers was launched!

A lot of new telecommunication, transportation, and electronic businesses have been launched from back rooms, back yards, and garages. To launch the American auto industry, Henry Ford worked with bicycles in a garage, while Olds and Bridger began their manufacturing industries in a shed. The young electronic experts, Hewlett and Packard, also began their innovations in a garage. The Wright brothers experimented in a garage before taking their flying machines into the air.

Western Air Express began operation in 1926 on the West Coast as an airmail service. In 1929, it carried nearly 22,000 passengers, who were required to wear coveralls, goggles, and helmets and to sit on folding seats on top of the mail sacks. Today, at many ranches around the world, modern "cowpilots" oversee their cattle operations from the air; to do so they own and navigate their own planes.

Humans get a lot of ideas for inventions from the animal kingdom. Several scientific studies have sought to discover how homing pigeons can get home. Some radar and laser inventions have grown out of such curiosity. (However, nobody has yet figured out how pigeons do it! And they have been flying home from great distances since before humans lived in caves!)

Several World War II pilots, reluctant to leave the air, took to crop dusting and then to founding commercial airlines; for example, Continental and the now defunct Frontier Company. Douglas, the founder of the McDonnell-Douglas aircraft and spaceship manufacturing company, got his start with nothing but a drafting board and writing tools in the backroom of a barbershop.

Men were not the only early flyers; women too have made a name for themselves in the air. Amelia Earhart's round-the-world flight, funded by Purdue University at a cost of $80,000, was a renowned pilot. Airmail pilot Katherine Stinson carried the mail by air in 1918 from Washington, DC to New York City soon after Western Air Express began. WASPS (Women Air Service Pilots) ferried fighter planes across both the Pacific and the Atlantic for delivery at the front lines. Other female flyers ferried supplies. At that time, however, women received no recognition, no military benefits, and no thanks. They proudly served, bonding with each other. Recently, Kelly Hamilton Barlow flew a tanker refueler during the Gulf War, with all benefits and due recognition and gratitude that her male counterparts received.

Besides the U.S. and foreign postal systems, there are private mail carriers. Federal Express, started by entrepreneur Fred Smith in the 1970s, also merged communications and transportation. People send and receive their documents and packages, which travel by thousands of trucks and hundreds of planes to and from over 90,000 pickup stations in the United States to the nearest airport. From these locations, all of their planes fly to Memphis for overnight processing and rerouting back to delivery points throughout the United States. Radio transmissions and computers with colored graphics to plot records track items in transit, made possible with bar codes stamped on the packages.

Planes must arrive in Memphis by 11 p.m. and leave by 1 a.m. to keep on schedule and keep up to the firm's promise of ". . . when it must absolutely positively get there overnight." During this two-hour window of time, workers in a 16-acre warehouse conduct electronic sorting operations, which works much like a telephone central switching system.

A dozen professional meteorologists advise air traffic operators on the weather and flight patterns. Fred Smith, CEO of FedEx, got his business idea in college when he observed the rapid changes in electronics and the equally rapid increase in the needs of people for fast deliveries.

Boeing's 777, put into flight in the mid-1990s, comes with a variety of customer services. From their seats, passengers can play video games, make catalog purchases by phone, and connect their laptop computers to the plane's telecommunications system. The 777 model airplane was designed entirely with the use of computer-generated designs—unlike the first airplane designed by the founder of the McDonnell-Douglas corporation, who simply used a drafting board.

Scientists dreamed of "seeing by telegraph" as early as the 1870s, but television was not launched until 1926, in London, by John Logie Baird. Television works by scanning a scene in lines and transmitting them in sequence as radio signals. The lines flash on the receiving screen so fast that the eye sees them as one picture. Since 1945, TV has become as important to communications as printing. Today, television makes it possible to link every nation with instant worldwide news, sports, weather, and entertainment coverage. Around-the-clock sports and headline news coverage is provided by such networks as C-Span, ESPN, TBC, Fox News, the BBC, and CNN.

With the passage of the Telecommunications Act of 1996 and the lifting of laws that formerly prohibited telephone companies from providing TV services and vice versa, a merging of these two major telecommunication systems should occur by the year 2000. It is beyond the imagination of most of us to predict what the twenty-first century will bring.

Activities for Section II

ACTIVITY II-1: CONDUCT COMPARATIVE INTERVIEWS

Name: _____ Date: _____

Background

Oral history is informal, personalized history. It is learned through visiting with and listening to old-timers talk about things the "way they were." With people from other cultures (foreign and domestic), we can learn about how things differ, right now, from our own experiences.

Read every Cave to Satellite section in this book before constructing interview questions. Technological background, both historical and present-day, will help you sound and feel more knowledgeable.

When interviewing seniors, ask about technological differences but don't forget the human and social implications. For example, how did they use radio as an information medium? What was it like to be on a party line, where eight or so other families could listen in on each other's private conversations?

Make clear comparisons between technology and the impact of telecommunication and transportation systems on social norms and how people live–both at work and at home.

Review the subtopics under "Understanding Ourselves" to get ideas about the interaction and interdependency of technology with social norms and habits. The social implications to be addressed should be those that occur(ed) primarily in the workplace but also in the home and in social groups to give you a feeling about "how things were."

Both types of interviews–with old-timers and with people who differ from you because of foreign or cultural reasons–are designed to help you develop human resources and to gather data from personal contacts. Like the POWs held captive for so many years in North Vietnam, we live with and learn from each other.

Directions

1. Meet in your groups. Select new management personnel—supervisor, recorder, and processor. The procedures for cooperative activities are the same as described in Section I. The supervisor leads discussion to reach consensus on the procedures to be used and the questions to be asked in the interviews.

2. Decide how to locate human resources for the two types of interviews. Start with personally known individuals—grandfathers and great-grandmothers, foreign students on campus, and business owners who represent ethnic differences. Other sources for old-timers are senior citizen living communities, and nursing homes. See also foreign exchange students and foreign or ethnic student organizations on college campuses.

3. Designate partnership teams to conduct the interviews. Each partnership, consisting of two to three people, conducts two interviews to collect comparative—similar and different—data.

4. Use the blanks to record notes and finalize the interview questionnaires.

Notes About Old-Timer (Seniors) Interviews and Questionnaires

Notes About Foreigner/Cultural Interviews and Questionnaires

5. The recorder summarizes the discussion and submits the notes to the supervisor. The supervisor directs the processor in preparing formal interview questionnaire forms.

6. The supervisor edits, approves the final copy, and transmits to the instructor a print copy of each questionnaire.

7. The instructor may recommend changes to questionnaires or procedures. When the instructor approves the revised questionnaire, you may proceed with the interviews according to the time line designated. It may be advisable to take an audiocassette recorder with you to record the interviews to save you from taking copious amounts of notes.

ACTIVITY II-2: PARTNERSHIPS–SKILL DEVELOPMENT AT THE COMPUTER

Name: _____ Date: _____

Directions

1. You will be summarizing your findings from the interviews you have conducted with senior citizens (old-timers). For the sake of convenience, you may wish to record your information in a separate category from your interviews with foreign students, people in business, and/or people on campus who represent multicultural backgrounds. (Optional: Use a typewriter if you do not have access to a computer and a word processing program.)

2. If you have access to a LAN, either on campus or at a business facility (see the tour activity in Section I), you and your partner may share information via the computer. (Otherwise, photocopy and share print materials.) Divide the input and composition in one of two ways: (1) one partner works only with old-timer data and the other partner works with foreign student/multicultural data; or (2) each partner works with one interview per document–one old-timer and one foreign/multicultural interview.

3. Compose in your own words the results of the interviews, describing what you learned and what surprised you most. You may want to list findings and then prioritize them in an outline form. Use the language correctly, verifying the accuracy of grammar, punctuation, spelling, and word choice. If you and your partner are working on a LAN, check each other's work through the system rather than by printout and in person. If no LAN is available, you may print, exchange printouts or photocopies, edit, revise, and so on. The result is that each partnership has the same copy of both compositions.

4. Share your notes and other information from your compositions with others in your group. Do this via the LAN or by printing and distributing duplicate copies to each group member. These reports should be retained in the individual portfolios.

5. The leadership personnel from all groups meet to summarize procedures and reach consensus on the most salient findings from

each report. The processor copies the MEMOHEAD (shell document) and composes a memo stating procedures and key outcomes, which are taken from the leader's notes. This memo is directed to the instructor, from the group, and is photocopied and distributed to group members.

6. Use the blanks below *before* your group leader meets with the other leaders. Individually list the key outcomes that you want the leadership team to consider when summarizing interviews. Share such outcomes with others in your group when you meet at a convenient time and place.

_____

_____

_____

_____

_____

_____

_____

_____

_____

_____

_____

_____

_____

_____

_____

_____

_____

_____

ACTIVITY II-3: DICTATE AND EVALUATE
PARALANGUAGE WITH A PARTNER

Name: _____ Date: _____

Background

You are an irate customer. You originally called a computer repair operator to make a house call to check your home laser printer. It wasn't working and you couldn't find the problem. She came and repaired the printer. However, she was there only 15 minutes and charged you $89. (This is her hourly rate, which she charges for anything from 1 to 59 minutes, because she "has to drive across town.") You are upset about the cost but mostly you are angry that she left greasy handprints on the desk and muddy footprints on your new carpet. The computer repair operator's business is a one-person operation (*sole proprietorship*). Instead of answering machine or answering service, she uses voice mail. You know that with this kind of system, you can talk for several minutes, so you decide to plan your complaints in detail.

Directions

1. Use the spaces below to compose a two- to three-minute message that you plan to dictate into a voice mail system. Use the language correctly (no obscenities, please). Speak clearly so your message can be understood—especially figures and proper nouns; e.g., your name, telephone number, address, and the price of the repair service.

_____
_____
_____
_____
_____
_____

_____

_____

_____

2. If you have access to a recorder or dictating machine, dictate your message. If not, meet with a partner, turn your backs to each other, and then rotate the reading of your messages. Express emotions via the paralanguage selected to accurately portray your feelings. Be ready to change moods, though. You might decide to start off polite and get gradually more distraught or to demonstrate the reverse. A range of emotions should be evident in your voice.

3. If you and your partner are using a recorder, each partner should listen to the other's voice in privacy. If no electronic device is available, take notes while listening to your partner dictate (with back turned to you). Use the spaces below to record notes while listening:

_____

_____

_____

_____

_____

_____

_____

_____

4. From your notes, evaluate the message that you listened to. Use the form that follows. Hold this form until the end of Section II.

EVALUATION CHECKLIST

Voice Mail Message Dictated by Partner

1. The paralanguage demonstrated the following emotions, as evidenced from the following type of sound signals:

Emotions Evident	*Sound Signals (Paralanguage)*

2. Evaluate the message on the basis of the five Cs, using the +, ✔, – method, where + = outstanding, ✔ = satisfactory or average, and – = poor/unsatisfactory.

   a. The message was *clear* (easy to hear)   _____

   b. The message was *complete*   _____

   c. The message was (eventually) *courteous*   _____

   d. The message was *correct* (see background)   _____

   e. The message was *concise*   _____

3. The message was incorrect, as follows: (Fill in the correct choice after each error, whether grammatical or word choice.)

Incorrect Word Choice or Grammar	*Correct Choice*

ACTIVITY II-4: BUILDING GOODWILL (PR)
IN A TELEPHONE MESSAGE

Name: _____   Date: _____

Directions

1. Take the role of the computer/printer repair operator who received the above call (Activity II-3) when checking his/her voice mailbox (use your own correct gender). Compose a reply, based on the assumption that you will get the customer's answering machine and have a mere 60 seconds to state your position clearly, accurately, and courteously.

2. Use the blank lines that follow to outline or compose your message. (No matter whether you would ordinarily and personally get angry about such a call, remember that you are a sole proprietor, in business to get and keep customers.) Think positive human and public relations.

_____

_____

_____

_____

_____

_____

_____

_____

_____

3. Dictate the reply into a recorder or dictating machine or by turning your back to your partner and rotating the reading of your reply messages.

4. Evaluate the reply on the basis of the five Cs and the ability to get and maintain goodwill (PR) for your business. Hold this form to submit to the instructor until you have completed all activities in the unit.

EVALUATION CHECKLIST

Telephone Reply Message to Promote Positive Human Relations

Directions

Use the +, ✔, − evaluation method, where + = outstanding, ✔ = average/satisfactory, and − = poor/unsatisfactory.

1. The choice of words, as follows:

   a. correct grammar   _____

   b. correct word choice   _____

   c. little or no slang   _____

   d. sentence structure   _____

   e. message made sense   _____

COMMENTS:

_____

_____

_____

2. The paralanguage style, as follows:

   a. pleasant, friendly   _____

   b. loud enough to hear   _____

   c. enunciated clearly   _____

   d. sounded in good mood _____

COMMENTS:

_____

_____

_____

ACTIVITY II-5: COMPOSING MESSAGES AND DICTATING

Name: _____ Date: _____

Background

Voice-activated computers represent another emerging and future trend. Imagine not keyboarding but dictating orally to enter data. Composing at the keyboard, as opposed to typing from print or script copy, is one competency; dictating is quite another composition competency. Without keyboards, we would be inputting everything to the computer by dictating.

Despite all of the technology, the findings from research studies conclude that about 85 percent of all materials are originated via handwriting. This figure may decrease as more executives and document originators become skilled at the keyboard. Yet, oral or dictation technology has been around for many decades and yet documents are still prepared by the manual method. With this activity, you will practice composing documents orally.

Directions

1. Use a dictation machine or recorder or dictate live to a partner.

2. Optional topics: the subject of your oral composition is taken from any of the topics discussed in this section (such as the importance of good human relations or effective oral communication). Enhance the topic by describing some related experiences that you, a classmate, a friend, or a family member have also had on this topic.

3. Play back your composition (or ask your partner to read it back to you) and make changes if they seem advisable. Dictate over the spots that you wish to correct or ask your partner to make changes in the original dictation.

4. Exchange cassettes or tapes with a partner. Listen to and make recommendations to your partner for improvement. Use the spaces below to record your recommendations:

_____

_____

_____

_____

_____

_____

_____

_____

_____

_____

_____

_____

_____

_____

_____

_____

_____

_____

_____

_____

_____

5. *Optional.* If you have access to a transcriber and time permits, transcribe the composition that your partner dictates. This requires that you keyboard the document. Then you may exchange hard copy printouts with each other to use for editing and evaluation.

ACTIVITY II-6: COOPERATIVE LEARNING–
CASE DISCUSSION

Name: _____ Date: _____

Directions

1. Keep the same leadership personnel–supervisor, recorder, and processor. Read the following cases before meeting with your group and add notations that represent your individual opinions.

2. Under the supervisor's leadership, the group discusses the cases toward reaching consensus. The supervisor directs the recorder in taking notes and summarizing ideas as the group reaches agreement.

3. The processor accesses MEMOHEAD from the disk and composes a memo–addressed to the instructor from the group–based on the recorder's summary of conclusions.

4. The supervisor proofreads the memo and makes recommendations, if any, for changes. The supervisor photocopies the final memo copy and submits the original to the instructor and a copy to each group member for inclusion in the individual portfolios.

5. The supervisor proofreads the memo and makes recommendations, if any, for change. The supervisor photocopies the final memo copy and submits the original to the instructor and a copy to each group member for inclusion in the individual portfolios.

Case Study 1: Can Young Families–Especially Women– 'Have It All?'

Lori Perez, wife and mother of three school children, works as a construction project manager for Construct, Inc., a small firm that operates out of Kansas City, Missouri. Construct does not do business with local firms or individuals unless they happen to be one of the SmartMart stores for whom Construct does all of its business.

Construct has a long-term contract with SmartMart to remodel and build new stores as they are designated throughout the United

States and Canada. However, there are another dozen or so construction firms who also build and remodel SmartMart stores. SmartMart lets out bids to these dozen construction firms so the latter will compete with one another in prices and deadlines. The construction firm that gets the contract is the one that comes in with the lowest cost bid that also promises to complete a quality job in a timely fashion.

Lori, her boss, and his son comprise the management team. Lori hired a business student graduate to do the books and serve as secretary. Before long, there was too much work for one office worker, so Lori hired a secretary as well. Jon Jordan is office manager/accountant and June Washington is secretary. Lori used to do the work of both before she took over as construction manager.

SmartMart alerts Construct about a store that needs remodeling or building. Each of the three managers works alone on individual projects to figure the cost of the job and the amount of margin (extra) the company will need in order to make a profit. This bid is approved by the management team before submittal to SmartMart.

What usually happens, though, is that Lori wants to see more than the blueprints that SmartMart has given Construct. So she grabs her always-packed overnight bag from the office closet and dashes out to KCI–Kansas City International airport.

In the destination city–which, to date, has included New York, L.A., Chicago, Seattle, Detroit, Miami, Dallas, and Quebec–she picks up a rental car and city map, unless of course someone from the SmartMart store chain has agreed to meet her. Meanwhile, the moment she decides to visit the site in person, Jon Jordan or June Washington quickly do the following:

- call the airline to reserve a flight ticket
- call the SmartMart store in (city) to alert them that Lori is on her way
- place calls to arrange reservations for her ground transportation (rental car) and hotel (if she will need to stay overnight).

Once in the air, Lori will verify the above arrangements by calling Jon or June, using the in-flight phone and her telephone credit calling card. She will also place other calls, to her boss or his son, each of whom may be anywhere else in the United States or Canada doing the same kinds of things that Lori does.

At the SmartMart site, Lori simply wants to get acquainted with SmartMart and local construction people in person, face-to-face. She smiles as she introduces herself, is attractively dressed, and uses the language or jargon of the construction industry. Her posture, body language, facial expressions, gestures, and paralanguage all speak of self-confidence and expertise. She knows her business and acknowledges that they know theirs.

Lori might leave town a mere six hours later or perhaps as long as three days to a week thereafter, depending on how many problems and obstacles occur to delay her departure. But by the time she leaves, she will have a good idea about the reputation of subcontractors and whether she can count on their promises. These subcontractors are local construction firms who will provide carpentry, plumbing, electricity, asphalt, roofing, and so on. Before submitting Contruct's bid to SmartMart, Lori wants to be sure of the prices these subcontractors will charge and the deadlines that they are willing and able to meet.

If all goes well and her phone calls to the office or home show that things are going well, Lori will return home the same day. When she dashes in the door, one arm full of groceries and the other extended to collect her children's school papers for parental review, her family won't even know—until she tells them—that she's been out of town! Megan might be mowing the lawn or vacuuming, Michael could be taking out the trash or making cookies, and Matthew is likely to be totally absorbed with a book or science project.

Lori's husband, Maynard Perez, firefighter and part-time tile installer for Lori's company, peels an orange and feeds sections to her for quick energy while they unload groceries and talk about their day. Maynard is what Lori calls a "professional sleeper," since he is awakened periodically throughout every night that he's assigned to work at the fire station and must be able to resume sleeping with little more than a tiny hitch.

It's a good thing that Maynard can stay asleep or go straight back to sleep, no matter the type of interruption, because the Perez phone is likely to ring off and on all night, every night, seven nights a week, 365 days a year! That's how much Lori is "on call." That's because SmartMart does not want to lose so much as one day's business, despite remodeling. They want no down time, so the construction crews work all night. They frequently run into problems. When they run into problems, they call Lori.

Besides bidding on construction jobs for SmartMart, that's what Lori does—solve problems. She mostly solves problems with the help of telecommunication devices—walkie-talkie, pager, cellular phone, and phones in cars, trucks, and planes. When she cannot solve problems by long distance, then she again dashes out to KCI and flies off to talk to people in person.

Sometimes when Lori has planned to be at a site no more than a few hours—and thus has not bothered to alert her family of her absence beyond a wee note on the refrigerator door—she ends up somewhere else. A call to or from June or Jon back in the home office may alert Lori to problems with remodeling jobs already in progress in other cities.

Whenever Lori's immediate or extended family members or friends want to know where Lori is, they call Jon or June, at the office or at their homes or in their cars (these phones are also provided by the company). June and Jon keep up with Lori's erratic schedule.

The reply might go like this: "Lori left Chicago to go to Seattle but she should be home by tomorrow night, unless of course she goes on to L.A. first. If you'll call either of us tonight or tomorrow, we'll know where she is and her ETA (estimated time of arrival)."

In response to queries about where all the Perez family members have disappeared, Jon or June might say: "Lori needed Maynard to lay tile in the store back east in Savannah. He exchanged firestation times with another firefighter and flew out this morning. The Perez children are with their aunt until their grandmother gets in from Texas. If you're calling about the picnic, don't worry, Lori says everybody will be back by Sunday afternoon in time to start the charcoal. But if they get in earlier, they'll be on the volleyball court after church."

Lori says the reason she travels to meet with people in person and not simply rely on telecommunications, is because of *the human factor*. "When I'm pleading with a carpenter to get him to meet his agreed-upon deadline and I'm standing right there looking up in his face, it's harder for him to hold out with a 'no' than it would be over the phone."

Later, in response to how she solves problems, she said, "I simply refuse to take 'no' for an answer. There's always some way around obstacles, some other way to do something." "If there's a truckers' strike, then perhaps a supplier can ship our building materials by train. If there's a flood, earthquake, or road construction underway that supposedly inhibits employees from getting to work, they can find a detour. If key personnel get ill, we'll call temps. You have to be creative to think of options—maybe a possible solution to every problem."

It appears that Lori uses whole-brain thinking to solve problems. From facts and figures, knowledge and experience that are all stored in her left brain, the right brain is able to retrieve ideas and options at random. Moreover, strategies that she uses at home are transferred to the workplace and vice versa.

At present, Lori has brought in 42 stores, every one on time. Her bonus (beyond salary) at the end of year number one in her new management job was substantial.

Apparently, some career people can combine work and play and give attention to family and recreation, all because of technological advances in both communications and transportation. Respond to the following discussion items, using the blanks to record notes and ideas.

1. List all of the telecommunication devices that Lori and others in the case use.

_____

_____

_____

_____

_____

_____

2. How has technology in transportation and communications changed jobs like the one Lori has—a job that requires a lot of

regular contact with people over long distances? Give examples from (a) your own experiences, (b) situations you have seen on TV, whether fact or fiction, and (c) circumstances you have heard about from human resources, including family members and friends.

_____

_____

_____

_____

_____

_____

_____

_____

_____

_____

3. How has technology contributed to changes in family life-styles, like that of the Perez family?

_____

_____

_____

_____

_____

_____

_____

_____

_____

_____

_____

4. What advice would you give to people who want to use office work as a stepping stone to a different or higher-level position as Lori did in moving into the position of Construction Project Manager?

_____

_____

_____

_____

_____

_____

_____

_____

_____

_____

ACTIVITY II-7: COOPERATIVE LEARNING–
EVALUATE OR MEASURE PROGRESS

Name: _____ Date: _____

Directions

1. Keep the same group leadership. Share and discuss portfolios.

2. Evaluate completed assignments on the major project.

Assigned Tasks and Person Responsible   Evaluation (+,✔,-)

_____

_____

_____

_____

_____

_____

_____

3. Make new assignments, using the spaces provided:

New Tasks   *Due Date*

_____

_____

_____

_____

_____

_____

_____

_____

_____

_____

4. Reach consensus on section objectives and learning outcomes. The supervisor leads discussion to reach consensus on learning outcomes. The recorder's notes are passed on to the processor who composes a memo for group distribution.

5. The supervisor is responsible for the accuracy of format and content, makes and distributes copies of the memo to group members, and attaches all individual members' work to the memo to be transmitted to the instructor. The supervisor also evaluates each group member confidentially, using the form provided. (Individuals tear out the form and give it to the supervisor.)

Section Objectives   *Learning Outcomes*

_____   _____

_____   _____

_____   _____

_____   _____

_____   _____

_____   _____

_____   _____

_____   _____

_____   _____

_____   _____

SUPERVISOR'S EVALUATION–SECTION II

Person evaluated: _____ Date: _____

Directions: use the +, ✓, – evaluation method, where + = outstanding, ✓ = average/satisfactory, and – = poor/unsatisfactory.

With this section, the group member was:

1. cooperative with co-workers   _____

2. responsive to assignments made by the group   _____

3. responsive to the supervisor's constructive ideas   _____

4. pleasant, cooperative, easy to work with   _____

5. dependable, attended class meetings   _____

6. dependable, attended out-of-class meetings   _____

7. responsible, produced work on time   _____

8. responsible, produced quality work   _____

9. reliable and willing to work   _____

10. positive team player who contributed greatly to the group   _____

SUPPORTIVE COMMENTS:

Evaluator's signature (confidential):_____

Bibliography for Section II

Baldrige, Letitia, *Complete Guide to Executive Manners*. New York: Rawson Associates, 1985.

Boeing Corporation. "Mid-Year Report to Stockholders," Seattle, July 1993.

Brothers, Joyce, "Why Husbands Walk Out," *Reader's Digest*, July 1987. (Sex as communication.)

"Building goodwill," *CBS News*, July 23, 1993. ("People not only want to buy good products, they want to buy good products from good companies.")

Charen, Mona, "C-SPAN: Where TV Has Never Gone Before," *Reader's Digest*, May 1992. ("Stay tuned and get hooked on democracy at work.")

Coffee, Gerald L., *Beyond Survival*. New York: G. P. Putnam and Sons, 1990.

"Courageous Women," PBS, October 27, 1993. (Women flyers in World War II.)

Crowley, Edward, and Jay J.R. Zajas, "Evidence Supporting the Importance of Brands in Marketing Computer Products," *Journal of Professional Services Marketing*, Volume 14(2), 1996, pp. 120-137.

"Generational humor," *Reader's Digest*, November, 1990.

Graf, David K., Church, Olive D., and Duff, Thomas, *Business in an Information Economy*. New York: McGraw-Hill, 1990.

Guisewite, Cathy, "Cathy," *Laramie Boomerang*. (Comic strip that treats gender differences with humor.)

Hairston, Barbara J., "Strategies for Developing Human Relations Skills," *Business Education Forum*, April 1987.

Hall, Edward T., *The Silent Language*. New York: Fawcett, 1959.

How the West Was Won (1962). (Some background on the Pony Express.)

"How'd They Do That?" CBS, September 19, 1993. (Federal Express.)

Illustrated Encyclopedic Dictionary, Vol. II, L-Z. Pleasantville, NY: Reader's Digest Association, 1987.

Interview with female accident victim, Corvalis, Oregon, July 1988.

Interviews with young entrepreneurs, among them Steve Jobs, PBS Special, "Young Entrepreneurs," December 1987.

Jennings, Peter (interviewing Bill Gates, Microsoft CEO, and John Malone, Time Warner CEO), ABC, September 29, 1993.

Ketcham, Hank, "Dennis the Menace," *Denver Post*. (Comic strip that treats generational differences with humor.)

Leibson, Beth, "A Low-Tech Wonder," *Reader's Digest*, July 1992.

Mamis, Robert A., "Born to Grow," *Inc.* May 1982. (Birth of Apple Computer.)

Moore, Richard G. and Scott Wilkinson, "Communications Technology," *Hospitality Research Journal*, vol. 17, no. 1, 1993.

Nietzsche, Friedrich. "Quotable Quotes," *Reader's Digest*, Vol. 135, No. 809 (September 1989) (see right-brain topics).

Ponte, Lowell, "In the Blink of an Ear," *Reader's Digest*, October, 1993. (Recent research findings suggest that humans have many more than five senses.)

Rather, Dan, and Connie Chung, *CBS Evening News*, July 23, 1993. ("People buy companies as well as products.")

"The Scientific American Frontiers," PBS, November 3, 1993. (On homing pigeons.)

Scott, Willard, *Today Show*, CBS, September 1, 1993. (The first telephone operator.)

Sheehy, Gail, *Pathfinders*. New York: William Morrow (Bantam) 1982.

_____ *Passages*. New York: Willam Morrow (Bantam) 1984.

The Sound and the Silence, TNT, July 19, 1993. (Two-part TV movie describing Alexander Graham Bell and his inventions.)

Taylor, Alexander L., "Striking it Rich," *Time*. (Interview with Steve Jobs about Apple Computer), February 15, 1982.

Tour of Western Heritage Center, Cody, Wyoming, 1989 (featuring Pony Express and other adventures of Bill Cody/Buffalo Bill, and the West).

Tours and interviews: Canada (1988); Mexico, Mexican manufacturers, and U.S. factories in Mexico (1984-85); England (1991), Europe (1992), e.g., businesses, industries, museums, art galleries; NASA (Houston, 1986); and Air Museum (Tucson, 1990).

Weber, Thomas E., "Cyberspaced Out," *The Wall Street Journal*, November 15, 1993.

_____, "Global Villagers," *The Wall Street Journal*, November 15, 1993.

Westward the Women, (1951). (Competition for resources and women on wagon trains heading west.)

Wonder, Jacquelyn, and Priscilla Donovan, *Whole-Brain Thinking: Working from Both Sides of the Brain to Achieve Peak Job Performance*. New York: Ballantine Books, 1985.

Zajas, Jay J.R., *Organizational Behavior, Managerial Systems and Communications in Two Urban Hospitals*. (Graduate School of Management: The University of Texas, Edinburg, 1979.)

Zajas, Jay J.R., "A Group Process Assessment for Interpersonal Growth, Communications and Managerial Development." *The International Journal of Management*, Volume 11(3). September 1994, pp. 772-777.

Zajas, Jay J.R., *The Marketing of Executives and Career Development Success*. MCB University Press, 1995.

Zajas, Jay J.R., *How to Strategically Plan and Prepare for Business Success*. (The Corporate Management Group, 1997.)

Zajas, Jay J.R., and Earl W. Brewster, "Beyond Goal Setting: Key Interpersonal Success Factors for Marketing Executives Today." *Executive Development Journal*, Volume 8(3). MCB University Press, 1995.

Zajas, Jay J.R., and Jann R. Michener Zajas, "A Conceptual Approach to Career Planning for Executive and Managerial Success." *International Academy of Management and Marketing, IAMM Proceedings*, April 1991, pp. 118-124.

Ziegler, Bart, "AT&T's Bold Bet," *Business Week*, August 30, 1993. (AT&T negotiations to purchase McCaw Communications.)

SECTION III:
BUSINESS APPLICATIONS
AND OPPORTUNITIES

Most careers today require some knowledge of telecommunications or bring people in contact with telecommunication systems. To do well in the contemporary business environment, though, one needs more than computer and telecommunication competencies. Knowledge of telecommunications, human relations, and communications is certainly helpful, but knowledge of these subjects alone is still not enough. To succeed in modern business, one needs to understand business applications and *how* economic opportunity affects people and markets around the globe.

One way to obtain an overview of the vast range of businesses is to scan the *Standard Industrial Classifications* (SIC). The SIC groups businesses by type of product. This section focuses on these 14 classifications. Another way to obtain an overview of the diversity of businesses today is to visit a large university, city, or county library and scan the reference books available on the topic "business." For example, *Hoover's Handbook of American Business 1997* gives in-depth profiles on 500 major U.S. companies, many which serve domestic, regional, and global markets. Another business reference book, *Hoover's Handbook of World Business*, discusses hundreds of companies headquartered outside of the United States. Combined with other reference books or other on-line electronic information services from companies such as Dow Jones, Dun & Bradstreet, and McGraw-Hill, Inc. (which publishes *Standard and Poor's Ratings* and *Business Week*), these sources, in tan-

159

dem with the SIC codes, provide an excellent overview of business companies. This section also examines how firms use telecommunications and some of the challenges facing individuals in today's job market.

OBJECTIVES

1. Discuss the major issues described in the unit and reach consensus on learning outcomes as compared with section objectives.
2. Interview people in a variety of local businesses (from several SICs) to identify how their firms use telecommunication systems and business principles.
3. Input interview data to a computerized database and share information with group members by using e-mail or fax.
4. Collect data on a variety of multinational businesses from several SICs and participate with your group in preparing a multimedia demonstration to share findings.
5. Using information from the two SIC databases, compose career advice and dictate a short report to your partner.
6. Participate with your group in discussing case studies.
7. Solve business problems and make economic decisions, using whole-brain thinking and one or more telecommunication systems.
8. Convene with your group to assess progress on the major project, assign new tasks and responsibilities, and reach consensus on learning outcomes in comparison with section objectives.

Chapter 7

Standard Industrial Classifications

Business firms, consumer goods enterprises, and nonprofit organizations are classified under several well-defined categories. The Internal Revenue Service (IRS) also uses these classifications when it requires entrepreneurs to report income from their small business operations.

The channels of distribution are reported with the standard industrial classifications (SICs). Buy-and-sell transactions take place along these channels and are conducted between and among companies as well as between companies and consumers. Both communication and transportation systems are utilized. Products are bought and sold using communication and record systems, whether conducted via oral, print, or telecommunication media. Goods are then shipped using private transportation systems or services such as Federal Express, UPS, or the public mail system.

Except for the single nonprofit classification, businesses in all of the other 13 classifications are in business to make a profit. Their income is derived from selling products. They must earn more money from sales than they spend on expenses or they will go out of business. Considering how individuals and families survive economically should lead to some understanding of how businesses operate.

For example, environmentalism deals with protecting the environment. Maslow's human need levels help us comprehend that humans too must be protected and cared for in order to survive. Thus, people do well to learn how to strike a balance: protect people and protect the environment. Human beings and the companies they represent serve each other in part by creating, producing, distributing, advertising, and selling products that others need and want.

Photo 7.1. *Chicago Sun-Times* Building

Large city newspapers like the *Chicago Sun-Times* are included in the communications SIC, along with television and radio stations and programming, printed
signs, publishers of books and magazines—in other words, things to do with the
distribution of news and data.

The survival decisions that people, businesses, and countries make are economic in nature. All other living creatures can live off the land, sea, or nature by following their natural instincts, or by going along with the cycle of life that promotes the survival of the fittest. Humans are different; they are more than animals because of their ethical, spiritual, social, and historical conscience. Humans must alter the environment in order to survive. Humans change their environment and help to change products from one form to another.

People don't want to just buy products, however. They want to buy *good* products from *good* companies. Companies that have demonstrated that they have a social and ethical conscience–care about people and the environment–are identified as "good" companies.

Products refer to both goods (tangible products) and services (intangible activities) that firms offer for sale to their customers. The *commercial or profit-making* sector includes all of the businesses that are in business to make a profit. The *public or nonprofit sector* includes all of the organizations that get their operating funds from some other source(s) than from sales, whether from taxes, membership fees, or donations. The classifications that follow include one public sector classification and 13 private sector classifications.

The U.S. Department of Commerce designates businesses by classification. Each subclassification is assigned a number. This section discusses the 14 primary classifications. They are presented relative to the *channels of distribution*–how goods get from their source to the customer.

GOODS (TANGIBLE PRODUCTS)

There are seven classifications under this section. These are as follows, based on their standard industrial classification (SIC): (1) extraction; (2) manufacturing; (3) construction; (4) transportation; (5) wholesalers; (6) retailers; and (7) utilities. Firms that go into business to deal with goods may expect to spend up to 50 percent of their income from sales on buying goods for resale or on buying goods to produce other goods. The remaining 50 percent of funds that come in from sales and earnings on investments are used

Photo 7.2. Construction Site

Many people—including engineers, architects, construction workers, and tele-communication operators—work together to bring construction plans to fruition.

to pay operational costs such as payroll, taxes, rent, and the expenses of doing business. Anything left after paying operational costs and taxes is called *profit or net income.*

Extraction

Under this classification are all the activities necessary to get raw materials off of or out of the land, sea, and nature. Thus, both agriculture and mining are subclassifications of this group. *Agriculture* includes farming for crops and produce, ranching, dairying, fishing, and lumbering. Ranching is the business of raising cattle, horses, sheep, ostrich, emu, goats, mink, etc. Huge feed lots for raising cattle and farms for raising dairy cows, turkeys, or chickens are often owned and operated by large corporations. Just a generation or two ago, this was not the case, as most farms prior to the 1950s were owned and operated by families.

Most people today know very little about agriculture, its social and economic significance, and particularly its link to human health and environmental quality. In addition to the farmers and ranchers who grow plants, crops, and raise livestock, agriculturalists include:

- researchers in universities and businesses who make scientific discoveries to improve agricultural technology
- teachers, extension agents, and journalists who communicate agricultural information and new discoveries
- managers, scientists and salespeople in companies who develop, prepare, and market agricultural products
- bankers, loan officers, and appraisers who make loans to farmers, ranchers, and agribusiness professionals.

All sorts of computer programs help agriculturalists make decisions. Using AGNET, a farmer can ask questions about how to salvage some of his damaged barley—would it be nutritious as feed for cattle? With telecommunications capabilities, agriculturists can get daily updates from their agri-bulletin board computer network.

All of the things that are extracted from the land are natural resources; they are also called *raw products*. Careful husbandry over animals and crop rotation to maintain soil quality help to preserve the land for agricultural products. As long as people need to eat food and wear clothes (e.g., leather, wool, and cotton products), there will be agriculture.

It took millions of years for fossil fuels (oil, gas, coal, etc.) to reach their present useful state. The depletion of these natural resources cannot be readily restored. That is why the world needs conservation as well as mining and other extraction activities.

Mining is the business of taking out of or off of the ground such natural resources as petroleum products, coal, uranium, gold, diamonds, sand, gravel, and much more. The Middle East is well-known for its petroleum products and South Africa for diamond mines, but many other regions of the world also boast an abundance of raw materials, with the United States at the top of the list.

As with most trade, price is a major factor in agriculture. For example, imagine the buy/sell telecommunication messages that are communicated around the world when OPEC (Organization of Petroleum Export Countries) makes decisions to raise or lower the price per barrel of oil, even by a few dollars. In the megalopolis areas where one city after another run together, e.g., Boston in the north through New York City, Philadelphia, Baltimore, Washington, DC, and Richmond in the south, many people commute long hours every day to get to and from work. The price per gallon of gasoline at the pumps makes a difference to their family transportation budget. In the West, where oil is also extracted, a drop in the price per barrel of oil means a reduction of services provided by every government bureau, school, and so on. Lower oil prices mean that lower and fewer taxes are paid to state governments, who must pay wages, fund education, maintain roads, and provide social services, etc.

In the eight-state Rocky Mountain region, nearly two-thirds of the 6,000 nonmetal mining companies are small sand-and-gravel firms. In some regions, coal mines operate the same way; for example, in Kentucky, over 200 of the 1,700 coal mines are family-owned operations. Not all mining operations are big businesses.

Manufacturing

Manufacturing is the process whereby natural resources and raw materials are transformed into other goods. Some of this output uses a direct channel of distribution—from manufacturer to consumer. A local cabinetmaker builds custom-order kitchen cabinets for local customers. Small operation manufacturers advertise in the local paper and Yellow Pages. Their customers sometimes contact cabinetmakers by leaving messages on an answering machine or with a telephone answering service where an operator takes and relays messages.

The majority of goods are manufactured in mass quantities. The channels of distribution vary, with many goods traveling a long route to the customer, through wholesalers, transporters, and retailers. Other goods take a shorter route because some large national and multinational firms own businesses or operate departments at every stage of distribution.

Some manufacturers sell their goods to other businesses who continue the transformation process, turning one type of good into another type. Wheat is a raw product (agriculture) that is transformed into flour. Some flour is sold to retail grocers but other flour is sold to bakeries, both large and small, who process flour and other ingredients into bread, rolls, etc.

IBM (International Business Machines) was once the richest company in the world but some key management decisions adversely changed this picture. Instead of manufacturing their own computer chips, they bought from Intel, which (because of the great increase in sales) made Intel one of the largest chip manufacturers in the United States. Instead of developing and manufacturing its own computer programming software, IBM bought from Microsoft. This strategy, among others, contributed to making Bill Gates of Microsoft one of the richest people in America in the 1990s.

The history of manufacturing and the history of unions developed along parallel lines. The more demands from customers for goods, the more manufacturing was needed and the more people were hired. In the early days of the industrial revolution, the wage-earners' job was not attractive because of unsafe and uncomfortable working conditions, long hours, few benefits, and low wages. With group protests that came from the formation of unions ("strength in numbers," "collective voice") emerged legislation to make these practices illegal and to thereby provide some measure of employee protection and economic coverage in the form of higher wages and more benefits. (See Maslow's basic and security/safety needs.)

Today, these things are happening in many countries around the globe. Poor facilities and low wages mean, to manufacturers, that the cost of production is drastically reduced. With low costs of production come low prices. People in countries where the use of technology and its impact on society and social legislation are just now emerging want and need to compete with technologically advanced countries. Third world people need jobs and good wages and a chance to survive and prosper the same as persons in more progressive countries.

Meanwhile, United States firms and other large manufacturing companies can ship raw products around the world to be assembled in countries that still pay low wages. This is cheaper than the companies manufacturing goods at home. American workers don't want to compete for jobs with foreigners who will work for less, but American consumers want to be able to buy goods at lower prices too. These are trade-offs.

Many years ago, "Made in Japan" meant poor quality but low prices. Today, thanks to Dr. Edward Deming and the quality management revolution, that statement stands for good quality. The four little dragons—South Korea, Hong Kong, Thailand, and Singapore—provided the low-wage competition to Japan that Japan had once provided the United States. As conditions and wages improved in these countries, other Southeast Asian countries, and some in South American and Central American countries, including Mexico also entered the manufacturing arena as competitors.

People who buy stock (shares of company ownership) are interested in companies from countries such as those described above. Stockholders who speculate (buy less-proven or riskier stocks) move their investments from company to company and country to country. With the revolution in telecommunications technology, communications, telephone, and cable television companies from every country are merging, buying each other out, getting in and getting out of business. For example, Phillip Morris owns many types of companies, including giant food processors, while tobacco is but one division.

For every major manufacturer, such as auto and airplane factories, there are approximately three thousand smaller firms producing the nuts, bolts, and other parts to go into these vehicles. Many companies that are large and multinational today started out small and local.

In his book, *Kitchen Sink Papers*, Mike McGrady described how his wife started her plastic see-through cookbook holder business in their basement with the help of their three children. When sales increased to the point where sufficient money was available, the company moved to a large brick building in their city's industrial region.

In Denver, another family known as the McFarlands designed and manufactured plastic flower pot watering bags in their basement. Once operational, they transferred the labor to ARC members—mentally or physically retarded adults who can learn small repetitive manual operations and thus find employment.

Debbie Fields made chocolate chip cookies and sold the tasty tidbits to neighbors at the age of 12. At 19, she opened a tiny 325 square-foot take-out shop, and ten years later, her chain had gone nationwide. She was worth over $55 million dollars. A wee tortilla factory in Cheyenne, Wyoming, expanded to tacos and went world-wide with their Taco John franchise.

Factories that produce consumer goods are generally called man-ufacturers and those who transform raw products into consumable food goods are called food processors. Both manufacturers and processors use telecommunication and computer programs to do business. They buy raw materials from businesses in the extraction classification and sell finished goods to other businesses including shippers, as well as, in some cases, to consumers.

As long as people need goods to survive (see Maslow's human needs), there will always be manufacturing. In a global economy, though, these goods and parts that are assembled into goods come from all over the world.

In former times, huge clerical staffs were needed to type pur-chase orders, sales orders, and invoices. Now, people use tele-phones, e-mail, fax, and computer programs to place their buy and sell orders, to send and receive bills, and to process checks in payment of bills.

Construction

Construction includes all of the building operations and their subfields that result in buildings, bridges, highways, homes, and parks, worldwide. See for example the case study in Section II. (Lori Perez described some of her adventures working for a small firm that specializes in one type of construction—building and remodeling retail SmartMart stores throughout the United States and Canada.) Notice that Lori started as an office worker before transferring to the job of Construction Project Manager.

Just about every business operates out of somewhere, even one's home or vehicle. The construction industry makes it possible for businesses as well as for families and government bureaus to have a home. The transportation industry also depends on construction because the world needs highways, bridges, and the like.

Transportation

Transportation includes all of the businesses related to the shipping of goods and people whether locally or around the world. Some shipping is done by planes and jets while much is done on ships, by ocean, sea, river, or lake. A great deal of shipping is done

Photo 7.3. Transportation

Packages and goods must be shipped, and people transported from their points of origin to their points of destination.

by trains and trucks. Trains travel on railroad tracks and trucks use the highways, byways, roads and streets. Travel agencies move people, whether for business or personal reasons, so they too come under the transportation classification (as well as under both business and personal services).

Dispatchers keep track of and are in constant communication with the people manning a company's vehicles. They do this by mobile phone, radio hookup, and CB (citizen's band). Data are fed into computers to calculate distances, the amount spent on fuel and time (equated with driver wages), and ETA (estimated time of arrival). The receivers of goods need to know the weight of goods and thus shipping costs to be charged to them, etc. The same communication modes and channels are used to report and deal with emergencies, whether medical, personal, or business.

As long as people need to travel and/or need goods to survive, there will always be transportation systems. It is difficult to imagine going faster or by different transportation modes, but as long as there are people with creative minds, new and surprising methods will keep emerging.

Wholesale Trade

Wholesale trade refers to middle or connecting activities along the channels of distribution. These firms buy from manufacturers and sell to other manufacturing or processing businesses as well as to retail firms who sell direct to consumers. Also under this classification are warehouses that store both specialized goods and a mixed variety of goods. Small manufacturers use these warehouses because it is cheaper than paying for the construction and maintenance of their own storage buildings.

Retail Trade

Retail trade includes the walk-in stores familiar to consumers. These stores are local independents, franchises, or members of a chain that operate nationally or internationally. From Quebec to Singapore, people recognize these brand names that illustrate the spread of franchises: Coca-Cola, McDonald's Hamburgers, Ford

Photo 7.4. Transportation Dispatch Clerk

Transportation and communication systems are related and often interdependent. Here a communications clerk, often called a dispatcher, tracks the movement of trucks that transport goods.

cars. Stores that are owned as one among many in a chain include Wal-Mart, Kmart, and Safeway.

Locally, people are familiar with the shops they most frequently visit. Local independent stores buy in small quantities from wholesalers, who buy from manufacturers, who buy from other manufacturers or direct from companies in the extraction industry, all of whom use transportation firms.

The channels of distribution are more direct with large companies that have organized businesses all along the channels. Texaco

(Texas Company), for example, has extraction operations, refineries (manufacturing) to transform the raw product into other products, vehicles to transport their products (at any and every stage), and service stations that sell their goods directly to the consumer.

Wal-Mart, Kmart, Safeway, and many other large firms also operate along several channels of distribution so as to deal in larger quantities at a time and to cut out the middle operations–decisions designed to cut costs. Part of these costs are then passed on to the consumer in the form of lower prices, which is one thing that motivates people to shop in their stores.

When you travel, particularly on interstate highways, watch for trucks whose signs illustrate brand-name products such as those mentioned above. Note freight trains as well. Semis piggyback on the flat cars of trains. Freight cars display company logos, often the name of the railroad (B&O, "Baltimore and Ohio"; UP, "Union Pacific," etc.), but when a large company owns its own freight cars, one will see these companies' names, too.

Bekins moves furniture for consumers, a process which is a direct channel of distribution. But Texaco, Safeway, and Wal-Mart trucks illustrate a crunching or bypassing of the channels. Texaco illustrates a company that operates extraction and manufacturing through shipping to the retail outlets that sell directly to consumers.

Utilities (Telephone, Electricity, Water, and Cable)

Utilities include electricity, gas, water, garbage pick up, telephone, and TV channel firms that provide people with basic- and security-level home protection services. (TV and telephone also contribute to satisfying our social, egotistical, and self-actualized needs for fun and knowledge.)

These operations use natural resources, among other things, to make our utility and communication services possible. It takes coal or nuclear power to generate energy for electrical power plants. Communication satellites and microwave dishes, electric poles and lines, cables and fiber optics, and a wide range of manufactured goods are used to bring into people's homes TV, electricity, and telephones.

Although TV cable companies are included under the utilities classification, TV stations and TV sets are not. Television sets are first manufactured, then transported and stored, then sold to retail outlets, and finally they reach consumers. TV stations and the programming they show are considered services.

SERVICES (INTANGIBLE OFFERINGS)

Most companies that deal with goods also offer services, but the services are usually designed to enhance sales, not to serve as the major sales product. For example, when ordering a computer program from Microsoft, the customer expects to get some support services—an 800 number to call to get free advice. But Microsoft does not sell the service unless it first sells the software product.

Service companies sell their services; they don't give them away. Their income statement generally does not reflect more than a 30 percent figure for cost of goods,* not the reverse as is often the case with the finished goods industries. However, their income statements usually show a higher percentage for expenditures than goods companies—especially for wages and supplies, and perhaps for telecommunications and other electronic services. Under this broad category, there are seven service classifications including the nonprofit or public classification. They include the following SIC areas: (1) communication, (2) professional service, (3) business and financial services, (4) hospitality services, (5) recreation and tourism, (6) personal services, and (7) public services.

Communications

Communications includes TV and radio stations and everything to do with "the word," whether printed or broadcast, such as book, magazine, and newspaper publishers as well as radio and television stations. Rupert Murdoch, owner of the Fox TV network in the United States, also owns a Hong Kong telecommunication service with the potential of well over a billion TV viewers throughout Asia.

---

*Cost of Goods Sold (CGS) is a generally accepted accounting term which differs from a finished "product."

Photo 7.5. Fiber Optics

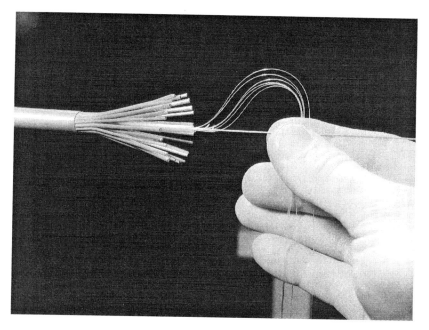

Six hair-thin single-mode optical fibers are at the heart of AT&T's cable. A copper cladding provides protection and strength to the cable core and electrical power for the undersea repeaters. Courtesy of AT&T Archives.

Companies that produce communications hardware are under the manufacturing classification. Anything that provides a communications service comes under this SIC. The variety of communication services is rapidly expanding as entrepreneurs with new ways of doing things open new businesses.

A married couple, Bill Terarca and Jane Strathman, each operate their own business out of their home. Tetrarca, who specializes in stringing up electronic networks for the health care and banking industries, and Strathman, who teaches corporate executives how to communicate more effectively, have two sets of clients. Thus, they require separate phone and fax lines and answering machines.

Professional Services

In most professional services, the owners typically have a minimum of a license, certification, or a bachelor's degree in a specified field (usually advanced degrees as well). Frequently, they must pass tests to get a professional license as entrance into their profession. Under this classification are all manner of medical doctors and clinics, hospitals, registered nurses, dentists, psychiatrists and so on, as well as attorneys, professional teachers, librarians, counselors, and the like.

This is one classification where laborers and other workers cannot move up the career ladder, even if ambition motivates them to improve their competencies. Rather, they must return to college to complete one or more professional degrees before they can enter careers at the professional level.

However, there are many support positions where technical competencies are of keen importance, such as knowledge of telecommunications, computer operations, and human relations. The professional service classification is generally one of "nurturing," so if helping others feels good one should seriously investigate or research this category.

Business and Financial Services

Business and financial services include firms that provide services to meet the *business* (not personal) needs of both business customers and personal consumers. Consumers have business or economic needs, such as getting their income tax forms prepared or a printed sign advertising a one-time garage sale. People run for office and use public relations firms and ad agencies to help formulate their political campaigns.

Financial needs prevail. People use banks, stock brokerages, credit unions, insurance agencies, real estate agencies, even pawn brokers. Businesses also need all of these services.

Hospitality and Recreation and Tourism Services

The "hospitality" segment is easy to visualize; the recreation and tourism components are less so. Hospitality refers to those services

Photo 7.6. Insurance Building

The headquarters of large financial firms, such as insurance companies, come under SIC of business and financial services. Many job opportunities for tele-communication, records, and other office positions are available.

that cater to guests and diners—hotels, motels, cafes, restaurants, taverns, and bars. These firms respond to people's most basic needs—to eat, drink, and sleep.

Recreation

Recreation includes the kinds of services designed to make people happy, to give them fun, entertainment, pleasure, excitement, culture, and competition. From bowling alleys and health spas to art galleries and symphonies, from exclusive world-renowned resorts to family camps, from the sports clubs located in metropolitan cities to intramural athletic competitions, anything relating to how people spend their leisure time is included in this classification.

Businesses also use some of these services. They send key personnel to meetings and conferences, which use hospitality and sometimes recreational services (as well as transportation, and the services of communications and business/finance). In providing training programs to improve employee competencies, some businesses plug into university, compressed video, off-site class or training offerings. Employers provide perks (rewards) to their employees for work well done and for helping to increase sales and profits, purchasing a variety of recreational and cultural services.

Tourism

Tourism includes all the efforts that communities—businesses, government, and concerned citizens—expend in order to bring tourists to one's city and state. Historical attractions may be supported by nonprofit agencies (see public services) or by corporations. Local businesses benefit from tourism, however, since people spend money wherever they go in order to meet their needs. The Wyoming Tourism Bureau estimates that for every 24-hour period that a family spends in the state (coming in, leaving, crossing it, visiting national parks and historical sites, etc.), every man, woman, and child in that family will spend approximately $75 each.

Hospitality services are also responsive to (and benefit from) people's basic needs too. Recreation and cultural services are responsive to (and benefit from) the social and physical needs for

Photo 7.7. Businesspeople at a Conference Meal

Hospitality services include hotels, motels, and restaurants, which are often used by business travelers and conferees.

fun and learning. Many other types of businesses, including retail stores, are responsive to (and benefit from) the human need to buy things—jewelry, perfume, petroleum products, food, clothing, repair services, medical services, TV and communication services, souvenirs, doodads, and more.

Personal Services

Personal services include all of the remaining services that people need in order to cope. A short list of examples includes: cosmetology and hair-styling salons, mortuaries, vehicle and appliance repair, home and business decorating, baby-sitting, yard and shopping services, Meals on Wheels (home delivery of meals), house and business cleaning, plant watering, house sitting, etc. Vehicle and appliance repairs are performed for businesses as well.

Public Services

Public services is the nonprofit classification. In addition to government (one out of four U.S. workers is employed by government), there are nonprofit organizations. They get their funds from dues, contributions, and endowments. People who belong to trade unions and professional organizations pay dues. The dues go to pay for employee wages and for operations to manage the organizations.

Contributions and endowments support numerous cultural and educational institutions. Museums, humanities, and art organizations that are not in business to make a profit come under this classification. Public schools are supported by government funds (taxes), proprietary schools are in business to make money, but some educational institutions are privately endowed.

Most public service offices, departments, agencies, bureaus, schools, etc., are government institutions and are funded by the taxes that hard-working taxpayers pay. Thus, elderly people sometimes do not vote for a school bond issue because they live on fixed incomes or would rather that public funds go to support the needs of the aged. Young people sometimes do not vote to extend social security benefits for the aged because they would rather that public funds go to support the needs of children and young families. Mostly everything in business or government is a trade-off.

Chapter 8

Basic Economic Concepts

Scarcity is one of the most basic economic concepts. There is seldom enough of anything for everybody, whether it be money, the assets that money can buy, time, space, talents, or personal competencies. The concept of *supply and demand* is closely allied with scarcity. If there were only 100 people living in the whole world, there would be enough of every natural resource for everybody because the demand would be very small in comparison with the supply. However, there would be few people to produce the goods and services that human beings want.

Numerous experiments are regularly conducted that use laboratory mice and rats. That's because mice and rats have some biological similarities to humans. When a bunch of rats are crowded into a tiny space, they will compete and finally go mad. Space is an economic resource—an asset. Two of the major world problems today are the population explosion and the depletion of natural resources, each which impacts the other. Many of our current social, economic, and developmental problems are interrelated to these two basic world problems. Even wars originate because a country's citizens run out of land (space) or want more even though they can survive with less.

If there were no scarcity or supply/demand problems, if every person, household, company, and country had every possible resource with which to satisfy every possible need and want, there would be less competition, and less unethical or criminal behaviors. But there are not (*unlimited resources*), so there is (competition).

About *competition*, it has been said: "Those who think that the competitive spirit is dead ought to watch the customers in a supermarket when a cashier opens a new checkout lane." The astute observer of human behavior often agrees. Competition over close-in parking spaces at malls, on college campuses, and the like reaches absurd levels. "Parking lot paranoia defies common sense yet it sometimes afflicts almost as many people as the common cold."

That which people must sacrifice (give up) in order to get what they want (choose) is called *opportunity cost*. In most democratic societies, almost anybody can be a millionaire—all one has to do is work hard for 50 years, save at least 20 percent of your income annually, and sacrifice a lot of everyday pleasures in the meantime.

Economics is based on balance: balancing the supply of goods and services (jobs, assets, etc.) against the demand; balancing the needs of the individual against the many—which results in making trade-offs; balancing the protection of the environment against protecting the needs and wants of humans.

Economic indicators include several barometers based on mathematics, statistics, and the gathering and reporting of conglomerate data. The *GNP* (gross national product) calculates the total goods and services produced by a nation in a certain year and can be compared with the GNP of other nations. The *consumer index* calculates changes in prices for consumer goods in one part of the country and world in comparison with others and from product to product and store to store. The *unemployment index* calculates the number of people out of work and looking from period to period. Other indexes tell the number of *construction startups*, the amount and type of *retail sales*, and so on.

A major theme of economics is the study of business. People need this because in businesses people design, produce, distribute, advertise, and sell the products that satisfy humans needs at all levels. Businesses create the jobs that employ people to produce the products and pay them for their efforts so they in turn can buy things that satisfy human needs.

Balance is the key to an understanding of how economic concepts affect humans. Feeling empathy for business comes from comparing the operation of businesses with the operation of households and individual resources.

BUSINESS AND ENTREPRENEURSHIP

Business owners are real people, just like employees and consumers. They seek to earn a living and gain a return on the investments of their money, time, and effort that they put into a business. If they did not put their money into the operation of their businesses, they could put their money into other savings and investment programs that would not require the expenditure of so much time and energy.

Stockholders are also real people who invest their money into the businesses of other people by buying stock (shares of the business) in the belief that the business will succeed, not fail (make a profit, not lose). From the profits of corporations that sell stock to stockholders come the dividends (portion of profits) that stockholders earn each period–quarter, year, etc.

Thus, neither profit, stock *dividends*, nor stockholders are negative words, they are words that describe what happens when real people put themselves and their money to work to meet a country's economic needs. The media, including some news anchors, movie, and TV plots would often have us think otherwise. Why pit management against employees, owners against consumers? People need each other.

Many organizations use SICs for clarification purposes. For example, the U. S. Internal Revenue Service (IRS) uses the SICs. When owners of small businesses process the income tax forms each year, they complete Schedule C for reporting income, expenses, and to show whether the firm made a profit or suffered a loss.

A major goal of business–usually stated first–is to satisfy customers' needs. If a firm's products do not satisfy customers, the customers will not buy them and the firm cannot meet its most important goal. The primary goal of business is to make sales at prices that will produce a profit so the business can continue, thus providing jobs and wages to employees and products to customers.

Telecommunications in Small Businesses

Small businesses use call forwarding (as well as answering machines, answering services, or voice mail) to reduce the expense of answering calls by their office personnel. Franchise and chain businesses, for example, can direct their inbound calls to a regional or central office for answering. The operator/owners of small businesses check in regularly to get their messages and customer phone numbers.

Gary first worked for an appliance repair shop, following the high school classes he took in auto mechanics, electronics, and computers. (Today's autos have so much computerized equipment in them that the old-style mechanic competencies are way out of date! To keep up, mechanics regularly attend classes offered by auto manufacturers and by trade schools and community colleges, whether trainees travel to classes or enroll via telecommunications.)

Working for someone else was not Gary's style but neither was managing all that equipment, the huge shop, and especially the number of support people in the office. He bought a van and emblazoned it with his company name and *logo* (symbol to represent his business). He equipped the van with the most essential tools of his trade, housing larger items in his garage. With an answering machine programmed with essential data, plus a message designed to advertise his type of service, he was in business.

He traveled to the homes and businesses of his customers during the day, checking his answering machine at noon and evening for messages he should return. Nights and weekends, he kept the books. To Gary, this chore wasn't tedious, it was exciting. It told him, on a daily, weekly, monthly, and quarterly basis whether he was making or losing money. How much money was coming in and from what type of customers for what type of appliance repairs? How much money was going out and to whom and for what?

His management decisions are based on the results of analyzing the accounting data. Accounting, it has been said, is "the language of business." Gary used a spreadsheet program at first, but then changed to a bookkeeping package specifically designed for small businesses engaged in appliance repair. He gets updates from the software company and calls them on their 800 number to get advice. His management decisions are directed to such issues as should he:

- increase or lower prices?
- look for suppliers who would offer him trade credit or continue to pay in cash?
- look for suppliers who would offer him lower prices but the same or better quality of product? Or would faster delivery be more important?

- spend more money on advertising? Advertise more often in both the local newspaper and on the local radio?
- change his method from getting calls from answering machine to answering service where a live person would field calls?

Plenty of small businesses are getting a good start because of the capabilities and versatility of computer and telecommunication systems. No matter what type of business they operate, would-be entrepreneurs should look into the possibilities of expanding their services with these options.

Business Opportunities

Home-based telecommunication firms are among those that are relatively new but growing in popularity. Imagine yourself contracting with several dozen companies under the manufacturing and wholesale trade classifications. They send catalogs to mail order customers. You type the mailing labels. As with Sherri with her cross-gluing business (see Case Study, Activity III-7), you would only make a penny or so per label, but it's volume that counts—the more labels, the more income.

Or suppose you are good at calculating income tax reports. Plenty of consumers have relatively simple reports to submit, but don't even know how to do that. You do it, for perhaps $50 to $250 per customer's IRS 1040 form. You do it at the computer and submit the form to the Internal Revenue Service via e-mail.

Maybe you have something to say or can collect the sayings of others on unique topics, enticing people to buy subscriptions. Publish a monthly newsletter—sell advice about how to make or save money, save a marriage, improve health, personality. Advertise in the certain magazines that cater to the type of customers who would want to read what you want to say. Charge maybe $18.95 per year for the paper. Distribute it by e-mail to customers who are on-line or otherwise via the U.S. mail.

How about a telephone answering service or teleconferencing service? Operators answer the telephones of dozens, perhaps hundreds, of small firms who cannot afford to hire their own office workers. Answer callers' queries from the client data that you access on your computer; take sales orders. Work with the telephone company of choice to determine how to set up conference calls.

Charge enough for your services to pay the bills plus allow for a small profit margin, your return on investment. This is the money you earn since you do not work for someone else at a wage.

Career Advice

Office work helps put employees in touch with insiders and outsiders in the industry via every type of communication method and system. Processing letters, reading documents that come in the mail or are already filed, talking on the telephone, and meeting people in person are all activities that help people learn about the specific industry in which they have found employment.

People make many types of career moves—upward, laterally, and sometimes downward on the career ladder—in order to earn more money but also to get more experience or have more fun or get more job satisfaction. Lori's experience (see her case in Section II) is just one example. A knowledge of computer and telecommunication technology is essential, however, whether one's goal is to break into the job market and remain at the entry level or use an entry-level job as a springboard to advance.

What Do You Think?
Review and Opinions

1. Name the classifications that deal with goods and give five or more examples from each. Of these examples, identify at least two local firms and two to three multinational firms. Discuss how telecommunications is or might be used in these firms.

    Compare the operations of firms that deal with goods with those that deal with services. As an employee, which type of classification most appeals? As a potential entrepreneur? Why?

2. Compare the parallel growth of U.S. manufacturing with the growth of unions in the United States. Then make comparisons with third world and technologically emerging countries that are becoming more competitive in the world market. Why are Americans afraid that their jobs will be lost to countries that pay lower wages while simultaneously wanting to buy products at lower cost from those same countries?

3. Discuss the following economic terms and give examples of their impact on W-I-S-H. W = Workers and Workplaces; I = Individuals; S = the broader Society of cities, states, nations, and the world; and H = Home and Households. An example follows for *competition*:

    W Job applicants compete to get jobs and when they get them, they also compete for promotions, raises, and so on.
    I Throughout one's school years, people compete to get on teams, to get parts in plays, a place in the choir or in the band, and for good grades. It hurts to fail or even come in second in a lot of competitions, but that's life.
    S Whereas, companies compete to get customers, towns and countries compete to get industries to move in and to attract tourists. Politicians also compete with each other for votes.

H Children compete for their parents' attention, for more space in a room they share with siblings, and over decisions about where limited money will be spent and how.

Use the model of WISH examples above to share your own for these economic terms: scarcity, opportunity cost, profit, risk, productivity, and incentives.

From Cave to Satellite

Weather satellites and balloons are equipped to send meteorological information to earth, transmitted to people's living rooms, using computer graphics to simulate clouds, rainstorms, etc. TV station helicopters hover over cities, reporting traffic patterns so commuters can avoid accidents. Banks and other financial institutions use electronic transfer to transmit funds instantaneously around the globe. Travel agencies book people into hotels and onto transportation vehicles throughout the world, using computers and telecommunications.

Medical personnel use computers and telecommunications to save and prolong lives, but also in cooperation with transportation systems. Messages are transmitted to speed paramedics to the scene of accidents to save victims. Meanwhile, paramedics and other medical practitioners speak rapidly into telecommunication devices to tell untrained people at the site exactly what to do to save a victim's life until the medical vehicle arrives.

Underwater missions to rescue crippled submarines use telecommunications between battleship and nuclear submarine. The small rescue subs tap out Morse code to keep in touch.

A CIA (Central Intelligence Agency) operative, working undercover and abandoned in the cold, rugged high country of Afghanistan, whispers into a communication device much like Dick Tracy's two-way wrist radio. His message is quickly relayed to CIA headquarters in Langley, Virginia. To reach the CIA, the message goes through a local station to a U. S. naval ship in the Persian Gulf and by microwave dish that is uplinked to satellite. It is then picked up by a U.S. Air Force jet–a McDonnell Douglas F-4G–out of a SAC (Strategic Air Command) base in Omaha flying high above the clouds and fast enough to break the sound barrier. The fighter pilot, preoccupied with an electronic surveillance mission, mistakenly relays the help-and-rescue message to NORAD (North American

Defense) under Cheyenne Mountain in Colorado Springs. Next, the message is correctly routed back across the North American continent to the East Coast.

A fast decision is made about how to rescue the operative and messages are relayed back the way they came (omitting the NORAD link this time and adding interceptive instructions to another fighter pilot). Meanwhile, the CIA man is shivering behind a rock outcropping, frightened that the moonlight will reveal his whereabouts and he'll soon be bushwhacked by native tribesmen.

Piloting a high speed jet (a versatile multimission aircraft), a pilot experienced in warfare takes off from Australia to coordinate with a sister aircraft (a combat Harriet Jump Jet multimission aircraft) out of Bangkok (Thailand). Within a few hours from the time he first radioed for help, the spy's rescue mission is launched!

By 1993, despite the end to the cold war, there were more spy satellites in space than ever before. The latest satellites are so powerful that they can see through dust, dirt, and even below earth!

Many nations have their own satellites, including spy satellites that are equipped to photograph tiny objects. It is hard to hide from each other these days. But things go wrong and wear out, including satellites. When a Chinese satellite fell to earth, NORAD monitored and traced its progress; it landed safely in the ocean with no internal damage. However, an American satellite also discovered that China was testing nuclear bombs. (If they develop full nuclear capability, many other countries may, and the possibility of another major world war occurring would increase.)

Dick Cheney, Secretary of Defense under U.S. President George Bush, said "The burden of defense (around the world) rests on the United States—the last remaining superpower." Despite the end of the cold war with Russia, the dismantling of their KGB (similar to the American CIA), and the destruction of a super Soviet spy satellite, U.N. and U.S. forces are dispatched around the world to help keep the peace—to Somalia, Bosnia, and Kuwait, for example.

Communication goes on all the time, between spaceships and earth, between submarines deep beneath the oceans between generals in the midst of war and government officials back home. Red-alert phones sit on the desks of top government leaders, who await calls to vanquish or negotiate with enemies or plain people at hot spots that keep cropping up somewhere on the planet.

Orbiting the earth are many spy satellites as well as communication satellites. Since spy networks are designed to collect information and interpret and transmit messages, it might be said that broadly speaking, they are all "communication satellites." These and many other sophisticated technological inventions have come to the consumer market because of the vast sums of government money that are spent on research and development. For example, a basic form of computerization was invented in the late 1800s, yet it took World War II and the needs of governments to compete before computers were refined so that businesses could use them after the war.

Why do we explore space? Why not? Humans have always been curious. Cave people explored beyond the next hill. Daniel Boone walked the land. Magellan explored the oceans. People look for new lands not only out of curiosity but also to meet their need to survive. We need new resources, raw materials, space, water. We leave one place and head for others to get away from despots and dictators, from cruelty and injustice. But–win or lose, fail or succeed–people thirst for independence and hunger to create things their own way. We want to govern ourselves, run our own businesses and make our own decisions. We long to explore our own inner capabilities as well as outer possibilities.

There are two great worlds operating within the world today. One might be called the *Super Overworld* and the other the *Super Underworld*. The Overworld consists of governments, big and small, but compared to the size of most businesses, they are big. To give an idea of the size of government in the United States, one out of four workers is employed by government–including local, county, state, and federal. Thus, government is big business. Its income is derived from all kinds of taxes, including personal and business income taxes.

The primary purpose of government, traditionally, has been to protect a country's citizens. Thus, we have military and defense programs and–at the state, county, and local levels–highway patrols, sheriffs, and other police officers. "Protection," it seems, has also come to include entitlement programs–welfare and social security, which nearly accounts for 50 percent of the national budget! Big bucks also get allocated for big programs, especially defense and space exploration.

The many *Super Overworld* departments, agencies, bureaus, and programs use sophisticated and expensive computer and telecommunication systems. These systems need people to operate them, so there are many technical jobs in government that require telecommunication and computer competencies.

The *Super Underworld* consists of all the crime, criminals, and criminal activities in operation at any given time around the globe. Just about every country has "organized" crime-systems in place that operate in as well-defined a fashion as any large business or huge government.

Multiply the organized crime groups by the many small-time crooks who operate outside of the legal system, and the result is plenty of illegal business operations that (although their activities may contribute to the economy) *pay no taxes*. There is a tremendous amount of trouble and turmoil associated with crime, not to mention the traumas that come to people and businesses because of violence and fraud.

There are also numerous types of white-collar and industrial espionage crimes. Many white-collar criminals use telecommunications equipment to break into and revise or delete computer files.

Drug dealing takes a lot of coordination between and among people in many occupations around the globe, from raising cocaine in South America (e.g., Colombia) or Southeast Asia, to transporting this and other drugs over water and air, by land and rail, to city distribution points, where it is further broken down (to diluted strengths) and passed around to small-time dealers. The communication systems to manage all these operations and the transportation systems to move them are huge.

The sophistication of telecommunication and computer systems placed into operation even temporarily by members of the underworld can disrupt business operations and personal lives. One type of "bug" (microsurveillance microphone) can be placed inside the telephone instrument, not only to overhear and tape phone conversations but also to record room conversations when no one has even picked up the telephone. Another type of device picks up the digits dialed so that surveillants (members of either the super over-world or the underworld) know what numbers are called.

Crooks and hackers get into telephone systems and computers to wreak mayhem. They sabotage records systems—sometimes to wreak vengeance but more often to steal—directly as in money, or indirectly as in information to resell. Computer hackers would not be able to get into and alter records systems were it not for telecommunications systems.

Think about this single illustration and philosophize with your responses: if there were no customers for drugs, there would be no drug sales, no drug dealers, no drug trafficking, and no need to spend vast amounts of tax dollars on eradicating the whole drug problem. The same can be said for any addiction, "imbalance," or "unhealthy" societal practice; for example, prostitution, gambling, or high-priced, black market rip-offs. Businesses, whether legal or illegal, moral or immoral, cannot sell what people do not want.

Review Maslow's hierarchy of human needs to see how some of the needs deemed immoral (by society) are met by the underworld. Where does greed come in? In response to security and safety? To "keep up with the Jones'," as in the social and ego levels?

With your TV viewing in this unit, watch the news *and* fictionalized stories (movies, etc.) for examples of how both the super overworld and the super underworld use telecommunications to make deals—good or bad, big or little. Note the use of all sorts of electronic devices and the link between telephones and computers.

Activities for Section III

Name: _____ Date: _____

Directions

1. Unless the instructor or course facilitator indicates otherwise, group roles (recorder, supervisor, etc.) should remain the same as with previous sections.

2. Listen to and view television shows to gather data about telecommunication systems and how they are used in business. *Enter SIC notations in the margins beside print clippings and notes from TV viewings.* These notations are in *addition to annotated comments to summarize highlights.*

3. Use some innovative approaches to collecting additional SIC data in person. "Let your fingers do the walking" through the Yellow Pages. Note local firms while on personal or household errands. Or take several driving tours through business and industrial neighborhoods.

Besides small, independent, local firms, look for large businesses—national or multinational firms. With a partner, group, or individually, choose two, or more of the following additional methods to collect and identify SIC data:

- Visit a stock brokerage or library and check out (buy or borrow) a copy of an abbreviation booklet. This directory lists alphabetically all of the two-to-four letter abbreviations used by the stock exchange and gives the full names of each company. Then when you only have abbreviations (e.g., IBM, CSX), you will be able to identify businesses by their full names. With this data, classify firms by their SIC.

- Look for various ways to find businesses–TV business shows, in the business pages of magazines and newspapers, or on the sides of trucks.
- Drive out to the edge of the city to a truck stop (cafe, gasoline station, etc.) or drive on an interstate until you come to a rest stop. Sit in the car and observe semis that park and drive by. Identify and note the companies they represent.
- Visit a train station or stop at a railroad crossing so you can watch freight cars go by and repeat the above steps.
- Watch the evening business report to define companies by their abbreviations.
- Read the financial section of major newspapers, such as *The Wall Street Journal*, *The New York Times*, *The Los Angeles Times*, the *Washington Post*, or news magazines such as *Forbes* and *Barron's*. Identify what companies do by any of these sources so that your records will be accurate.

4. The ability to identify companies from their names is based on experience and knowledge. IBM stands for International Business Machines. Even if you did not know the full company name, you probably know that IBM manufactures computers.

What about a company like CSX, though? This company represents a merger of several other types of companies. CSX now deals with railroads in the United States and, internationally, with real estate, energy, and computer and telecommunications technology. Relying on group knowledge may produce more extensive and accurate information than working alone to decipher the type of companies you see represented by various means.

Look for a minimum of one company example per SIC. You might want to compete with other group members to see who can fill out their list the quickest with the most accurate data. Or cooperate with your group's members and compete as a team with other groups. Use the spaces and pages that follow as a journal to record what you see and learn, as noted under each SIC (some examples are given to get you started).

Extraction–mining: (Texaco, Kuznetsova Loggers)

_____

_____

Extraction–agriculture: (Hillside Farms Dairy, King Ranch)

_____

_____

Manufacturing: (IBM, Sony, General Motors, Woobee Knit Shop)

_____

_____

Construction: (The House Coat–painting, Spiegle Builders)

_____

_____

Wholesale Trade: (Waco Cold Storage Locker, ABC Distributors)

_____

_____

Transportation: (Salt Creek Freight, B&O Railroad, Delta Airlines)

_____

_____

Retail Trade: (Kmart, Safeway, Moeller's Boutique)

_____

_____

Utilities: (Pacific Power, Northern Gas Co., TCI Cablevision)

_____

_____

Communication Services: (*The Washington Post*, Delmar Publishers, Watmore's Advertising Agency, Aspen Software, FOX TV Network, NBC)

_____

_____

Professional Services: (Coates Clinic, Finemyer & Associates)

_____

_____

Business and Financial Services: (Key Bank, Machalek Real Estate, State Farm Insurance, Roberta's Secretarial Service)

_____

_____

Hospitality, Recreation, and Tourism Services: (Hilton Hotel, O&S Guest Ranch, Yellowstone National Park, Cowboy Bar, Seattle Symphony)

_____

_____

Personal Services: (The Hair Port, Stitchin' Post–custom sewing, Kleaner Korner)

_____

_____

Public and Nonprofit Services: (United Way, Salvation Army, Red Cross, Boy Scouts, American Heart Association)

_____

_____

5. Meet with your group to share new portfolio news (added since the close of Section II). The supervisor leads discussion as each member shares new information. Opinions about the most accurate SIC designation for each business may differ. If so, reach consensus through discussion and by referring to directories and other notations.

6. The recorder takes notes and the processor composes a memo from these notes to summarize and report findings to the instructor. The supervisor proofreads the memo and makes recommendations, if any, for revision. Hold for transmittal until all activities have been completed from Section III.

ACTIVITY III-2: CONDUCT INTERVIEWS WITH LOCAL BUSINESS OWNERS

Name: _____ Date: _____

Directions

1. The supervisors of all groups meet to divide the list of SICs. If there are three groups, then two groups will work with five SICs and one group will work with four (total of 14).

2. Within each group, four or five classifications are divided among partners so each partnership is assigned to interview no more than two or three business owners. Use personal knowledge, a walking or driving tour, or the Yellow Pages to select businesses within your designated SICs. (See also Activity III-1 to identify local businesses from the total list.)

3. Use the document provided by your course facilitator or one of your own interview documents to record your SIC (Standard Industrial Classification) questions. Allow space on the document so you can enter answers from personal interviews.

Topics to address in the questionnaire include some major business principles as well as how the firm uses telecommunications. Examples are listed below. Use the spaces that follow to compose any notes or information that you may find helpful.

     a. Company name and how it was determined (such as from the owner[s] name, something clever, etc.):

_____

     b. Company logo (how and why the design, if any):

_____

     c. Product (good or service):

_____

_____

d. SIC (you will probably have to fill this in, since the business owner may not know):

_____

_____

e. Product sold locally, nationally, or worldwide?

_____

_____

_____

f. Channel(s) of distribution (where and how the firm gets its major products–from what other companies; and where, besides to the consumer, do products go next):

_____

_____

_____

g. Transportation system(s) used (to get goods shipped to the local firm, if the firm deals in goods instead of services):

_____

_____

_____

h. Telecommunication system(s) used (to make buy-and-sell transactions, and for conducting any other type of business):

_____

_____

_____

_____

i. Marketing methods (to advertise locally or to broader markets):

_____

_____

_____

_____

j. Does the firm use telemarketing and if so, to local or to broader markets?

_____

_____

_____

_____

_____

k. Does the firm employ local office personnel or do they rely on telecommunications for part of their support service (i.e., do they use an answering machine, an answering service, or voice mail to record calls from customers)?

_____

_____

l. Business structure (sole proprietorship, partnership, or corporation):

_____

_____

m. What are the typical costs of doing business? For example, cost of goods sold (wholesale prices of goods bought that are resold), rent or mortgage payments, utilities, employee wages, advertising (marketing), insurance, transportation, communication or telecommunication costs, miscellaneous, etc. (Find out what goes into miscellaneous or that you did not account for, such as under "etc." If possible, get percentages—the percent of total sales or income that goes for buying goods at wholesale prices, and for total expenses plus key expense items such as wages and marketing.):

_____

_____

_____

_____

_____

_____

_____

_____

_____

_____

_____

_____

_____

_____

_____

_____

---

4. Arrange to conduct interviews by calling or walking into the establishment. Ask to speak to the manager or owner. Explain that this is a class project and arrange a time that is convenient for both of you and that allows from 30 to 40 minutes of conversation.

Note that if you plan to *electronically record the interview*, you must explain this procedure to the interviewee. If the owner(s) agree and you have the equipment, use a *cassette recorder*.

5. Organize your handwritten notes or listen to the recorded interview to see if you clearly understand what was stated. Call the interviewee(s) if you need to clear up any questions before proceeding to the next activity.

SUPERVISOR'S EVALUATION–SECTION III

Person evaluated:_____ Date_____

Directions: use the +, ✔, – evaluation method, where + = outstanding, ✔ = average/satisfactory, and – = poor/unsatisfactory.

In contributing to the development of the SIC1 database, this group member:

1. was present and on time for small-group meetings   _____

2. contributed his/her fair share to interview ideas   _____

3. met with the interviewee(s) as scheduled   _____

4. collected usable interview data   _____

5. was responsible to group members   _____

6. was amenable to the supervisor's suggestions;
   e.g., corrected errors, responded to ideas   _____

7. was accurate in finalizing her/his share of the database _____

8. overall, was cooperative, pleasant, dependable   _____

SUPPORTIVE COMMENTS:

Evaluator's signature (confidential):_____

ACTIVITY III-3: PARTICIPATE TO PREPARE A MULTIMEDIA DEMONSTRATION

Name: _____   Date: _____

Directions

1. The purpose of this activity is to develop a multimedia demonstration representing only those classifications for which you and your partner were personally responsible (see the previous two activities). Bring your portfolio to a group meeting. The portfolio should by now be annotated with SIC notations.

2. Brainstorm to decide what type of media you will use in preparing a demonstration to be presented to the full class; for example,

- A simple collage of pictures representing your designated SICs could be prepared for poster or bulletin board.
- Prepare a series of transparencies for overhead projection.
- A camera with slide film may be used to shoot photos of the local businesses.
- Similar to the above, but using a videocamera. A group member or the school's media resource center might have one. For this plan and the slide series idea above, you also need to check out the appropriate equipment from the resource center—slide projector and screen or television set with VCR.
- The most sophisticated multimedia demonstration uses the computer with a variety of other input devices and methods.

3. Discuss with your instructor or group members ideas about how to prepare for and present a class demonstration. Arrange your schedule with the instructor for the class presentation.

4. Use the spaces provided to record notes at each of the group's planning and work sessions. (The evaluation is conducted by the instructor at the time of the presentation.)

_____

_____

5. Use the spaces provided to record notes about the *other groups' demonstrations.*

_____

_____

_____

_____

_____

_____

_____

_____

_____

_____

_____

_____

_____

_____

_____

_____

_____

_____

_____

_____

_____

_____

_____

_____

_____

_____

_____

ACTIVITY III-4: PARTICIPATE
IN DISCUSSING CASE STUDIES

Name: _____ Date: _____

Directions

1. Read the cases that follow and record notes that reflect your own opinions *before* joining group members for discussion.

2. The supervisor leads discussion toward reaching consensus about personality types who are more suited to work for themselves than to work for others in a typical 9 to 5 job. (No consensus should be reached regarding individual opinions about yourself.) The recorder takes notes and from these notes, the processor prepares a memo. Directed to the instructor, this memo reports discussion.

Case Study 1: I'll Never Leave My Home!

Sherri Paduchi was married to a creative man, Guy, who preferred creating musical pageants for church at no pay than going out to work for others. With babies coming fast, Sherri did not want to leave her home to earn the family's living, so she started not one but several home-based businesses over the years. Gail or Guy spearheaded the following projects with the help of each other and their growing children:

- They glued wee crosses onto biblical bookmarks for a religious bookstore–income: one penny per cross. The family developed efficiency methods, using tweezers, glue-soaked sponges, and time-and-motion savings, so that they could glue from 5,000 to 10,000 crosses per day ($50 to $100). But that took many boring hours every day and little time was left for everyday living.
- They opened a cleaning service, catering to private homes and businesses, which was hard work and boring, but paid some of the bills for a few years. It was so boring and hard, though, that after a while Guy mostly slept in while Sherri dragged the chil-

dren off to help her clean. Feeling guilty, perhaps, Guy went out to market the business into big bucks by bringing in big clients: churches, school gymnasiums, and finally an entire airport, with firms like TWA and Delta paying the tab. Now, though, they had many employees and multiple personnel problems and it all became just too big a nuisance.

- They sold Shaklee products, both directly to the customers who came to their home store and indirectly through the distributors who signed on with them. Guy found a creative outlet in running the training sessions for new distributors and composing and publishing a monthly training and sales newsletter. But they got so excited about the program that they went into debt buying and stocking inventory and providing costly incentives to their distributors, which meant they had nothing with which to pay their own bills. So they had to back off and find something else to do.

- They organized a musical group and got a number of bookings and even some major concerts. They rented a performance/production facility and produced cassettes to sell. It was a lot of hard work, but fun, especially when they recruited Guy's two sisters and their husbands into the band and later all of their growing children. But the production and marketing costs overran the income and they could not clear enough money to support even one family, much less three.

- In between their semi-successes and major fiascos, Guy picked up odd jobs in painting and carpentry. They purchased cheaply a four-story house because there was very little of the house left after a major fire. Over the years, Guy gradually turned room after room into livable quarters, which doubled in use as both home and businesses—the Shaklee store and distributor training classroom, rehearsal hall for the musical group, and a preschool.

- Sherri, who had been pursuing a degree in elementary education when she married, opened a preschool in their home. One group of a dozen or so tiny tots enrolled in the Monday/Wednesday class and the other group in the Tuesday/Thursday class. Sherri charged $1 per hour, per child. Some children stayed five hours, others six, and still others as long as eight hours. The income paid the monthly mortgage and utilities and put some food in the cupboards, but allowed for little else.

- One night, after being struck head-on by a drunken driver, Guy sustained fatal injuries. After Guy's tragic death, Sherri continued with her two major businesses—selling Shaklee (but no longer recruiting or training new distributors) and operating the preschool. Money was tight. The oldest two children took one, two, even three part-time jobs, while the youngest took children into the home to earn money from baby-sitting.
- Sherri remarried, this time to Blair McDonald, a man who was partially disabled from an industrial accident. Blair cannot hold a job all day, not as a manual laborer, which would put his back and legs into painful condition, and not in a white-collar office job, which would knock his back out completely from sitting all day. He has creative talents, too, one of which is professional photography.

Blair is also a great handyman and keeps himself occupied around the big house repairing things that had gone untouched for awhile. The savings that he brought to the marriage went for two things—first, to pay off the home mortgage and second, to buy into a partnership whereby his firm would produce how-to videos for the home handyperson type of customer.

Blair can vary the type of work he does during the day so as to relieve his back and legs. He is his own boss—well, partially. His partner, a slow-working perfectionist, likes the production end of the business. Because of his physical impairments and his interests, Blair runs the outside errands. He is in and out of the shop and his van all day, meeting with businesspeople—bankers, accountants, advertising agency reps, and telecommunication personnel.

The how-to video company needs an 800 number so it can advertise in catalogs and magazines for home repair buffs. When customers want to buy a video, they call Blair's 800 number, where operators from a telephone answering service answer queries and take sales orders.

The telephone companies do not automatically provide an 800 number to everybody who asks, even people who operate legitimate businesses. Credit ratings must be checked and collateral put up, as with any supplier who provides trade credit, before an 800 number is approved.

Blair's van has a telephone and he wears a beeper on his belt so Sherri can call her husband at any time, no matter where he is. Sherri often needs Blair to help her at home—either with the noisy bustling preschool-age children or the telephone that rings all day long from Sherri's Shaklee customers or Blair's business contacts. She also fields Blair's calls, in between everything else.

1. What type of personality traits suggest that people should work for themselves instead of working for someone else in a typical 9 to 5 job?

_____

_____

_____

_____

2. Suppose that your type of personality and human needs suggest that you seek the security of a regular paycheck instead of entrepreneurship. However, you cannot find a job anywhere. Would you be interested in exploring entrepreneurship? Why or why not?

_____

_____

_____

3. Many young mothers work out of the home. What is your reaction to Sherri's plan—that she work at just about anything inside the home but will not leave her children to look for work else-where? (You will recall that she spends many of these home business hours involved with one or more businesses and not directly and exclusively with her children.)

_____

_____

_____

_____

4. Although Sherri kept saying (when interviewed), "I'm not very creative myself . . . ," she seems to be attracted to self-defined "creative" men. What is your opinion about how she adapts to their personalities—their inability or unwillingness to work for others?

_____

_____

_____

_____

5. About 98 percent of the 16 million or so businesses in the United States are small businesses. There is a trend among women and minorities to start their own businesses. With telecommunications, many more home-based small businesses are emerging. Meanwhile, many large companies are opening branches in other countries or transferring tasks from this country's employees to employees who live elsewhere around the globe.

Comparing these statements with the innovativeness of Sherri and her husbands, what predictions would you propose about the extent and type of small enterprises that are likely to be created over the next decade?

_____

_____

_____

_____

_____

_____

_____

_____

_____

_____

_____

Case Study 2: Home-Based Software Company Posts $1.2 Million

A woman walks into a small room where a row of 16 computers wait anxiously for someone to press a key that will rid the monitor of its flashing "Welcome" sign. She begins to answer questions given by the computer about her TV viewing habits, favorite games, pet peeves, and so on.

This is not a game nor a political poll. This is a job interview. The computerized interview is the brainchild of Brooks Mitchell, owner of Aspen Tree Software in Laramie, Wyoming. His company, that posted $1.2 million in revenues and a 50 percent pretax margin a few years after launch date out of his home, was featured in *Forbes* magazine.

Mitchell has designed job interview and other software programs for such companies as Marriott, Neiman Marcus, Corning, Foley's, and American Express. He describes himself as "a man who never fit into any organizations but able to predict who would."

Mitchell can't abide sticking to the prescribed business dress code of button-down shirt, tie, and suit. He prefers western wear and likes to drift through small Wyoming towns setting up a karaoke machine in a strange bar and playing guitar to the accompaniment of young and old-timer cowboys.

He majored in personnel management and was hired once by a West Virginia garment manufacturer to reduce their high turnover rate among sewing machine operators. After interviewing in-depth those who quit and those who stayed, he noticed that the better sewing machine operators weighed over 300 pounds and were not likely to own a car. Armed with such data, he hired a computer hacker to design a program to score an applicant's answers. Then he discovered that job applicants were more likely to admit to the computer if they intended to stay only a few months. The garment company soon cut its turnover rate in half.

1. What kind of personality and pet peeves do you have? For example, are you more or less likely to adapt readily to working for someone else, including following their dress code and other job performance and behavioral requirements?

_____

_____

_____

_____

_____

_____

_____

_____

2. A number of vignettes appear in this section that describe entrepreneurs and their enterprises. See for example, the SIC descriptions of extraction, manufacturing, and communications, among others. Review the topics in Section I about home-based businesses—those that use telecommunications and those that can be classified under the communications SIC, as in this case. Report your reactions (both thoughts and feelings) to these stories. Notice that the following two categories allow you to report both positive and negative reactions. Sometimes we learn as much about ourselves when analyzing what we dislike as what we like.

POSITIVE REACTIONS:

_____

_____

_____

_____

_____

_____

_____

_____

_____

_____

NEGATIVE REACTIONS:

_____

_____

_____

_____

_____

_____

_____

_____

_____

_____

3. What does the information that you reported above tell you about yourself? Would you prefer to work for someone else or be your own boss? Can you handle risk? Do you find it exciting? Or would you prefer the security (Maslow's second need level) of a regular paycheck? Report your reaction below and give a rationale.

TENTATIVE DECISION AND RATIONALE:

_____

_____

_____

_____

_____

_____

_____

_____

_____

_____

ACTIVITY III-5: PROBLEM SOLVING
WITH WHOLE-BRAIN THINKING

Name: _____ Date: _____

Background for Economic Decision Making

Few, if any, solutions produce only advantages and no disadvantages. Every decision comes with a trade-off or opportunity cost. This opportunity cost or group of disadvantages may be worse than the original problem. So the goal is to select the best solution.

The charts that follow illustrate the economic principles of choice versus opportunity cost. The choice is stated in the left-hand column and the items sacrificed are on the right. The first chart describes a family decision and the second a national one.

ITEM CHOSEN	ITEMS SACRIFICED
Purchase a car for Junior	Savings for Junior's college
	Family room for family
	Vacation for family

ITEM CHOSEN	ITEMS SACRIFICED
Reduce the national deficit	Raise for seniors on social security
	Aid to two starving nations
	Repair highways and parks
	Build new schools

Directions for Individual Decision Making

1. Use the charts that follow to construct your own decisions regarding the following economic assets—money, time, and space: (a) what you will do with $15,000, (b) how you will spend the next year of your life, and (c) what you will do with one additional room to be added to your dwelling.

MONEY–What I will do with $15,000

CHOICE	SACRIFICED

TIME–What single special thing I will do next month

CHOICE	SACRIFICED

SPACE–What I will do with one extra room

CHOICE	SACRIFICED

2. Use the chart to make a real-life decision that is your own.

CHOICE	SACRIFICED

Directions for Group Decision Making

1. Meet in a full class session. Choose a facilitator, who leads a brainstorming session on operating four businesses. Review the topic in the section entitled "Business Opportunities."

2. Create T-charts on a chalkboard or newsprint, on which to list advantages and disadvantages of each of the four types of telecommunication businesses described in the section.

3. One recorder records ideas and one processor composes a memo to report group consensus. Proofread, correct, and hold.

ACTIVITY III-6: GROUP MEETING TO REACH SECTION CLOSURE

Name: _____ Date: _____

Directions

1. Reconvene a meeting with your group. Bring your file or portfolio that should include printouts of all documents created and received over the course of Section III.

2. The supervisor leads discussion and the recorder takes notes to reach group consensus about the learning outcomes in comparison with section objectives. Use the spaces provided to record ideas and notes:

Section Objectives   *Learning Outcomes*

_____   _____

_____   _____

_____   _____

_____   _____

_____   _____

_____   _____

_____   _____

_____   _____

_____   _____

_____   _____

3. Verify the completion of tasks on the major project.

4. Use the spaces provided to designate new tasks and people:

Tasks	Person Responsible	Due Date

5. The processor composes a memo from the recorder's notes. The memo, directed to the instructor, lists the attachments and states progress on the term project. Attached to this memo are all documents and reports (not already submitted to the instructor) that represent individual and group work on this section.

6. The supervisor evaluates each group member confidentially and submits this form to the instructor. (Submit evaluation form to supervisor.)

SUPERVISOR'S EVALUATION–SECTION III

Person evaluated:_____ Date:_____

Directions: use the +, ✔, – evaluation method, where + = outstanding, ✔ = average/satisfactory, and – = poor/unsatisfactory.

With this section, the group member was:

1. cooperative with co-workers   _____
2. responsive to assignments made by the group   _____
3. responsive to the supervisor's constructive ideas   _____
4. pleasant, cooperative, easy to work with   _____
5. dependable, attended class meetings   _____
6. dependable, attended out-of-class meetings   _____
7. responsible, produced work on time   _____
8. responsible, produced quality work   _____
9. reliable and willing to work   _____
10. positive team player who contributed greatly
    to the group   _____

SUPPORTIVE COMMENTS:

Supervisor's signature (confidential):_____

Bibliography for Section III

Adams, Nathan M., "Cocaine King: A Study in Evil," *Reader's Digest*, December, 1988.

Barnes, Fred, "Victory in Afghanistan: The Inside Story," *Reader's Digest*, December, 1988. (Using telecommunications to facilitate war and espionage activities.)

Brinkley, David, and Sam Donaldson, *This Week with David Brinkley*, ABC, October 24, 1993. (Interviewing Dick Cheney, U.S. Secretary of Defense under President George Bush.)

Cheney, Richard, former U.S. Secretary of Defense under President Bush, interviewed by David Brinkley and Sam Donaldson, *This Week with David Brinkley*, ABC, October 24, 1993. ("The burden of defense around the world rests on the United States as the last remaining superpower.")

Chervenak, Larry, "Hotel Technology at the Start of the New Millennium," *Hospitality Research Journal: The Futures Issue*, vol. 17, no. 1, 1993.

Chiles, James R., "To the Stars," *Reader's Digest*, December 1988.

Church, Olive D., *Crackers*. Cincinnati, OH: South Western Publishing Company, 1994.

_____, *Entrepreneurship Step-by-Step*. Portland, ME: J. Weston Walch, 1986.

Clancy, Tom, *Clear and Present Danger*. New York: The Berkeley Publishing Group, 1989. (Well-researched techno-thriller about technology in battles.)

_____, *Patriot Games*. New York: G. P. Putnam's Sons, 1987.

"Cocaine and the CIA," *60 Minutes*, CBS, November 21, 1993.

Dobbs, Lou, *Money Line*, CNN, November 4, 1993. ("With the underground economy, the United States loses over $150 billion in unpaid taxes each year.")

Downs, ABC, November 22, 1993. (The Navy spent billions of dollars during the Cold War; now they use the equipment to track and save whales.)

Downs, Hugh, and Lynn Sherr, *20/20*, ABC, July 30, 1993. (Addressed working conditions of the early industrial era and some child labor laws that followed.)

"Global Mafia and Technology," *Newsweek*, December 13, 1993.

Gray Lady Down, (submarine rescue using telecommunications between ships, shore, and submarine), *Encore* (The Mirish Company, 1978).

Gumbel, Bryant, *The Today Show*, NBC, July 21, 1993.

Hamilton, David, "Restricted Access," *The Wall Street Journal*, November 15, 1993.

Hoover's Handbook of American Business 1997, edited by Gary Hoover, Alta Campbell, and Patrick J. Spain. Austin, Texas: The Reference Press, Inc., 1997.

Hoover's Handbook of World Business, edited by Gary Hoover, Alta Campbell, and Patrick J. Spain. Austin, Texas: The Reference Press, Inc., 1997.

Investing in the Future: Germany's New Federal States. Bonn, Germany: Federal Ministry of Economics, March 1992.

Jennings, Peter, *ABC News*, September 17, 1993. (American spy satellites discovered China's nuclear bomb testing.)

Keller, John J., "Net Assets," *The Wall Street Journal*, November 15, 1993.

Lewyn, Mark, "Catching the Next Technology Wave," *Business Week*, August 30, 1993.

Lumpkin, Marc, "Forbes Magazine Features Innovative Laramie Computer Firm," *The Laramie Daily Boomerang*, August 6, 1993.

_____, "Wyoming Investment Author Discovers Faded Highway in 1936 Olds," *The Laramie Daily Boomerang*, October 28, 1993. (Home-based author uses telecommunications to gather information while living and working in Wyoming.)

McCarroll, Thomas, and Sandra Barton, "New Star Over Asia," *Time*, August 9, 1993. (Media baron Rupert Murdoch bought a hot TV service in Hong Kong; Murdoch also owns the U.S. FOX TV network.)

McNichol, Tom, "Fire Your Boss and Work for Yourself," *USA Weekend*, July 16-18, 1993.

Owens, Gwinn, "Spaced Out," *Reader's Digest*, September, 1990. (Paranoia over competition for parking spaces in U.S. mall parking lots.)

Peters, Thomas J., and Robert H. Waterman, Jr., *In Search of Excellence*. New York: Warner Books., Inc., 1982. (Lessons from America's best-run companies.)

Rather, Dan, and Connie Chung, *CBS News*, July 23, 1993. (People want to buy products from companies that can demonstrate that they have a social conscience.)

Rolston, Don, "World Food Day," *Wyoming Livestock Roundup*, October 10, 1992.

Samuelson, Robert J., "How Our American Dream Unraveled," *Newsweek*, March 2, 1992.

Schrader, Richard K., "Air Mobility Command," *Air Combat*, September/October 1993.

Schwartz, Evan I., "The Shaker-Uppers at AT&T," *Business Week*, August 30, 1993.

Thomas, Craig, *The Last Raven*. New York: Harper PaperBacks, 1990. (Well-researched espionage novel.)

Winter, Barbara, *Making a Living Without a Job*. (Interview about her book, see McNichol, Ibid.)

"The Wireless Warehouse," *Home Office Computer*, June 1993. (Advertisement about automating a warehouse to reduce staff and speed production.)

Wise, David, "Closing Down the K.G.B.," *The New York Times Magazine*, November 24, 1991.

Zajas, Jay J.R., *Achievement, Motivation, Employment, Job Satisfaction, and Socio-Economic Status of Doctoral Business Administration and Education Graduates: A Comparative Analysis*. University Microfilms International Press, 1985.

Zajas, Jann R. Michener, and Jay J.R. Zajas, *Effective Planning for the Success Oriented Manager* (The Corporate Management Group, 1996).

Ziegler, Bart, "AT&T's Bold Bet," *Business Week*, August 30, 1993. (AT&T negotiations to purchase McCaw Communications.)

SECTION IV:
DEFINING AND USING
TELEMARKETING

One of the most familiar examples of telemarketing is the telephone call that rings in the homes of consumers, often during the evening hours. To telemarketers, this is known as an outbound call. From the consumer's viewpoint, this is often seen as the undesireable side of telemarketing. Another common use of telemarketing is the inbound call, which callers make when they place a call into a company. For consumers who enjoy shopping from home by telephone or computer, this is often seen as a time-saving benefit of telemarketing.

Television is the medium used for TV advertising, known as commercials. Print media are also used to market products. These advertising methods are often combined with telemarketing procedures because ads regularly list the telemarketing firm's toll free 800 or 888 number; or they may provide a 900 number, which must be paid for by the caller.

Telemarketing methods are based on a company's need to market their products. Marketing is based on psychology and sociology—the ability to understand people, their needs, and how to reach them through effective marketing. Besides technology, marketing uses the fine arts, the things that help to promote products and entice an emotional right-brain response from potential customers.

Numerous innovations using technology and the merging of technology have produced new businesses and new ways to market products around the world. Creative employees and creative entrepreneurs are producing new companies and creating new jobs unheard of just a few years ago.

OBJECTIVES

1. Discuss the major concepts described in the section and reach consensus on learning outcomes.
2. Collect and report on advertisements from print and broadcast media that represent the use of telemarketing by multinational organizations.
3. Identify the country of origin of manufactured clothing or other consumer goods and personalize the experience with reactions to advertising and marketing.
4. Conduct simulated telemarketing activities to demonstrate how to effectively handle outbound calls.
5. Conduct simulated telemarketing activities to demonstrate how to effectively handle inbound query or service calls.
6. Participate with your group in discussing case studies.
7. Convene with your group to assess progress on the major project and assign new tasks and responsibilities.

Chapter 9

Defining Telemarketing

Telemarketing is the offering of goods and/or services by telephone, fax, television, computer, or other electronic media. Telemarketing procedures generally involve the use of telephones and computers, with operators taking messages and orders and trying to make sales. Television and Internet e-mail marketing are other uses of telemarketing.

Free-to-caller 800 and 888 numbers are the most popular direct means for consumers to use in contacting firms, whether to ask questions, get information, or actually buy products (tangible goods or intangible services). Understanding the use of 800 and 888 numbers introduces a range of other topics, such as the use of 900 numbers, the handling of outbound and inbound calls, the coordination of broadcast and print media with telephone procedures, some legal ramifications and illegal scams, and telemarketing occupations and competencies.

THE USE OF 800 AND 888 NUMBERS

For wide-market advertising, such as that found in national print matter and on television, firms often list their 800 or 888 toll-free numbers. For printed ads, firms might include a coupon that can be mailed or an address to whom customers may write. However, telecommunications has replaced written and mailed correspondence to such an extent that providing free long-distance telephone calls has proven to be much more effective in getting customers to make contact.

Telemarketing operators, switchboard operators, receptionists, and secretaries are often the first company representatives that

Photo 9.1. Telephone Use

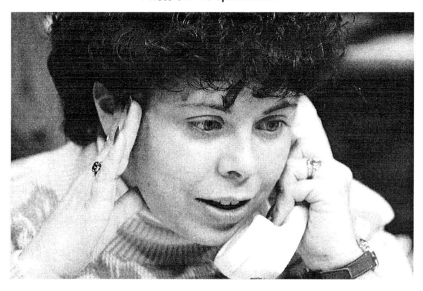

Telemarketers, receptionists, and other office workers often spend a majority of their work day on the telephone communicating with customers, prospects, and information seekers.

potential customers reach. Thus, every incoming call represents a chance to make or lose a sale, to promote or harm the business.

To stay in business, companies must sell their goods and services. They must reach customers, promote their products in a manner that will demonstrate how their products can satisfy the needs and wants of customers, and make sales. Every query or request for service is an opportunity to make a sale.

Companies pay for their 800 or 888 numbers, usually with a large monthly fee based on the number of calls they anticipate receiving (rates will change when the number of calls increases). Their credit record is checked before approval of a toll-free number is granted. Since paying for toll-free numbers is an expense of doing business, every firm's telemarketing staff must be as effective as possible when handling calls.

THE USE OF 900 NUMBERS

Firms who make 900 numbers available actually earn income from inbound calls. Some firms and individuals have no other business to conduct, no other sales to make, other than the information they provide over the phone. Calling a 900 number can cost anything from a very small price to a high price per minute while on line. Consumers need to be aware of such costs per minute and what they are getting for their money when they place long-distance calls to 900 numbers.

A TV station, political campaigner, or a research firm that conducts public polls might charge a minimal amount, such as $.25 to $.95 per minute. Their purpose is not to make money on such calls (realize a profit beyond expenses), but rather to gather information—for the purpose of conducting research. One may watch TV shows that invite you to call in with Yes or No replies, tell who you will vote for, or provide the organization with other data. Call if you like, the charge will appear on your telephone bill.

Those who are in business to make money from calls may provide a variety of services, some of which are pornographic. Like it or not, pornographic and sexual fantasy calls usually go for the highest rates, sometimes $9 or more per minute! The marketing and economic principles at issue here are "whatever the traffic will bear" and "supply and demand." If there is a big demand for such calls, then the company providing such pornographic information can charge exorbitant rates and still get customers. The same can be said for some money-making schemes—many people will pay dearly to get financial advice. Since financial advice can rarely be provided in a few minutes of costly long-distance calls, there are fewer such services.

Of course, not all 900-number calls are erotic. "What the traffic will bear" means that the price is determined by estimating the attractiveness of the service or information and the number of people who are willing to spend that amount to call. This catch phrase is used in marketing to establish prices for all sorts of things in comparison with determining customer demand.

One example of information available from a 900 number is Yel-Low Talk, which also offers print directories of telephone numbers. (One criteria of legitimacy is the cost: $.95 per minute is probably okay; $19 per minute is excessive.) By dialing their $.95-per-minute 900 number, you can get (as advertised) "Fingertip secrets you should know," including information about lifestyles, horoscopes, sports, television and movies, health and fitness facts, and even how to minimize taxes or burn up fat.

HANDLING OUTBOUND CALLS

Telemarketers may work out of their homes, using their home phones in the late afternoon or early evenings to call consumers at home. This was the method often used in the early days of telemarketing. A similar plan has a marketing representative ("rep") come into a town for a month or so, hire temporary telemarketers to work from many phones out of one or more hotel rooms. The rep is also available to make personal contacts, preferably sales, to interested local customers.

Lately, numerous telemarketing companies have sprung up who do nothing but place outbound calls and take inbound calls for their business clients. One example is the firm Sitel, which is headquartered in Omaha, Nebraska. There, operators place both outbound and inbound calls. In the dozen or so branch offices scattered throughout rural areas in Nebraska, South Dakota, Kansas, and Wyoming, only outbound calls are made.

Sitel personnel say they opened branches in this part of the country to accommodate farm wives and college students who need and want part-time jobs. Other reasons, suggest Sitel, are that people in this region generally demonstrate the traits of honesty and responsibility–otherwise known as the "work ethic"–and also have clear speaking voices with little or no accents. Because Omaha is in the Central Time Zone, it is also less expensive and easier to make long-distance calls from this region; easier, because whether calling east or west, there is no more than two hours difference in time zones.

Telemarketing firms get business clients who prefer not to hire their own telemarketers for big sales campaigns. When General Motors introduced its credit card, outbound *telephone service rep-*

resentatives (TSRs) in several midwestern branch offices placed the calls. Sitel contracts with General Motors for this service.

Training Procedures

Many telemarketers get a full week or more of training, using the telephone and the computer simultaneously. With the computer, they pull up various scripts that the business client has provided for the telemarketers to use. The telephone service reps (TSRs) read scripts off of the screen into the telephone. There are many options, though, about which the TSRs must make decisions. If the called person wants more information, then the TSR branches to one option on the menu of scripts. If the potential customer has objections about which they want reassurance, the TSR branches to another script option, and so on. The training procedures cover these

Photo 9.2. Telemarketers in Training

Telemarketers in training "on the floor" at Sitel celebrate when they learn to effectively relate to, and satisfy, customers.

options, using the equipment and software, practicing courtesy and correct language, and keeping computer and manual records.

Another essential part of the training session is to learn about the company that TSRs will be representing once they are on the telephone. They hear lectures about the firm's products, reputation, and preferences in handling calls. For each business client, there is a specific training session, so ideally each session is personalized for each client.

On the Floor

When TSR trainees have completed their training, they move onto the busy, buzzing, active telemarketing floor. Here there are dozens, perhaps hundreds, of telephones, each in its own cubicle that is also equipped with computer, forms, and supplies.

At Sitel, a supervisor or team leader works with about ten people per team. Instead of having individual quotas, there is a team quota. For example, the team might be expected to make ten or more sales per hour (which still equals one sale per individual team member per hour). Occasionally, someone will have bad luck while another TSR will hit a winning streak. The team approach helps its members develop loyalty to the team and to the team's sales goal. The leader dashes back and forth to see how everybody is doing and to keep a running tally of sales on a writing board. This adds excitement to the process and helps to motivate team members. If the team meets its goals with 20 minutes to spare, they get a 20-minute break. They still get a ten-minute break at least once every two hours but the time benefit helps push them to meet goals and thus helps to please every team member.

Suppose the business client publishes and sells magazines. The client wants the telemarketing company to sell more subscriptions. Established customers will be invited to renew their subscription and also to order additional magazines. TSRs like this type of call. It is known as calling a "warm" customer—one who already has purchased something from the company. With the magazine, the TSR has only to build on prior customer satisfaction with an already accepted product.

Another type of warm customer is someone who often purchases a variety of products from a company. Generally they already been

Photo 9.3. Telemarketing Floor at Sitel

Telephone service reps (TSRs) and other telemarketers often support each other with humor, goodwill, and positive attitudes.

won over to that company's reputation and the type and quality of its products. In this case, TSRs encourage the purchase of additional products.

The business client usually provides one or more types of mailing lists, such as for warm or established customers. These are called "mailing" lists because, in addition to a telephone number, the business client has the customers' addresses from previous orders of goods shipped. Other lists are of "cold" customers—people who have never purchased products from the business client, although they may have been approached at some time via telemarketing or mass mailings (through "junk" mail, advertisements that arrive unsolicited).

Some organizations establish individual quotas instead of group quotas on an hourly or work session basis. At Washington State

University in Pullman, Sean Vincent manages 75 to 85 part-time college student TSRs. They face each other in cubicles that contain four telephones. Although they do not have a group quota, they cooperate to provide each other with moral support and helpful suggestions. TSRs start at minimum wage but nightly bonuses provide monetary incentives to meet quotas. Raises for outstanding work can also double the entry-level wage.

Nonprofit organizations such as colleges and universities use telemarketing to contact alumni and friends to invite them to contribute funds in support of their alma mater. Few colleges can manage on their limited budgets without regular contributions and significantly large endowments. Thus, telemarketing can serve to help nonprofit institutions as well as large multinational business conglomerates.

Evaluation

Evaluators or monitors regularly listen in to telemarketing operators. The performance evaluation form or process may be quite complex, covering everything from polite manners and correct language to knowledge of the product and use of the technology. A poor evaluation typically leads to a conference between the TSR and the supervisor and recommendations for how to improve. Failure to improve leads to eventual dismissal, sometimes sooner than later if the infractions lend themselves to losing sales or customer rapport, or fail to conform to company rules and regulations. Because of the challenge inherit in telemarketing roles, turnover is sometimes higher than in most non-sales positions.

COORDINATING PRINT AND BROADCAST ADVERTISING WITH TELEMARKETING

Major marketing campaigns coordinate all advertising and selling activities, such as:

- television commercials
- magazine and newspaper advertisements

- mass mailings to households (and/or to businesses, if the product is appropriate for business use)
- telemarketing efforts
- personal visits from sales reps

When General Motors launched its credit card campaign, they advertised in all these media simultaneously. The sales gimmick or benefit to entice customers away from other credit cards was a discount on a General Motors vehicle. Purchases charged to the credit card go toward building an account fund for that purchase.

Open a magazine, there was a General Motors credit card ad. Open your mail box, there was a General Motors credit card ad. Turn on TV, you saw and heard another credit card pitch from General Motors. Answer the ringing telephone, and there was a TSR promoting the General Motors' credit card. Voila!–A General Motors marketing campaign blitz.

Magazine, newspaper, and mass mailing print advertisements usually contain 800 or 888 numbers. Television commercials for direct-order products and TV shopping channels include toll-free numbers. Catalogs–of which there are over 10,000 on the market– include 800 and 888 numbers. Billboards on the highway and hand flyers distributed locally may also include such toll-free numbers. People use these toll-free numbers to ask questions and to order products. When they contact a firm by telephone, it is called an inbound call.

HANDLING INBOUND CALLS

When people use 800, 888, or 900 numbers to ask questions and place sales orders, they often reach telemarketing sales representatives (TSRs) who are prepared to fill out sales orders immediately. Other inbound calls are to request information. Inbound TSRs also have menus of scripts to provide them with the answers to just about any type of query related to the business clients and their products.

With some systems, the callers may be put on hold temporarily because all operators are busy. That's when the inbound caller has reached the voice mail system, often with a menu of options to enter by pressing a number on the phone or else they will hear music while waiting a few moments for a human operator (TSR). Even with the latter method, an automated voice will return every few seconds (from one-half to three-quarters of a minute) to courteously invite the caller to continue waiting.

For the General Motors marketing blitz, all inbound calls went into the Omaha office of Sitel, Inc. Sitel hired over three thousand telemarketers just to handle General Motors' inbound calls alone. Such telemarketing processes and marketing campaigns can create many new jobs, whether permanent or temporary. When one business client is satisfied or moves from a "blitz" phase to a more stable, steady, and continuing marketing phase, telemarketers move on to train for and respond to another client's marketing needs.

Another type of inbound call does not usually generate sales, at least not directly. Operators often receive queries. They must be able to read their product data—either from printed manuals or a computer script—to answer intelligently.

For companies to keep customers happy so they will keep on buying products, support service must be provided. Suppose that a customer fails to receive an order, or perhaps a product fails to function properly. Maybe the customer cannot follow the instruction manual. All of these people place calls to companies to ask for help or to register complaints. Somebody must answer the telephone, transfer calls, and help to see that the customer is satisfied.

A common type of product complaint call, especially when technology is involved, is a request for service or service information. The operator must be able to transfer the customer's call to the appropriate department or service person. Service operators take these calls. A typical example is a computer software company. Service and instructor personnel walk the customer through his or her manual while the customer is on the line. Typically, the customer may be asking questions and listening to the replies while trying to read the manual, take notes, or manipulate the computer to debug the program.

Satisfied customers become "warm" customers when they buy products more often than any other category of customer. They tell their friends about how pleased they are with certain companies and specific products. These people and many others place inbound calls in order to buy. When marketing campaigns are coordinated with television, whether products are offered on the TV shopping channel or via commercials elsewhere on local, network, or cable TV programming, customers call in to make purchases. Operators record and process these sales orders.

LEGAL ISSUES AND TELEMARKETING SCAMS

Whether purchasing products from a TV commercial, a TV shopping channel, or in response to a telemarketing call to the home, buyers generally have up to three days to change their minds. That is the law.

Since the proliferation of telemarketing, other legal issues have emerged. Consumers can request that their names be removed from mailing and calling lists. They can request TSRs to discontinue calling. TSRs cannot discontinue calling unless they keep records—flag the called person's name in the computer so that every other TSR on the network will see this warning beside the name of anyone who has previously registered such a complaint. Even though a TSR fails to flag the name, the telemarketing firm is still liable if unwanted calls are made after complaints have been registered.

Citibank's telemarketers dialed the wrong number when they called consumer advocate Michael Jacobson more than once in 1993. He had been waiting to test a law against unwanted phone solicitations. Jacobson told Citibank twice not to call again with its offers of credit card discount services. The third time, he sued in small claims court and won a $750 settlement. Jacobson had been keeping a "tele-nuisance list" since the Telephone Consumer Protection Act went into effect in 1992. Says Jacobson: "The key thing is not to hang up on a telemarketer, but to say, 'Never call me again,' and keep track of who called and when." Jacobson is cofounder of the Washington, DC based Center for the Study of Commercialism, a group dedicated to ending excessive marketing.

Telemarketing is relatively new. There are a lot of untested situations emerging and those yet to emerge may end up in court as the basis for some future legal precedence. As these precedences from court cases begin to proliferate, there will be many more laws associated with telemarketing procedures and careers. As a consumer, watch for those laws that will protect you. Although the majority of businesses and individuals are honest, some are not. Telemarketing firms should train their employees about such laws so as to protect their company and better serve their customers. For both consumers and telemarker, keeping abreast of the new laws can be very beneficial.

One criminal group used religion as their gimmick to attract participants. The group called itself the Christian Value Firm, using outbound calls to tell people they had won $20,000. The glitch in the con game was that people had to put up $579 in so-called "charges" in order to collect. Senior citizens were often targeted in this telemarketing scam, with 600,000 potential victims, before the perpetrators were finally caught and sentenced to 18 months probation. The fraudulent scheme came to light after a number of victims reported their suspicions. Some of the victims had placed inbound calls to the number they were given, only to hear this automated report: "The number you have tried to reach is no longer in service."

Home alone, a Tennessee youngster answered the phone and heard this message: "Answer the following question and you can win a trip to Hawaii: What is the name of Batman's car? Just dial this 900 number with your reply." He did, and then dialed a second 900 number that the first 900 number's automated voice directed him to call. Eight months later, instead of a free trip to Hawaii, all his parents had received was a $120.72 telephone bill.

Everybody knows that 900 numbers cost money but that 800 numbers are free—or are they? Some information providers have sought to fool the public by switching from 900 to 800 numbers—with a gimmick, called the "800-number callback scam." When you call them, your telephone number shows on their computer screen. Then the company calls you back—collect! And this was legal because you supposedly requested the collect call in order to get some information. The Federal Communications Commission—the legal agency responsible for watching the telecommunications business—proposed new regulations to cover this type of unethical contingency.

Billed as entertainment on the Fox network, *America's Most Wanted* show has brought tips from everyday citizens about criminals, thus leading to their subsequent capture, arrest, and incarceration. Even fellow criminals reported on an inmate about to be released when his face appeared on the screen in connection with con games and telecommunication scams.

Some con artists boldly advertise their telemarketing schemes in local papers. Many local papers have responded by inserting warning ads under their personal columns—the category under which many of these con games appear in the print media. (Just because an ad appears in a paper does not mean that the paper has verified the honesty of the advertisers or stands behind the ad's offerings.) Consumers do well to remember the Latin phrase *caveat emptor*, which means "buyer beware." Because of the increase in fraudulent business practices, consumers do well to call their local Better Business Bureau to check out claims or offers that sound too good to be true. A good rule of thumb is this: If an offer sounds too good to be true, it probably is! Here is an example of an ad designed to warn readers about the possibility of fraud:

> This classification may contain ads for conversation or recorded messages through the use of telephones. Calls to such numbers result in a charge to the calling phone number. These telephone related services are telecommunications and are regulated by the Federal Communications Commission. Complaints may be directed to the FCC, 1919 M Street, N.W., Washington, DC 20554.

TELEMARKETING OCCUPATIONS

Salaries are commensurate with the duties assigned to a wide range of telemarketing occupations. Entry-level TSRs may earn little more than the minimum hourly wage. However, there are many opportunities for promotions and raises. Notice with the Sitel example earlier that a team leader supervises about ten TSRs and the monitors evaluate TSR performance. These people are not hired from outside but are promoted from within; they already understand how their telemarketing firm functions.

In the midwest, a young college student started part-time as a TSR to help pay his and his wife's college expenses. Before graduating, he had been promoted to assistant manager and upon graduation, accepted a full-time job as the department's telemarketing manager.

Some people report a lot of job satisfaction with TSR positions and remain in this or similar jobs, advancing, in time, to senior levels. Even the TSR job attracts two types of personalities: the extrovert enjoys the challenge of making outbound calls and trying to make sales with both warm and cold customers; the more introverted personality is happier taking inbound calls, answering queries and transferring calls to service personnel.

Other TSRs advance to become team leaders or monitors. Both of these jobs involve as much communication and human relations skills as that of the TSR but contacts are internal rather than external. Supervisors and monitors work with fellow employees, not with business clients or customers.

Marketing reps work with companies to attract their business as clients; they work with external clients. Personnel managers and trainers work with fellow employees; theirs are internal positions.

Any occupation that deals with the public—warm or cold customers—may be said to include telemarketing competencies. These occupations include secretaries, receptionists, switchboard operators, local or traveling sales reps, advertising agents and account executives, telecommunication entrepreneurs, and so on. People who use the telephone in connection with marketing, and who otherwise work with human and public relations, are, generally speaking, involved with telemarketing.

TELEMARKETING OPERATOR COMPETENCIES

Above all else, the TSR must be competent with the language. During the oral interview, it will be immediately apparent whether the applicant can meet this criteria. A review of telephone manners and consideration to others in Sections I and II suggests that no matter how frustrated or irritable the customer may be, the TSR must be courteous. Correct grammar must be used at all times. They should avoid, for example, *he don't, it don't, she don't* or *they was, ain't,* or double negatives such as *I don't got no* or *he don't know nothin'.*

Being courteous and patient are both very difficult sometimes. People on the other end of the line can be rude, unfeeling, stupid, or obscene. Telemarketers do not have to accept obscene language. They should politely state their unwillingness to listen. If they must stay on the line and the person persists in haranguing them, a supervisor should be told immediately. The supervisor, monitor, or team leader may take over the call or direct the telemarketer to hang up.

Lord Chesterfield said, "Most arts require long study and application, but the most useful of all, that of pleasing, requires only the desire." When you understand that others, like yourself, have human needs and are frustrated when these needs cannot be met, it will be easier to be patient. Once you understand and can care about others, it's easy to develop the desire to be nice. That's all that manners and courtesy are about–being considerate of and polite to people.

Although computer literacy is an important competency, most software programs typical of the TSR position are user-friendly. The training session teaches TSRs everything they need to know technically about the software used. Attitudes cannot be so readily learned. Besides courtesy and patience, those who get the jobs are those who are enthusiastic, eager to learn, and eager to please both the customers and the business clients. This type of applicant can demonstrate interest in and loyalty to both the telemarketing firm and the business clients, as well as the ability and willingness to cooperate with others in a team setting. Those who demonstrate the work ethic with a record (including references who will speak for them) of honesty and responsibility are as important as all other attributes. These attitudes are demonstrated by the habits that follow an individual, from establishing a record of promptness and attendance in school to every job, no matter how menial, that one ever holds. Getting work done thoroughly and submitting it on time, whether homework or job assignments is how one demonstrates promptness, quality production, and honesty.

Chapter 10

Essential Marketing Concepts

Telemarketing functions are part of the total marketing picture. This section presents some essential marketing concepts, including human needs, the marketing mix, the store mix, human demographics, the life cycle of a product, the marketing niche, competition, and risks.

HUMAN NEEDS

People usually will not buy what they do not want or need. A basic purpose of marketing is to communicate, to share with people the information they need about the product to enable them to decide whether they want or need it. Another purpose may be to create or stimulate one's desire for something. Thus, marketers need to understand people's generalized needs, which means looking anew at Maslow's hierarchy, as described in Section II.

Animals do not have economic needs; people do. Animals have fur, thick hides, or other natural devices to keep them warm; people must rely on their clothing or protective sheltering to endure bitter cold. Animals forage for food in the wild, whether by eating vegetation or by satisfying their hunger from killing and eating each other or, when domesticated, by getting fed by humans. Animals have many more biological instincts than do human beings. In modern society, most humans go to school, go to work, earn money, and buy products; animals don't.

Re-create the levels of human needs and imagine the wide range and huge number of products it takes to satisfy these needs. Many supermarkets alone may contain 20,000 or more products, not all of which are food products.

Marketers have learned to gear their advertising campaigns in terms of satisfying human needs. Thus, advertisements (and TSRs) speak of benefits or satisfiers rather than of products themselves. Note from the following list how this may work (Maslow's need levels appear within parentheses):

- *sex appeal*—get it, keep it, improve it, in order to get a mate, keep a mate, improve a marriage, have a family, dispel loneliness, have fun, and so on (addresses basic, security, social, and some ego needs)
- *health, diet*—get healthy, keep healthy, improve health, live longer, live better, do more, have more. Diet goes along with health in looking and feeling good but diet also goes with sex appeal in getting and staying slim, fit, and attractive to others (addresses basic, security, social, and ego needs)
- *money*—get it, keep it, save it, invest it wisely and make it increase, buy products, improve one's station (prestige and status), get more, have more, help others, and contribute to society (addresses basic, security, social, and ego needs)
- *fun, including exercise*—have some fun, relax, enjoy life, be happy, socialize, laugh, feel good, share with others, etc. (addresses social, ego, and some self-actualization needs)
- *control, power*—get some control over oneself and one's own life, get some power over others including at work and possibly in the home or in relationships (addresses ego, security, and social needs)
- *status, prestige*—to improve one's self-image and one's image in the eyes of others (friends, family, neighbors, co-workers, society at large) as in purchasing a fine house in the "better" or "best" neighborhoods, the fanciest car, the most costly clothes; having jewelry, traveling to exclusive resorts, getting accepted into expensive, exclusive clubs; getting one or more college degrees, preferably from exclusive and expensive (as in "ivy league") schools; getting promotions, prestigious titles, a big office with a view and fine furniture (addresses ego, social, and security needs)
- *self-improvement, education*—get a job, get a better job, increase one's creativity, skills, and knowledge, earn more money,

improve relationships and marriage, learn hobbies, make and keep friends, have fun, get control or power, feel good about oneself by being able to help others to achieve new and better accomplishments, or any combination of these activities (addresses self-actualization, ego, and social needs).

When you know the above things about people, you'll have a better idea about how to make a sales pitch. Get people's attention about how your firm's or your business client's firm can satisfy any one or more of the above needs and you're well on your way to closing a sale. What's more, you'll understand better the nature and sequencing of statements in sales scripts. Moreover, entrepreneurs who understand the spectrum, or range, of their customers' needs will have a solid foundation for advertising or promoting their business.

THE MARKETING MIX

Telemarketers should use the "five Ps" as a means of remembering the marketing mix. These five Ps consist of product, place, price, promotion, and people.

The *product* is the line of goods or services to be offered for sale. It or they must be something that people want and need. An individual who is thinking about opening a business will not succeed simply by choosing a product that pleases him or conforms to his aptitudes. The product(s) must please and satisfy customers. If there is no perceived need, no purchases will be made; if no sales, no income from which to pay expenses; if no profit, no business; if no business, there will be no jobs for employees.

The *place* is where customers can go to shop or how they can otherwise avail themselves of the product. Via telemarketing, customers can get the product by ordering over the telephone. For physical locations where customers walk in to purchase, the place can be one of the most important decisions that entrepreneurs make. For mail-order and telemarketing firms, the physical location makes little difference other than to the employees who work there.

The *price* is the amount customers will have to pay in order to get the product that will help to satisfy their human needs. Because

Photo 10.1. Mr. Lenox Church, Sales Rep

Here, Lenox Church is equipped with his firm's sales materials in his briefcase as he rents a car in Kansas City, Missouri. He is here to call on contacts, or "warm" customers.

there are so many varieties and quality and prestige levels of the same or similar types of products, there are just as many price variations. Experienced shoppers are often comparison shoppers. They quickly discover what their local stores charge for a product compared to stores in neighboring communities. They check catalog prices, TV shopping channel prices, and the prices offered by telemarketers who call their homes and places of business.

A high-quality product—or one that, through advertising, is made to appear as a quality product—commands a higher price. Goods that cost more to produce typically command higher prices in order to cover production costs. However, one must remember the phrase, "what the traffic will bear." When customers perceive, again through advertising, that buying one product over another provides prestige and status, those whose prestige need prevails will pay top dollar–the highest price they can possibly afford.

Prices are determined in dozens of ways, but perhaps the three most common are based on production, prestige, and competition.

Production plus pricing means that careful accounting is performed to determine the exact cost, per unit, required to produce a product before adding a small margin out of which to pay taxes and realize a profit.

Prestige pricing is based on charging a high price in order to attract people who actually want to pay high prices and also on producing high-quality items that sell in the finest, most exclusive shops.

Competition pricing may include production-oriented pricing but beyond that, is based on what the competition is charging. Big, large volume firms, particularly those that offer a variety of goods and services, can more readily decide to fight the competition by offering lower prices than can small firms or firms that do not diversify (by offering a variety of products). During these price wars, firms generally lose money because they cut prices below the production cost levels. They cannot do this for long or they will go out of business; unless of course, they have plenty of other products on which they can temporarily raise prices to cover losses on the lower-priced items.

The *Promotion.* This is the advertising campaign, the firm's plan for communicating to potential customers how the product can satisfy their needs and wants. Again, review Section II, for the explanation of left- and right-brain functions. The words used to describe a product are left-brain oriented, particularly when describing factual, logical benefits of a product.

The pictures, music, and any other art form(s) used in the campaign are right-brain oriented. Also, when words are used seductively, in whispers and with emotion, using emotional adjectives and verbs, the right hemisphere as well as the left hemisphere of the brain responds.

TV promotions obviously make good use of right-brain options—photography, music, objects, dance, emotional paralanguage, etc. TSRs on the telephone must rely on their paralanguage (shown in Section II), since they have only their voice and their language on which to rely. (Until such time when picture phones and video phones become common; then the whole telemarketing game will change anew!) Magazine layouts use color as well as black and white photography; newspapers, generally, rely more heavily on black and white pictures and graphics. Computer-generated graphics can be used in TV commercials and with magazine ads as well as in presentations. (The innovative job seeker might create a resume with colored graphics to depict, say, a variety of experiences, type of education, and more!)

Under this topic, marketers must bring to bear every possible means of communicating to people the benefits of one's product and eliciting from them both rational and emotional reasons why they should buy. Psychology, technology, language, and the fine arts all converge in developing effective and successful ad campaigns.

The *people* who work in all the jobs related to marketing and telemarketing, including research and selling, are responsible for seeing that a product reaches the market and is advertised in a manner that will encourage customers to buy. Only several years ago, the following phrase was common in business: "Build a better mousetrap and the world will beat a path to your door." No longer. There are so many people, so many products, and so many places and ways to buy, that few if anybody can possibly find out about a new or improved product unless it is effectively marketed. The better mousetrap will never sell unless *people* advertise and sell it.

THE STORE MIX

Closely aligned with place, the store mix refers to the stores in the same neighborhood as one's own store. Will a pet shop go over well in an industrial community consisting of warehouses and shipping depots? No, because pet customers will not likely venture into such a neighborhood. A pet shop located next to a cinema, toy store, or video arcade might do well.

In telemarketing, the store mix concept refers to how, where, and when advertised. A TV shopping channel groups like products together–in the same hour or time slot; much like locating a pet shop next to a toy store, video arcade, or cinema. In TV advertising, the store mix concept refers to careful selection of the show(s) on which to place one's commercials.

Would one advertise denture cleaners during a Saturday morning lineup of cartoons? Of course not, such an idea is absurd. Less obvious are the more subtle choices. Thus marketers must know not only something about human needs but also about human demographics.

HUMAN DEMOGRAPHICS

Demographics is the study of populations and their characteristics. Marketers and sociologists identify people not only by their physiological and psychological needs, as Maslow did, but also by such things as gender, age, education, occupation, income, location of residence, and socioeconomic class. People with prestigious occupations, education, income, family background, and place of residence could also be categorized as upper class. They are the ones telemarketers target for high-priced and prestigious products.

Older people buy products that children and adolescents do not; teenagers want products that their parents do not. Women and men want different products as well as some of the same things.

Since the 1960s, Americans have been admonished not to discriminate, which is pretty much the same thing as not being *able* to *differentiate*. Marketers must be able to categorize people in a generalized sense. If they could not tell the difference between what one group of people is likely to want compared to another, their marketing plans would go awry. They might advertise Barbie dolls during the late night shows or denture cleaners during Saturday morning cartoon shows. TSRs would get mailing lists of working class people to whom to pitch Rolls Royce automobiles. Wheelchairs could be targeted for marathon runners. Season tickets to the Seattle Symphony or to London's Royal Opera House might be pitched to the impoverished (try bread and warm clothes first).

Stereotyping, however, is not the same thing as developing the ability to differentiate. Some old-timers like rock and roll music. Some bartenders and bowlers enjoy opera and classical music. Many minorities play golf and tennis and many Anglos eat tortillas, hot peppers, and spicy fried chicken. Some wealthy, well-educated doctors and lawyers living in fine homes drink beer and watch baseball and some school dropouts on welfare appreciate beautiful sculptures, paintings, classical music, and architecture.

THE LIFE CYCLE OF A PRODUCT

A product typically goes through four phases from birth to death. Each phase has a nickname, which may be easier to remember than its real name. Refer to Figure 10.1 for an illustration of the typical product life cycle.

FIGURE 10.1. The Four Phases of the Product Life Cycle

- *Star* (introduction phase)—a big marketing budget puts the new product in all the media; see, for example, the General Motors advertising blitz when they introduced their credit card. It is during this phase that telemarketing firms are likely to get the client's business.
- *Cash cow* (growth phase)—the product is known and has been accepted by people in various market segments (demographic groups); it is profitable, getting sold, and bringing in money.

During this phase, a telemarketing firm might continue to hype the product, but the client does not spend as much money on the advertising campaign. In other words, prior advertising is now paying off, and the firm is reaping cash benefits as a result.

- *Problem child* (the mature phase)—sales begin to wane, it may be costing more to produce the product than the revenue it generates in from sales. Marketers must decide what to do with the problem child product. Researchers and developers may come up with a way to improve or redesign the product. If it is to be retained among other products, marketing efforts may have to be renewed. If so, telemarketing firms will again be asked to launch a big new campaign to accompany a total blitz program in various media simultaneously.

- *Dog* (declining phase)—whether or not a new marketing program was launched, the product was improved or not, the product may still have passed into disfavor. When was the last time you saw or heard an advertisement for the hula hoop or Rubik's Cube? When a product no longer brings in money, it is usually pulled from the market. It's a dead duck. Even if some customers still want it, they can't get it in the primary retail market.

Firms are constantly analyzing their products to determine at which phase a product is in the product life cycle. Then they must make decisions about what to do with it—improve it, advertise it, or kill it and replace it with something else. Thus business is neither static nor stable. Something new and different is happening all the time.

MARKET NICHE AND MARKET SHARE

Companies often develop a market niche, to address the needs of a particular target market. A *market niche* is a segment of the market in which a firm maintains a dominant position. When Apple Computer came out with the desktop personal computer (PC) in the early 1980s, it was a new innovation (a star). Apple went after (targeted) the school market and before long every school in the United States wanted Apple computers. Soon, Apple controlled the school market as their dominant market niche.

Radio Shack, a division of the Tandy Corporation, then came out with their desktop computer. By then, there were a dozen other computer manufacturers, but Apple and Radio Shack each had a market share of about 30 percent each. *Market share* is the percent of the total market (for a given product) in which a firm sells its products and/or controls. However, within a few years Big Blue (IBM) entered the desktop computer market as a major competitor.

COMPETITION

International Business Machines (IBM for short and Big Blue as a nickname) was once the largest, richest company in the world. When they entered the desktop computer market with their Personal Computer (PC), it was a significant market share challenge to both Apple and Radio Shack. People were already familiar with and trusted the name IBM, so if IBM made computers, they must be good—that was the idea. IBM blitzed the media with advertising, and soon Apple and Radio Shack lost the high percentage of market share they previously had enjoyed.

Competition is always one of the biggest risks in business (see the topic on pricing) earlier in this section. Competitors battle it out to control a bigger segment of the market, and one way they compete is to lower prices. Price wars among the airlines and among oil companies are well-known to consumers. Big companies with a diversified product line can weather the storm of low prices that are below the *break-even point* (point below which the company now loses money; is not meeting its expenses, not making a profit, going "into the red," etc.); small companies or companies with only one or a few products cannot.

Telemarketing firms feel the backlash from price wars and other competitive battles when their business clients reduce the telemarketing services they are willing or able to buy. Telemarketing firms also experience competition from each other when other telemarketing firms start into business, move into the same locale, cut the prices they charge to business clients or take clients from another firm—all of which diminishes the market share held by other established firms.

RISKS OF GOING INTO TELEMARKETING
(OR ANY OTHER) BUSINESSES

A telemarketing manager will appreciate knowledge of and sympathy with some of the risks involved in running a business, any business. Most of these have been discussed in this section but not necessarily from the point of view of risk, as follows:

- *Competition risks*–there are risks which originate from new businesses or from new products and new marketing campaigns of existing businesses which are in the same or similar product lines.
- *Risks from undercapitalization*–insufficient money was available to launch the business initially so when the competition cuts prices, launches new products, or new advertising campaigns, there is not enough money to fight back (in the same or in different ways). When products are in their problem child or dog phases, there frequently is a lack of money to cover the expenses, including wages, and to maintain business during slow periods. The firm goes under (closes, goes belly up, files for bankruptcy, or sells out) because they cannot generate enough income to pay for everything.
- *Personnel and management problems*–the firm has not hired the best people at the best wages (for the company) and the employees do not have the best attitudes, including the work ethic. Management does not make the best decisions. In other words, it is an internal people problem resulting from ineffective selection and/or poor management.
- *Physical, disaster, and criminal risks*–fire, flood, hail, earthquake, tornado, hurricane, wrecks and accidents, and crimes from both external and internal sources. Businesspeople can purchase insurance policies against many of these potential risks. Hiring honest employees, training them well, establishing effective internal control measures, and protecting facilities against crimes and disasters are other precautions.
- *Legal risks*–there are so many laws of which business people must be aware; still, consumers, employees, and general passers-by may sue a firm. The cost of doing legal battle, just to defend oneself in case of lawsuits, can be exorbitant. Knowl-

edge of the specific laws that deal with an industry, the purchase of some types of insurance policies (such as malpractice for medical personnel), proper training, supervision, and caution are the best advice.

In summary, going into business is a risky business! Plenty of money is spent annually by the vast majority of businesses to keep themselves out of trouble and to get themselves out after they've gotten into trouble. Employees who understand these risks are more sympathetic to the needs of business and management, and are generally more willing to do their part by being productive, honest, and responsible.

Chapter 11

Innovations and Technology
from Around the World

The ability to readily communicate with people around the world, to promote products, to discover cultural differences, and to succeed in the competitive global business market have been greatly impacted by changing technology and twentiety-century innovations. Nothing man-made is perfect; in this world there are problems to solve, obstacles to overcome and conquer. From around the globe, here are some samples of technological and telecommunications innovations and their impact.

A MULTIUSE TELEPHONE

Instead of a paper folder in the desk drawer of some hotels, the guest accesses services via the telephone. On this type of phone is a statement: "Touch any button for access to a world of services." It has a consumer keypad, a phone pad, and a credit card slot. This innovation combines the technologies and functions of telephone, computer, telemarketing, shopping, and paying for something immediately, whether they be goods, services, or information.

If the hotel TV is hooked to channel services, one might be able to get the weather report there, so why use the phone? People make such either/or decisions (in this case, using the TV vs. the phone) on the basis of curiosity, necessity, or simply because they want to. For such things as the local or national weather, or a stock market report, for example, pressing one number produces a menu from which to press additional numbers as options. Before receiving the desired information, though, the customer must first enter a PIN number–whatever that number may be. Buying products from the computerized catalog, provided via telephone, leads to entering one's credit card in the slot right on the phone. Other numbers on the phone pad lead one through the following menu, some of which are local and inhouse calls while others are long distance:

restaurant information	FedEx overnight delivery
nightlife	pizza delivery
events and attractions	car rental
sightseeing and tours	travel information
local transportation	news
health and fitness	stocks
business services	sports
flowers and gifts	horoscopes
catalog shopping	weather

PHOTO MACHINES IN MALLS

Remember the small photo booths into which one could step, assume a silly pose, punch a button and, a few moments later, out would pop one's picture? Now, with computer graphics, the process is more sophisticated with a variety of other options. One can get a personalized greeting card from Hallmark, with a picture and a message of one's own composition. Or a person can choose to have his or her picture printed on a $1,000 bill, a "Wanted" poster, on a country western or gangster scene, or on the front page of a newspaper.

ON-LINE, ON CABLE, OR IN PRINT

Instead of or in addition to getting a printed telephone directory, a disk directory is available to use at the computer. Although it is still possible to order printed transcripts of such TV shows as *Eye to Eye*, *Prime Time*, *20/20*, and the like, now a video of the complete show may be ordered. A toll-free number is provided for quick purchase but one must have a credit card to pay. Music tapes, cassettes, records, or compact disks may be purchased by phone, mail, or fax. Consumers may also order small strange appliances, clothes, jewelry, spa equipment, computers, stereos—the list is seemingly endless.

Perusing print matter, computer matter, video matter used with VCR and television, and listening to TV as shows are viewed are among the many ways of getting information fast. Ads appear in the print matter, commercials, on video, and on TV. With over 10,000 catalogs available to home shoppers, consumers can browse, compare product features, and read print matter before ordering. The use of the 800 and 888 numbers helps to link this method of shopping to telemarketing.

GLOBAL ECONOMIC AND MEDIA ACTIVITIES

In the global business market, adversities and opportunities come in all seasons, shapes, and sizes. Some choices are good, some are less so. Some opportunities are fads and will soon disappear, others will make life better and be around for years. Some changes frighten people, such as the loss of jobs due to downsizing, layoffs, corporate mergers, acquisitions, and obsolescence. Other changes, such as cable and satellite TV, modern subway and railway transportation, reduced airfares, fuel-efficient automobiles, and new wonder drugs are welcome changes. Because of accelerated changes in telecommunications and technology, the innovations and culture of the most progressive economies in the world (such as can be seen with the Japanese, American, and European markets) are being absorbed in part by other nations and cultures. One example of this is the U.S. television and entertainment industry. Other examples are the Japanese automotive and electronic industries.

U.S. TV and Films—World Leaders Among World Players

Each year after the American television networks announce their new fall programs, hundreds of TV executives from around the world descend on Los Angeles for what has become known as the L.A. Screenings. What the foreign programmers (electronic-age pilgrims) watch in Burbank will show up eventually in Bonn, Bombay, Valparaiso, or Vladivostok.

In the United States, entertainment is the second biggest export after aircraft. Fifty-seven percent of the movies shown in France come from the United States, but the French have to pay an extra charge at the box office, which goes to subsidize French filmmakers.

An individual traveling the world, will see, among local programming, reruns, often black and white, often violent or silly, of U.S. TV shows (e.g., *I Love Lucy*, *The Dick Van Dyke Show*, and *Dallas*). Nowadays, new shows are also on the menu.

With interactive TV and the new generation of television capabilities, where up to 500 channels are possible, Americans are also able to get plenty of opportunities to view programs from around the world. Numerous channels for specialized tastes are also among the innovations, such as sports, weather, finance, news, travel, golf, or fishing channels, and even channels that allow the viewer to sit in on the U.S. Senate and House of Representatives. One finance channel advertises itself as "Money all day, talk all night." Translated, that means up-to-the minute U.S. stock market and other financial news in the daytime, stock market and monetary news from other stock markets (e.g., London, Tokyo) at night, and talk about money and finance all night.

Entertainment, including classic films and modern movies, on demand, is another innovation. Pay TV by ordering specific movies and paying for them with credit card over the telephone, such as in hotels, is a popular consumer choice.

Helping people navigate their way through all these TV channel options to decide what they will view is another new industry. Computer disk directories, print directories, and TV channel directories provide information from which to make decisions. How these descriptions are written and how they are rated (such as from one to four stars, as in TV movies) is another means of advertising shows versus downgrading them. New ratings are being promoted on a volunteer basis by Hollywood and other film and entertainment producers to warn parents or other viewers of the violence or adult content in films or television shows. These are just a few of the innovations in the U.S. film and television industry, some of which will have global influence.

A New Star Over Asia

A single satellite orbiting high above the equator suddenly became one of the world's most coveted media properties. Partly owned by a Hong Kong company, the satellite has a simple function: it transmits a service called STAR TV (Satellite Television Asia Region). STAR TV brings such Western TV fare as the BBC (British Broadcast Company) and American programming such as *Lifestyles of the Rich and Famous* and MTV to impoverished slum dwellers in Cairo and the nouveaux riches in Zhangzhou. The reason for the value of STAR is its potential market: three billion people—two-thirds of the world's population!

In 1994 a bidding war among giant international media companies ended with Australian media baron Rupert Murdoch (who also owns the U.S. Fox TV network) emerging as the winner. He beat out Britain's Pearson PLC as well as America's Time-Warner and Turner Broadcasting. About a year later, the American company Time Warner acquired control of Turner Broadcasting. Television viewers from Israel to India, from Japan to Singapore, can tune in. At first, only affluent Asians who traveled or knew English could effectively access STAR, but now satellite dishes can be found on the roofs of remote farmhouses as well as on urban apartment high-rises.

Societal and cultural influences generally follow technological achievements. It is common to find teenage girls in China wearing lipstick and youth throughout Asia copying clothing styles and other fads from U.S. movie and MTV stars. American culture and other cultures from around the world proliferate because of the media. Meanwhile, the most upwardly mobile group in the world seems to be the Asian middle class, the biggest market for media of all kinds.

The Swedish Trade Council

The Swedish Trade Council announced a new way for American businesspeople to communicate with Sweden regarding trade and investments. Their number, 1-800-SWEDEN4. To introduce their new number, the Swedish Trade Council, together with Scandinavian Airlines, offered a pair of round-trip tickets to Stockholm to three western U.S. chambers of commerce whose members made the most use of the service during the fall months of 1993 and 1994. Incentives or inducements such as this encourage the promotion of cultural and business exchanges on a global basis.

Stock Markets

The New York Stock Exchange and Chicago's Board of Trade are not the only places where people can buy and sell stocks, bonds, and commodities. The London and Tokyo exchanges are also well-known, but there are many other players on the global financial scene. Moreover, one need not travel to visit a stockbroker in person. A variety of discount brokers provide limited exchange services. Since they do not gather financial data with which to advise their customers, but merely provide the buy-or-sell electronic linkage, they can discount the rates that they charge.

Stockholders around the world can therefore buy and sell holdings at any time, around the clock. Orders taken at 3 a.m. on a Sunday morning will be processed as soon as whatever stock market handles the proposed issue is open.

Tourism Packages

To attract visitors (and thus shoppers), Shanghai and Beijing in China and Tahiti and Bora Bora in the South Pacific have offered tourists discounts and travel packages. (A package may include air and ground transportation, hotels, some meals, and associated amenities such as tips, taxes, and perhaps tour guide and tour bus fees). Airlines make more money with full planes, especially on intercontinental flights.

China as an Emerging Economy

By the early 1980s, China was sending ads to America's business magazines and newspapers. China also invited U.S. businesses to advertise in their publications and via their telemarketing and television media. The Shanghai Securities Exchange is booming, the Chinese are buying—that's over 1.2 billion consumers. Some things in China have not changed in over 4,000 years; others seem to be changing every few hours. These changes are mostly in technology and telecommunications.

A Pepsi Promotion Misfired in the Philippines

A magic number, 349, printed inside a Pepsi bottle cap would win its holder a one-million peso (about $40,000) prize. A computer error produced 800,000 winning numbers instead of 18. Explaining that their company did not have the $32 billion it would take to pay off that many winners didn't help. The promotion quickly turned into a nightmare. Disgruntled "winners" banded together in protest groups, fanning anti-Pepsi flames at frequent demonstrations and marches. More than 22,000 people holding the 349 number filed 689 class action or individual civil suits seeking damages, as well as 5,200 criminal complaints that alleged fraud and deception. The company paid out $10 million in providing 500 pesos ($20) in goodwill prizes to winners but the local trade committee still faulted Pepsi with "deceptive advertising."

NEW JOBS EMERGING, OLD JOBS DISAPPEARING

Those who drop out of school without getting occupational competencies, can always get a service job in a fast-food restaurant, right? Not always. Some of those are disappearing too, together with even more manufacturing jobs.

In Tokyo, customers can walk into a clothing shop and find not one single human person to wait on them and not one single rack of clothing ready to peruse, try on, and possibly buy. Instead, a computer talks to customers, inviting responses by menu. Customers enter replies to every facet of their physical dimensions and then choose fabrics and colors from computer graphics and store samples to the price range they prefer. A credit card is entered to pay. In 10 to 20 minutes, out pops the completed article of clothing!

Somewhere behind the scenes in the retail clothing establishment, with no more than a tiny handful of people to oversee all operations, lasers have cut the garment from whole cloth, and computer and sewing technology have commingled to produce an original, customized garment. A computer program informs the customer what is owed by simultaneously recorded data to tell the retail store owners their cost, expenses, and profit.

In a fast-food restaurant in Europe, customers are also greeted by a talking computer and video screens—with no humans apparently around. Customers enter what they want to purchase with a variety of condiment options, pay by credit card, and their order comes out. Somewhere about, a shift manager and several assistants supervise the operation and its technology, while making business decisions about inventory, purchases, operational supplies, maintenance, and cleanup.

In a global economy driven by competition and technology, as old jobs disappear, new ones emerge. People in these new jobs need to have some technical competencies and, most essential, good interpersonal or human relations skills. Equally important, however, they must understand that life is not a group of separate compartments of knowledge but is an interdependent interlocking system of how things work and why. For example, what was once viewed primarily as fine arts is an integral part of many other things—including marketing and telemarketing—that use the media for communicating and promoting.

Knowledge that once was the bailiwick of accountants, financiers, and economists must be understood by marketers, telemarketers, and anybody else who would seek to communicate in business. The business climate of the twenty-first century will require managers, employees, and entrepreneurs to merge technical and telecommunication systems, with knowledge, competencies, and talents.

What Do You Think?
Review and Opinions

1. Describe the similarities and differences between outbound and inbound calls from the standpoint of a telemarketing firm (not from a consumer viewpoint). Which personality type might find each of these TSR jobs appealing? Which personality type are you? What purpose does telemarketing serve in a major marketing campaign?
2. Discuss each of the marketing concepts and explain how they apply to and impact the telemarketing of products; for example, the marketing mix, the store mix, the life cycle of a product, market niche and market share, and the human topics of demographics and needs. Describe how psychology and sociology support the field of marketing and state how a knowledge of marketing is essential in modern business.
3. Share any interesting, unusual telemarketing activities and experiences from around the world, whether from this section, from personal experience, or from recent information gleaned from TV viewing and reading.
4. Discuss occupations and typical competencies needed for telemarketing and marketing jobs. Brainstorm to generate ideas about possible jobs that are only now emerging or have not as yet emerged in comparison with jobs that are disappearing.

For example, how might people with backgrounds in psychology, sociology, and the fine arts find a market niche (type or cluster of jobs) for themselves? How has technology changed the job market and how much do you think you should know about telephones, computers, and television in order to be technologically literate in business?

In the next section, careers will again be discussed, including possibilities related to virtual reality. For now, think about contributions from musicians, performers, writers, photographers, artists, and the like, as well as competencies from business, economics, finance, math, language, and human relations. Use the spaces provided to record notes from the brainstorming session:

_____

_____

_____

_____

_____

_____

_____

_____

_____

_____

_____

_____

_____

_____

_____

_____

_____

From Cave to Satellite

In ancient civilizations, people drew pictures on cave walls to convey messages. Art, including architecture, was the first form of media.

One of the characteristics of old European buildings is that they contain many priceless historical artifacts. Most of these ancient structures were built to last. Many are traditional, fanciful, and spectacular. Britain, France, Spain, and many of the great European nations built great buildings and palaces because they could. Governments and religions were run not by huge bureaucracies but mostly by a handful of rich and powerful men. They collected taxes and tithes, held the money, and decided how funds would be spent. Instead of dispersing tax dollars to support the masses, they chose to preserve their legacy or heritage with great buildings, sculptures, and the commission of portraits and statues.

Long before the slave trade began in the Middle East and Africa, it was the practice to bring home as slaves any of the victims from those countries that a nation's military forces conquered. During the 167 years it took to build St. Peter's Cathedral—the largest cathedral in the world—Rome's population was approximately half citizen, half slave. The slaves of those bygone days represented many colors and races. These factors didn't really matter; getting conquered and vanquished did. Slaves worked inside and outside for little or no pay under the harshest of conditions and with bare minimum support only. Outside workers in Rome and elsewhere were compelled to work constructing these great buildings that have lasted in some cases more than 2,000 years.

Today, these great buildings and landmarks serve as marketing devices. They advertise countries and cities, making them well-known and appealing to visiting tourists. Visiting tourists spend money; they buy goods and services. Tourism today is the number-three industry throughout the world. Where, for example, are these famous landmarks—St. Peter's Cathedral, the leaning tower of Pisa, the Eiffel Tower, Big Ben, the Great Wall, the Taj Mahal, the Empire State Building, the Brandenburg Gate, the Sphinx?

Certain symbols and emphases have come to represent certain ideas: growing vines for life, a snake for danger, dead foliage for death, or a young voluptuous woman and a strong virile man which may symbolize life and the perpetuation of the human species. These are among the major things that people think and worry about, which represents several needs on the first three levels on Maslow's hierarchy.

Early Dutch painters included the above symbols and others in their paintings to convey values and emotions. Some artists included Roman, Grecian, or ancient symbology or other cultural background from prominent civilizations in their works of art to brag of their sophistication and status. The message told viewers that the painter had traveled to Rome, the center of Western civilization's sophisticated culture and fine arts.

Artists have always painted for a number of reasons: to develop and display their talent, to communicate emotions and messages, to describe what they see to others, and to earn a living from the sale of their paintings. They paint landscapes, seascapes, still lifes, and abstract and impressionist works.

But before there was photography, artists were also employed or commissioned by the state—governments of the countries and the fiefdoms—to record events and portray them in paintings. Just as famous people today seek exposure through photography and printing or broadcasting of their photos in the media, the would-be famous people of yesteryear also wanted their images known; they sat to get their portraits painted.

In contemporary times, these great paintings hang in world famous art galleries, in the castles and palaces of the world's few remaining monarchs, and in the mansions of the very wealthy. Today the photos of everyday people can be found hanging in their homes on their walls and mounted in their photo albums. Tourists returning home drag out and show to their friends the slides they took while abroad and, lately, people record events on tape using video cameras.

The Mona Lisa, hanging in The Louvre in Paris, is a small painting that, without proper advertising, might have remained insignificant and unknown. In addition to effective marketing, the economic principle of supply and demand applies to renowned paintings—because they are few in number, their value skyrockets. People buy famous paintings by long-dead artists for their beauty but also because of the prestige of owning such expensive treasures. Moreover, they buy and sell art because of the investment potential. If a painting is valued at a million dollars today, it might sell for two million in the near future.

Major themes of days long gone by, depicted in paintings by the old masters, were pretty much the same as they are in today's media. They also appear pretty much in the same order of frequency as in days of old, namely (after commissioned portraits): nudity, love and family, religion, war and misery, major historical and political events, and leaders or celebrities depicted at work and play.

A philosophical question has been asked throughout the ages: "Which comes first, art or life?" Translated, this means the following: Does the media depict and reflect what is happening among people in real life? Or, does the media's perspective influence people to think and act as "mindless robots" by conditioning them as the media sees fit?

People who visit a variety of art galleries, particularly those that display the old masters, will see both nudity and violence—the latter often depicting battles and crimes of many centuries past. Artists portray subjects that people are interested in. These themes were and still are popular because of their significance to human survival, as depicted in Maslow's hierarchy of human needs.

Marketers know these things or they hire people who are knowledgeable in the liberal arts and behavioral sciences. The soft teddy bear with the trusting innocent face is the logo for Downy fabric softener. The dough boy is the symbol for Pillsbury. Fresh fruit advertises Fruit of the Loom underwear for both men and women. Other symbols, such as the skull and crossbones warn consumers of poisonous ingredients, especially to children.

Except for advertising, it sometimes seems that today's media news describes predominantly bad news; good news seems rare. Not all news is bad, though. Walt Disney merged the fine arts, including writing with technology, to create magic in his commercial enterprises: Disney cartoons and films (see for example, *Santa Claus–the Movie*) and in the three-dimensional Disney theme parks. At Disneyland and Disney World, all human senses are invoked while visitors are given sensational thrills on the rides. At Epcot Center, people's minds expand as they are captivated by experiential knowledge.

Ancient Babylonians put their information in vessels of baked clay. The Egyptians wrote on papyrus, the Romans on parchment and untanned leather. Medieval monks copied prayers and bibles on paper once the secret of paper-making had been learned from the Chinese. Until the printing press was invented, the main forms of communication were speech, drama, and art.

In the 1040s in China, books were first printed from individual clay characters held in an iron frame. Metal type was used in Korea around 1400. The process—letterpress printing with locked in raised letters that could be inked—was invented independently in Europe around 1440 by Johann Gutenberg of Mainz, Germany. The development of lithography in Germany (1798) made it simpler to reproduce color pictures and, in 1895, the engraving of copper plates was adapted to reproduce photographs, by etching light and shade onto the plate in a series of dots.

With printing, literature advanced. Contemporary students of literature read and analyze what are known as the classics. Perhaps they are classic because the values espoused have endured. Or could it be that few people of long ago could read and write and the technology was so limited that few books were printed? Once printed, they must also be advertised and distributed via transportation systems. In modern society, literature includes thousands of novels, nonfiction books, and hundreds of feature films and documentaries produced every year.

Before videos, silent pictures, moving pictures (nicknamed "movies") and communication satellites, there was photography. Before photography, there was art. Before television, there was radio. Before radio, there were newspapers and the pony express. Before compact disks, there were eight tracks and cassettes, and before these there were records and phonograph players. A wide variety of mediums have been used to produce commercials and advertisements, from moving pictures to newspapers, radio, television, computers, and the Internet. With the sophistication of modern graphics, art, and music technology and the wide variety of media available (print, radio, TV, electronic mail, direct mail, telemarketing, etc.), marketers and advertising tycoons today have tremendous opportunities to communicate with their audience.

All of these things, advanced by technological developments, have merged to produce the marketing components that elicit right-brain emotional responses. Their purpose is to persuade and to promote. They persuade people to think and behave in certain prescribed ways—to promote products whether they be goods, services, or ideas. People view, read, listen, and feel. They are moved to respond, to form value judgments, and to buy. It has always been thus. Even religious organizations are especially adept at marketing their theological or educational products, at eliciting emotional responses to their doctrine and values through the use of inspirational music and the poetry of scripture to stir the soul.

Regardless of the media used, or the type of technology available, advertisers and marketers have addressed prospects and customers with products and services to meet almost every level of human need. From primitive art forms on cave walls, to newspaper, radio, television, telemarketing, and computer media, trillions and trillions of messages have been sent to inform, persuade, or otherwise communicate. With the sophistication of modern technology and telecommunications, one message is clear: The proliferation of the electronic advertising age is here to stay!

Activities for Section IV

ACTIVITY IV-1: COLLECT AND REPORT ON ADS AND COMMERCIALS

Directions

1. Using magazines, catalogs, flyers, junk mail, and newspapers, identify and clip (or photocopy) ads that contain 800 and 900 numbers. Include multinational or foreign companies and record the country of origin.

2. Repeat the above task, using TV commercials. Take notes on what you see (or record on videotape) from commercials that market products from multinational or foreign countries.

3. Mount clippings and photocopies (of ads in print copies that do not belong to you) in your portfolio or save in a folder.

4. Retain the same leader, recorder, and processor in your groups unless informed otherwise. Use the spaces below to record findings from group analyses of the ads reported in your portfolio. View TV commercials from video and share print ads. The group looks for and records examples to support ideas taken from the section. See the list of checkpoints that follow:

Left-brain use of symbols and/or words: _____

_____

Right-brain use of:

    music _____

    art _____

performance (acting/dance, etc.) _____

computer-generated graphics _____

Human need(s) addressed: _____

_____

5. The leader facilitates discussion of materials collected individually and analyzed collectively in comparison with section topics on marketing.

6. The recorder summarizes notes from the discussion.

7. Discuss the findings of the group and write a brief summary about what the members learned concerning advertising and marketing. Rate each of the ads for their overall effectiveness and give a rationale explaining why certain ads were better than others.

8. Share your summary report with the others in your class, or with your instructor, facilitator, or employer. Compare your ratings and/or observations with your peers and/or colleagues.

ACTIVITY IV-2: USE SCRIPTS
TO HANDLE OUTBOUND CALLS

Background

Together with a partner you will simulate how to handle outbound telephone calls to SmartMart, a business client. This firm has stores scattered throughout the United States and Canada (see also the case study in Section II). SmartMart sells software programs of all kinds–those used by businesses and those used by consumers. Games are especially popular with children, teens, and young adults–the company's best market niche (see the demographics topic).

Now they have developed a marketing campaign to blitz the media. The telemarketing program has coordinated with their print and broadcast media advertising. You are employed as an outbound telephone sales representative (TSR).

Directions

1. Refer to instructions or suggestions that may be provided by your course facilitator. You will have several script options for placing outbound calls, for example to warm customers versus cold customers.

2. Exchange roles with your partner so each of you have an opportunity to attempt to make telephone sales. One of you will use the telephone scripts while the other partner plays the role of the called person. The called person is at home during the evening. This person should turn his/her back to the caller. You should be able to hear but not to see each other.

3. Review all scripts before placing the first call. Meanwhile, the called person reviews the print copy of possible replies as given to you by your instructor (the TSR should not be able to anticipate which role the callee will play during each of the simulated calls).

4. From the script options suggested, you will know that a warm customer will already own one of SmartMart's computer programs. Your job thus is to sell the customer on another program.

One cold call will be to a person who has a computer, knows how to use software, and is interested in purchasing more–but not necessarily a program by SmartMart. Your job is to sell this person on the company's reputation and the follow-up services, refunds, etc., that are possible from buying SmartMart products.

One cold call will be to a person who has never heard of Smart-Mart and does not own any games or business or consumer software. During the conversation with this person, you will discover the extent of his/her knowledge and interest in computers and programs. You will then decide which script option to use in talking with this person.

5. The partner playing the called person evaluates the performance of the TSR, using the following evaluation form.

6. Exchange roles, with the called person receiving new information from the instructor about how to respond to the telemarketing operator.

7. Each partner evaluates the other on the form provided. Hold these forms until the end of the section before submitting them to the instructor.

EVALUATION OF OUTBOUND TSR CALLS

Name of TSR: _____ Date: _____

Directions: Use the +, ✔, – evaluation method, where + = outstanding, ✔ = average/satisfactory, and – = poor/unsatisfactory.

Left-brain factors

1. The TSR spoke clearly, could be understood   _____

2. The TSR used correct grammar   _____

3. The TSR made correct word choices   _____

4. The information given sounded correct   _____

5. The data given sounded logical, rational   _____

Right-brain factors

6. The emotions in the paralanguage were appealing   _____

7. The tone of voice enticed my interest and made me want to purchase something from SmartMart   _____

8. Colorful and descriptive adjectives and verbs were clearly stated and made the offer attractive   _____

9. I wanted to buy something from this caller, even if I were not interested in buying anything from SmartMart   _____

10. This caller sounds like a very nice person   _____

COMMENTS *(suggestions for improvement)*:

Signature of evaluator: _____

ACTIVITY IV-3: USE SCRIPTS
TO HANDLE INBOUND CALLS

Background

You are a TSR assigned to handle inbound calls for your telemarketing firm's business client, SmartMart. From the 800 number that appears in every print ad and TV commercial, people call in to ask questions and sometimes to place sales orders. Besides choosing from a variety of script options on your disk to enable you to answer effectively, you will also process sales orders when customers want to buy.

Directions

1. Together with a partner, you will play roles of TSR and customer, exchange roles, and evaluate the caller in the TSR role.

2. Refer to suggestions or documents that your course facilitator may provide you. Such suggestions or documents will delineate your scripts. When simulating phone calls, turn your back to the person you will be working with so you can hear but not see each other.

3. Use the evaluation form that follows or one suggested by your course facilitator. Also refer to the sales order form that follows for ideas and suggestions. Your course facilitator may suggest other copies of scripts or you may use the sales order form that follows.

4. Discuss with your partner the evaluations of each other from both types of calls—outbound and inbound—and suggest ways that you can improve your telephone manners.

5. Hold the sales and evaluation forms until the end of the section, when they will be submitted to the instructor.

SMARTMART SALES ORDER FORM

Customer's Name: _____ Date: _____

Address: _____ P.O. no. 1001

_____

ORDER DATA

Stock no.	Item Description	Number ordered	Unit cost	Total cost

EVALUATION OF INBOUND TSR CALLS

Name of TSR: _____ Date: _____

Directions: Use the +, ✔, – evaluation method, where + = outstanding, ✔ = average/satisfactory, and – = poor/unsatisfactory.

Left-brain factors

    1. The TSR spoke clearly, could be understood   _____

    2. The TSR used correct grammar   _____

    3. The TSR made correct word choices   _____

    4. The information given sounded correct   _____

    5. The data given sounded logical, rational   _____

Right-brain factors

    6. The emotions in the paralanguage were appealing   _____

    7. The tone of voice enticed my interest and made me want to purchase something from SmartMart   _____

    8. Colorful and descriptive adjectives and verbs were clearly stated and made the offer attractive   _____

    9. I wanted to buy something from this caller, even if I were not interested in buying anything from SmartMart   _____

    10. This caller sounds like a very nice person   _____

COMMENTS (suggestions for improvement):

Signature of evaluator: _____

ACTIVITY IV-4: PARTICIPATE IN CASE DISCUSSIONS

Directions

1. Read the cases as directed and record your own opinions and responses before meeting with your group for discussion.

2. Retain the same leader, recorder, and processor as before. The leader facilitates discussion, the recorder takes notes, and the processor composes a memo to report group consensus in response to the questions posed at the close of the case.

3. The leader proofreads the memo and makes recommendations, if any, for revision. Hold the memo until the end of the section.

Case Study 1: Designing Products and Packages

To help marketers design more eye-catching products and packaging, an image design computer system can simulate what a shopper should see when strolling through a supermarket. Designers at Levi Strauss use this type of program to experiment with the look of different fabric textures and patterns on three-dimensional images of jeans designs. All this is done before the jeans are produced.

Aerospace and automobile companies also use three-dimensional imaging programs to simulate the look and design of automobile and airline interiors. Now, they can design everything else on computer without resorting to a drafting board at all. These three-dimensional systems have revolutionized and improved the designs of countless products.

1. Review the variety of devices and systems described in the third part of this section. Discuss all of these and more, including the three-dimensional system above and news of other recent devices.

2. What do these things tell you about how industries are changing? Share opinions about how you think jobs are changing.

_____

_____

_____

_____

_____

_____

_____

_____

Case Study 2: Using the Information Highway

Jonathan Grant of Texas is a person on the cutting edge of the new technology. He likes the idea of an interactive, wireless, on-line, on-demand portable computer technology that provides both information and entertainment. To keep current in the newest state of the art technology, Jonathan leased a sophisticated laptop computer from AT&T, which included a pen-driven EO screen, cellular phone, fax, modems, and a host of convenient telecommunications features. This system is referred to as the EO personal communicator laptop, and Jonathan is pleased with it. Following are some of the things Jonathan has used his computerized device for so far:

- He took notes straight on the pen-based EO screen while attending a seminar in San Francisco.
- Without leaving his seminar chair, he scanned an urgent e-mail request from his office.
- He then cross-referenced related subjects, still from his chair at the seminar.
- He responded to the e-mail received with a response over the EO's cellular phone.
- While out house hunting with his wife, they received a fax from a real estate agent that described details of the houses they were headed to see.
- He and his wife used the EO to jot down highlights and impressions of each of seven different houses visited.
- Still enroute, they looked up the house owners' names on the EO, called them on the cellular phone, and ended up making an offer on their first choice–all within a few hours.

Jonathan loaded his EO with these options: 64 megabytes of memory (RAM), an internal modem, a 2.4 gigabyte hard drive, a cellular phone, and an extended battery. Jonathan says he's had great service with his EO system. Also, he says, "When I call in to AT&T on their toll-free customer service line to ask a question, they answer it immediately. They even follow up a week later to see if everything worked out."

The growing two-way flow of voice, pictures, and data has immense implications for retailing. In the upcoming decades and beyond, shopping will involve fewer trips to the mall and more pushbutton, on-line ordering as home delivery systems and cable shopping channels proliferate. AT&T is at the forefront of the trend toward "stores without walls." Technically, of course, AT&T is not a store at all (although it does have neary 400 phone center stores in 44 states that carry its entire product line). However, in the mid-1990s, AT&T was by far the number-one telecommunications retailer, with sales of hardware, systems, and financial services accounting for 28 percent of its $65 billion in annual revenue.

Since 1989, AT&T has been the leading retailer of corded and cordless phones, as well as answering machines. Other products include videophones, NCR notebook computers, the EO Personal Communicator (which also faxes), and the universal calling/credit card. AT&T provides brand recognition and high quality.

1. In your opinion, what are the advantages of owning computer telecommunication devices similar to the one used by Jonathan Grant? What are some of the disadvantages?

_____

_____

_____

_____

_____

_____

_____

2. Share knowledge and experience of the devices listed or described in the case as well as others that have not been mentioned—in the case or the section. How has technology changed in your lifetime? Discuss a few of these changes.

_____

_____

_____

_____

_____

_____

_____

_____

3. Discuss how these devices, if any, might be used in your business to enhance and make more efficient its communications and marketing functions. What is the most beneficial electronic device that your business uses? Why?

_____

_____

_____

_____

_____

_____

_____

_____

_____

ACTIVITY IV-5: FINALIZING THE TERM PROJECT: PLANNING THE PRESENTATION

Directions

1. From the individual or team assignments made in Section III, verify that all tasks have been completed. Individuals or partnership teams should volunteer to complete any last-minute details. Plan how these remaining tasks will be accomplished, by what deadline, and who is to be responsible for each task. Record notes below:

UNCOMPLETED TASK   DEADLINE   PERSON(S) RESPONSIBLE

_____

_____

_____

_____

_____

_____

_____

2. Review the term project activity in Section I to get ideas about how your group's presentation to the full class will be made. Verify with the instructor the date when your group will present this project to the class. Use the spaces below to establish a work plan:

TASKS TO BE COMPLETED   DEADLINE   PERSON(S) RESPONSIBLE

_____

_____

_____

_____

_____

_____

_____

ACTIVITY IV-6: COMPARING LEARNING OUTCOMES WITH SECTION OBJECTIVES

Directions

1. The group leader facilitates the section review and the discussion, supervises the assembling of each member's activity materials for submittal to the instructor, and directs the recorder and processor in their tasks.

2. The recorder takes notes during the discussion, which is designed to reach consensus on learning outcomes in comparison with the section objectives. The processor composes a memo to report learning outcomes to the instructor and the leader proofreads and makes recommendations, if any, for revision.

3. When all work is completed, the leader evaluates each group member, using the form that follows. If you are not the leader, remove this form and submit it to your leader. Data entered on these forms are confidential. Include all work completed by group and individual members during this section and submit the packet to the instructor.

LEARNING OUTCOMES	SECTION OBJECTIVES

SUPERVISOR'S EVALUATION– SECTION IV

Person evaluated: _____ Date: _____

Directions: use the +, ✔, – evaluation method, where + = outstand-ing, ✔ = average/satisfactory, and – = poor/unsatisfactory.

Within this section, the group member was:

1. cooperative with co-workers   _____

2. responsive to assignments made by the group   _____

3. responsive to the supervisor's constructive ideas   _____

4. pleasant, cooperative, easy to work with   _____

5. dependable, attended class meetings   _____

6. dependable, attended out-of-class meetings   _____

7. responsible, produced work on time   _____

8. responsible, produced quality work   _____

9. reliable and willing to work   _____

10. positive team player who contributed greatly
to the group   _____

SUPPORTIVE COMMENTS:

Supervisor's signature (confidential): _____

Bibliography for Section IV

Bishop, Jerry E., "Helping Hands," *The Wall Street Journal*, November 15, 1993. (The swift exchange of data over the networks has been a boon to scientific researchers all over the world.)

Brokaw, Tom, *NBC Nightly News*, July 24, 1993. (Telemarketing scam.)

Carnevale, Mary Lu, "World Wide Web," *The Wall Street Journal*, November 15, 1993.

Chamber of Commerce News, *The Laramie Daily Boomerang*, October 10, 1993. (Swedish Trade Council's 800 number.)

Comfort Inn Motel, Denver, November 24, 1993. (Phone services including credit card slot to order products.)

Crowley, Edward, and Jay J.R. Zajas, "Evidence Supporting the Importance of Brands in Marketing Computer Products," *Journal of Professional Services Marketing*, Volume 14(2), 1996, pp. 120-137.

Daggett, William, "The Many Innovations in Retailing Today," presentation at Western Wyoming College, Rock Springs, Wyoming, September 23, 1993. (No humans; shop for shirt/blouse to order on demand in Japan.)

Didson, Reynolds, "The Boy Who Heard the Future," *Reader's Digest*, July, 1993.

Duston, Diane, " 'Don't call back' means 'don't call back,' " *The Laramie Daily Boomerang*, December 17, 1993.

Edwards, Tamala, "Marketing: Numbers Nightmare: A Pepsi promotion misfires in the Philippines," *Time*, August 9, 1993.

Eye to Eye, CBS, July 29, 1993. (Order cassette by phone with credit card instead of writing for a print copy.)

Fenner, Elizabeth, "AT&T: The Store without Walls," *Money*, December 1993.

Graf, David, Olive D. Church, and Thomas B. Duff, *Business in an Information Economy*. New York: Gregg/McGraw-Hill Publishing Company, 1990.

Gumbel, Bryant, *Today Show*, August 20, 1993. (Personalized greeting cards– Every consumer can become a personal marketer.)

Hafner, Katharine M., "Computer Graphics are Animating Another Market," *Business Week*, March 16, 1987.

Harriss, Joseph, "A Parisian Love Affair," *Reader's Digest*, March 1989. "How Competitive is America?" Council on Competitiveness report, Washington, DC, 1988. (Private sector leaders assess U.S. performance.)

Illustrated Encyclopedic Dictionary, Volumes A-K and L-Z. Pleasantville, New York: Reader's Digest Association, 1987.

Jennings, Peter, *ABC World News*, ABC, September 29, 1993. (News about the popularity of the QVC-TV Shopping Channel.)

Kahn, Alfred, *Nightly Business Report (NBR)*, PBS, September 3, 1993. (Telephone and cable company highlights.)

Kuralt, Charles, *CBS Sunday Morning*. "Postcard from Shanghai," CBS, September 12, 1993. (Booming economy and modern transportation and communication systems in China.)

_____, *CBS Sunday Morning*, January 2, 1994. (Orthodox monks make icons.)

Lipman, Jean, Elizabeth V. Warren and Robert Bishop, *Young America: A Folk Art History*. New York: Museum of American Folk Art History and Hudson Hills Press, Inc., 1986.

Lord Chesterfield, "Quotable Quotes," *Reader's Digest*, December 1991.

MacNeil-Lehrer News Hour, PBS, August 10, 1993. (Creativity and entrepreneurship make a good match.)

McCarroll, Thomas, "Television: New Star Over Asia," *Time*, August 9, 1993.

McNichol, Tom, "The Rise of Ho-Ho-Home Shopping," *USA Weekend*, December 17-19, 1993.

North Park Pioneer Museum, Walden, CO. (Short-wave and ham radios, wax cylinder, Edison phonograph, music box over 200 years old; U.S. mail post office manufactured by the Sadler Co., Washington, DC, Indianapolis and Kansas City, Missouri.)

Pekas, Mary D., *Basic Telemarketing: Skills for Sales and Service Productivity*. Eden Prairie, MN: Paradigm Publishing International, 1990.

Personal column, *The Laramie Daily Boomerang*, regularly appearing editorial.

Prial, Frank J., "Freeze! You're on TV," *New York Times Magazine*, September 25, 1988.

Rather, Dan, "Dan Rather in China," CBS, September 7, 1993. (Chinese economy booming, low flight fares to attract winter tourists, and ads in U.S. business magazines from China businesses.)

Reader's Digest, "Notes from All Over," November, 1990. (Cooperative learning in industry.)

"Reclaiming the American Dream: Fiscal policies for a competitive nation," Council on Competitiveness, Washington, DC, 1989.

Royko, Mike, "Telling off Telemarketers," *Reader's Digest*, April 1993.

Sitel, Inc., telemarketing firm, several tours, interviews and observations, Omaha, Nebraska and Laramie, Wyoming, January and February, 1994.

Slutsker, Gary, "The Company that Likes to Obsolete Itself," *Forbes*, September 13, 1993.

Smith, Harry, *CBS This Morning*, CBS, August 6, 1993. (800-number call-back scam.)

"Style," CNN, November 20, 1993. (Architectural design started out as media.)

Sutton, Remar, "Dial '900' for Trouble," *Reader's Digest*, August, 1991.

Tempest, Rone, "American TV: We Are the world," *Reader's Digest*, July, 1993. (Telemarketing and marketing via TV commercials.)

Tours and observations, among others, 1986-1996:
Art Institute of Chicago
Brandenburg Gate, former Checkpoint Charlie, and Berlin Wall
Buffalo Bill Museum, Cody, Wyoming (Native American art and artifacts as
well as cowboy and western art)
Cathedrals, castles, palaces and government buildings in Mexico, Europe,
British Isles, Berlin; the Kremlin, Russia; St. Peter's, Rome; St. Paul's,
London; Notre-Dame, Paris; Prince's Palace, Principality of Monaco;
Buckingham Palace, Windsor Castle, Canterbury, England; Mad King Lud-
wig's storybook castle, Neuschwanstein (Disneyland castle model)
Dallas Art Gallery
Denver Museum and Art Gallery
Egyptian Museum, Berlin (famous bust of Nefertiti; pharaoh days)
Gallery of Fine Arts, Florence; Michelangelo's David and Moses famous
sculptures; Sistine Chapel, Forum, Colosseum, Rome
Historical Museum, Geneva
The Lion of Lucerne, world famous monument which symbolizes Swiss hero-
ism and is hewed directly into natural rock
London art galleries and museums
The Louvre, Paris (Mona Lisa, many Old Masters' works, include sculpture)
Metropolitan Museum of Art, New York City
Museum of Modern Art, Boston
National Gallery, Berlin (includes Asian, African, Indian art)
National Museum, Zurich
Nelson Art Gallery, Kansas City, Missouri
Opera de Paris, Bastille
Principality of Liechtenstein (buildings and sites)
Rijksmuseum, Amsterdam–Dutch paintings, history from prehistoric times,
masterpieces by Rembrandt, Vermeer, Frans Hals; Dutch sculpture, Asian
Art (except Islamic)
Royal Opera House of London
St. Mark's Square, Clock Tower, Doge's Palace, Venice
Uffizi Gallery, Florence, Italy

Vincent, Sean, Telemarketing Manager, Washington State University, interview
covering telemarketing procedures in a nonprofit organization, January, 1994.
"The Wireless Warehouse," *Forbes*, August, 1993.
Zajas, Jay J.R., *Achievement, Motivation, Employment, Job Satisfaction and
Socio-Economic Status of Doctoral Business Administration and Education
Graduates: A Comparative Analysis*. University Microfilms International
Press, 1985.
Zajas, Jay J.R., "Integrating the Marketing Concept Through Strategic Analysis
and Management," American Business Women's Association, Presidential
Forum, September, 1992.
Zajas, Jay J.R., "Strategies for Enhancing Your Executive, Personal, and Career
Development," *Business Perspectives Journal*, Volume 6(4), 1993, pp. 2-6.

Zajas, Jay J.R., "Strategy Formulation: How Customer Responsive Is Your Firm?" *Executive Development Journal*, Volume 6(5), 1993, pp. 18-21.

Zajas, Jay J.R., "The Marketing of Executives and Career Development Success," *Executive Development Journal*, Volume 8(3), 1995.

Zajas, Jay J.R., and Earl W. Brewster, "Beyond Goal-Setting: Key Interpersonal Success Factors for Marketing Executives Today," *Executive Development Journal*, Volume 8(3), 1995.

Zajas, Jay J.R., and Harold Cates, "Current Trends and Challenges in Marketing and Executive Candidate," *Health Marketing Quarterly*, Volume 13(3), 1996, pp. 2-12.

Zajas, Jay J.R., and Edward Crowley, "Brand Emergence in the Marketing of Computers and High Technology Products," *The Journal of Product & Brand Management*, Volume 4(1), 1995.

Zajas, Jay J.R., and Jann R. Michener Zajas, "A Conceptual Approach to Career Planning for Executive and Managerial Success." *International Academy of Management and Marketing, IAMM Proceedings*, April 1991, pp. 118-124.

Zajas, Jann R. Michener, and Jay J.R. Zajas, *Effective Planning for the Success Oriented Manager*, (The Corporate Management Group, 1996).

Zajas, Jay J.R., and Lawrence P. Zotz, Jr., "Integrating Customer Satisfaction into the Strategic Marketing Plan," *Journal of Customer Service in Marketing and Management*, Volume 1(3), 1995, pp. 50-66.

SECTION V:
RECORDS SYSTEMS
AND TELECOMMUNICATIONS

For organizational, reference, and analysis purposes, it is essential that businesses have a method, or system, for recording and classifying actions, decisions, and transactions. One of the ways businesses keep organized is through the maintenance of a viable records system. Records are the life-blood of any organization, from huge governments and multinational conglomerates to households and the individuals who must keep track of what they are doing. Records, provided that they are organized properly, are the present, past, and future of civilized society.

Records management is related to telecommunications because so much of what businesses do now is not only computerized but also is available and transmittable over telecommunication systems. Records management is related to telemarketing because every sales and purchase transaction and every attempt to turn a cold customer into a warm customer must be tracked, recorded, and filed.

Data that are filed, whether by manual, electronic, or telecommunication means, must be readily retrievable. If we could not quickly access the data that are filed, these data might as well be sent to the dump and never stored at all. Since we must be able to retrieve data quickly from many types of sources and from all over the world, we must learn how to use specific rules, methods, procedures, and systems which have been developed.

OBJECTIVES

1. Discuss major section topics and draw comparisons with issues presented previously to identify how these topics are related.

2. Collect and share broadcast, print, and interview news that illustrate the interdependency of records, telecommunication, and telemarketing systems.
3. Access database documents and update records for customers, employees, and citizens.
4. Participate in group activities to demonstrate the simultaneous management of records and human relations.
5. Participate in discussing cases.
6. Cooperate with your group to complete and/or present the term project.
7. Reach consensus in comparing learning outcomes with section objectives, finalize the portfolio, and conduct evaluations.

Chapter 12

Records and Telecommunications

The Global Positioning System (GPS) is an innovative development of the twentieth century. This little electronic device is a sophisticated computerized radio receiver that uses information from orbiting satellites to calculate position, speed, altitude, and distance to destination. Pilots use them to stay on course while in flight, which is very helpful when flying during poor visibility conditions.

The GPS can immediately identify latitudinal and longitudinal coordinates and tell pilots and others exactly where they are on earth. One may never get lost again! When Mike Fraser recently went snorkeling off Campbell Island—a mere speck of land between New Zealand and Antarctica—he was attacked and lost half his arm in the jaws of a shark! By the time he had fought off the vicious predator and swam the 40 yards to shore, he had also lost about half of his blood!

Mike and his companions were over 400 miles from the nearest hospital, there was no airstrip on the island, and a boat would take three days to reach them. A co-worker ran 300 yards up a hill to a small hut equipped with first-aid kit and a VHF radio.

After a five-hour flight, Mike's rescuers aboard the Squirrel helicopter knew that the only thing standing between them and an icy death was their tiny craft and Grant Biel's skills as a navigator. To locate Campbell Island at night, Biel planned to rely on the Squirrel's GPS. But that night, the GPS satellites were taken off the air for routine repositioning in space. Panic ensued! At last, halfway to the island, Grant Biel saw black numbers again flashing on the tiny GPS screen. Because Mike had a GPS transmitter, he was able to be located and rescued.

Photo 12.1. Medical Records

Every industry has a need for records, and in most cases, these are confidential. Every major metropolitan newspaper and many smaller newspapers regularly list vacancy after vacancy in their classified help-wanted columns for medical records personnel because there is such a demand for medical record keeping.

The Global Positioning System provides a variety of benefits as an innovative satellite tracking system. As illustrated in the previous example, it can be helpful to pilots for determining their location (as well as the location of others). It can also be used as a tracking device to help keep aircraft on target with their anticipated destination point. Anytime a pilot deviates from his or her flight coordinates and goes off target, the GPS informs the flight crew and gives directional input to the pilot for making corrections in the current flight pattern. This tracking function can be especially helpful in poor visibility conditions, or when the pilot experiences difficulty with the plane's navigational instruments. Some of the downsides to the GPS occur when the tracking satellites are temporarily deactivated for repositioning or maintenance, or when the GPS is used for illegal or unethical purposes.

What does the GPS and its sophisticated technological capabilities have to do with records? It demonstrates the interaction and interdependency of two or more major systems; in this case, the gathering and transmittal of precise information (also the link with a transportation system to physically rescue Mike). Because of its use as a tracking system, the GPS is really a technological method for advanced electronic record keeping.

Records management makes possible the systematic gathering, organizing, storing, and fast retrieval of data. *Telecommunications* makes possible the systematic and rapid, almost instantaneous, transmittal and receipt of data over distance. Now, these systems have merged. Records management also applies to telemarketing. Gathering data by whatever means is called *research* but with telecommunications, the access to data is faster and provides a far bigger pool of information.

TELECOMMUNICATIONS AND RECORDS

Many documents are still stored manually, using file cabinets, file folders, printed labels, and hard copy papers. Often these are merely backups for the records that are stored electronically.

Labels and Directories

Every database that is meant to be retained can be accessed by someone on-line but only if a systematic method for storing and retrieving is used and shared with those on the network. Thus, record keepers name files (whether manually or electronically) and create directories so people can find what is stored.

Passwords

Every time that every person sitting at a computer saves a document, it is stored until such time as it is deleted (or disaster such as an electrical outage accidentally deletes data). Any data stored by computers that are connected to networks (LANs or WANs) become part of a total telecommunication system. These data are then available to everyone on the networks, world wide, provided they know the passwords to admit entry into the system and that they can follow the directory to lead them to what they want.

Devices

Any telecommunication device, from pagers to personal digital assistants (PDA), that are designed to communicate messages provide more ways to generate data. Records result from the generation of data, whether transmitted or received; whether numeric, alphabetic, or musical.

The transmittal of music is another example of the need to create and record data such as vocal and instrumental music. Digital Music Express (DMX) is programmed so firms can pipe into their organizations any of 30 different categories. The purpose of DMX? To soothe as in a dentist's office, to entice happy feelings as in the Christmas music that promotes gift buying or contributes to increased productivity among employees.

Pagers do a lot more now than just beep. Many new services are transforming paging from a system that transmits phone numbers to one that carries full-blown text messages and other data. One can now get stock-price updates, news flashes, sports scores, and the like. Numeric pagers communicate in code. For instance, 32, 42 could mean "return to the office." Alphanumeric pagers communicate using both words and numbers; thus they cost more but provide more services.

Nearly all pagers receive radio waves using a crystal that is ground at the factory to resonate at a set frequency for a specific network. Switching carriers is sometimes difficult because of long-term user agreements. (With cellular phones, one can choose a preferred phone company carrier, such as AT&T, Sprint, or MCI.)

To get Americans comfortable with the idea of sending messages by radio, Motorola set up several networks for receive-only e-mail and, with IBM, for two-way wireless messaging. Paging didn't exist in Brazil until Motorola arrived to install a paging network.

PDAs and other communicators, such as Apple's Newton and AT&T's EO personal communication systems, lack traditional keyboards. Instead, they rely on handwriting recognition systems or touch-screen keyboards. Another device, the Altair Plus II wireless LAN, can operate at speeds of 5.7 megabytes per second, more than fast enough to handle compressed video transmissions. The chart in Figure 12.1 summarizes information about devices and systems and how they work.

TELEMARKETING AND RECORDS

A quick overview of telemarketing generally reveals what must happen to make both outbound and inbound calls worth the effort and expense of doing business this way. Telemarketing sales reps (TSRs) place outbound calls from mailing or calling lists. However, somebody had to first gather, record, and make available those lists.

Records must be kept of calls placed and sales made. These data are transmitted to the departments where action is taken—goods are shipped or information, service, or ideas are provided. Sales records are meshed with accounting records. Management makes decisions based on sales made and sales lost and on numerous other financial records that emerge from the TSRs' calling activities.

Complaints must be recorded and these data transmitted to others. Files must be flagged so that no future calls are placed to people who request that they not be called again.

Records must be kept of inbound calls. These data are also transmitted to those who need them—such as employees in the marketing department, the advertising and sales offices, and/or the accounting division, etc. People representing environmentalism, consumer advocacy groups and religions, hobbies, lobbies, and special interest groups place a variety of inbound calls. Their needs must also be acknowledged. One way that organizations can do this is by recording and keeping records.

Figure 12.1. Staking Wireless Claims

System/Players	How It Works	Implications
ENHANCED CELLULAR Baby Bells, AT&T (through McCaw Cellular), GTE, Sprint, others	By adding radio equipment and moving to digital technology, carriers can greatly expand number of customers they can serve.	Ubiquitous coverage, established customer base, but warring digital standards and patchwork ownership make it tough to provide seamless nationwide roaming.
ENHANCED PAGING Most Baby Bells, SkyTel (MTel), PageNet, EMBARC (Motorola)	New technology added to the radio-based systems will allow two-way paging, so customers can acknowledge receipt of a page.	Old but still popular, reliable, and cheap; adding limited two-way capability may spur further growth.
SPECIALIZED MOBILE RADIO (SMR) Nextel, CenCall, Dial Page	These local voice dispatch networks, used by truckers and taxis, will be converted into cellular-like systems through new digital technology from Motorola.	Handles voice and paging messages in one pocket-size phone. It also allows easy nationwide roaming. But digital cellular could catch up.
RADIO-BASED DATA NETWORKS ARDIS, a joint venture of Motorola and IBM; Ram Mobile Data	Nationwide system of radio towers sends text to handheld computers.	Sends long data files efficiently and cheaply by transmitting them in bursts or pockets. But it faces competition from cellular and SMR, which also offers voice calling.
PERSONAL COMMUNICATIONS SERVICES (PCS) Likely players include Baby Bells, GTE, long-distance carriers, cable-TV operators, startups	Like cellular, but uses lower-powered radio transceivers spaced closer together, for higher capacity and presumably, lower customer costs.	PCS operators can overspend for air rights, and they must catch up with other wireless providers.
SATELLITE American Mobile Satellite, Orbital Communications, Iridium (consortium including Motorola, Sprint, and Sony)	Will use relatively inexpensive satellites to send and receive voice and/or data to handheld devices around the country or the globe.	Expensive to put in place, which results in costly rates; rise of seamless cellular networks limits its appeal.

Government agencies and political parties conduct surveys and polls. They invite people to call in to register their votes, opinions, queries, suggestions, and complaints. Records are also kept.

DATA COLLECTIONS AND DATABASES

An overview of the vast amount of information available in databases follows. These data are available to people with access to computers, computer networks, and telecommunication systems. How did all these data come to be collected? Many people are involved with the collection, computer entry, and managing of these billions of records. Many new career options are in fact emerging as the result of these developments.

Accessing Databases

A review of databases in Section I introduces this topic. From personal use of cyberspace by cyberpunks (or techno-nerds) and telecommunication entrepreneurs to members of government bureaus and multinational organizations, people are accessing the Internet.

The Internet is a vast network of computers that within a few years will reach an estimated 100 million people worldwide. People on the Internet can download information to their own computers or browse through documents while on-line.

The Internet got its start as a way to link universities doing defense research, but the network has expanded far beyond its origins. It has evolved from a purely academic forum into an on-line community of, for example, gourmet cooks with recipes to share, computer-wise kids with games in mind, anarchists, neo-Nazis, Zen Buddhists, the White House, and the Library of Congress.

With the merging of systems, the Internet's capacity has expanded to link it with networks built by the telephone and cable TV industries. Recently, due to increased demand, government agencies began scrambling to make their information available on the Internet.

Photo 12.2. Innovative Record Systems

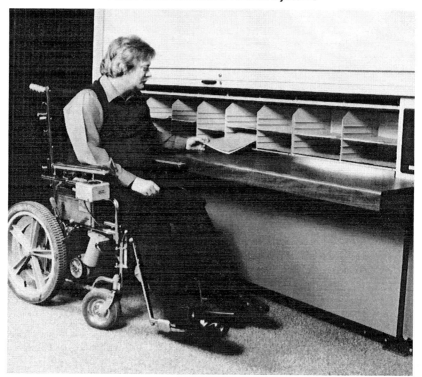

Innovative filing systems allow the files to come to the file clerk rather than the reverse. Here, the person who is accessing files need not walk around, reach up, or reach down to retrieve manual hard copy files. Whether paper, cards, or microfiche records, they come to him.

Examples of Governmental Use

The Federal Bureau of Investigation (FBI) can stalk criminals down a different kind of main street—the information superhighway. FBI agents expanded their search for the Unibomber who was for years out to get computer buffs, computer companies, aircraft and airline industries, and university researchers. The bombings began in 1978 and continued through the mid-1990s. The FBI placed notices on the Internet using a computer owned by the National Aeronautics and Space Administration (NASA).

Like the role of the TV show, *America's Most Wanted*, the FBI hoped that some people on the Internet might have clues that would bring down the Unibomber(s). The Internet notice read: "Internet users are precisely the type of individuals that to date have been victims of explosive devices." The notice further advised that users were not being asked to put themselves in harm's way, but were encouraged to come forward with information. Such notices were helpful in the eventual capture of the alleged notorious Unibomber.

The Internal Revenue Service (IRS) trains agents to battle an increasingly popular weapon of tax cheats: the computer. Although the computer has made the task of detecting tax evasion more difficult, once a scheme is uncovered, the technology "makes it easier for us to pull the case together," said the IRS's assistant commissioner for criminal investigation in Washington. Instead of engaging in the laborious task of searching invoices manually, the IRS reverses the method and uses their own software to unravel records. The IRS seizes computers, programs, and records when they suspect fraudulent activity.

Government Data Collections

Unlike businesses, governments do not exist to make money but to spend it. They spend money to protect and help citizens. Military defense, law enforcement, and protection against crime and criminals involves the expenditure of money and manpower, including the collection and management of records. Instead of producing industrial and consumer goods, local and national governments collect, use, and produce information and services. The following is a small sampling of the U.S. federal government's vast databases:

- Justice Department—over 200 data systems and 200 million records with data on criminals, criminal suspects, aliens, people linked to organized crime, securities laws violators, and "individuals who relate in any manner to official FBI investigations."
- Treasury Department—over 900 data systems and 1 billion records of files on taxpayers, foreign travelers, people deemed by

the Secret Service to be potentially harmful, and dealers in alcohol, drugs, firearms, and explosives.

- Health and human services—over 700 data systems and 1.5 billion personal records including marital, financial, health, and other data on recipients of Social Security, social services, Medicaid, Medicare, and Welfare benefits.
- Defense Department—over 2000 data systems and 300 million records pertaining to service personnel and people investigated for such things as employment, security, or criminal activity.
- Department of Transportation—over 300 data systems and 40 million records including information on pilots, aircraft and boat owners, and all motorists whose licenses have been withdrawn, suspended, or revoked by any state.
- Department of Commerce—over 100 data systems and 500 million records, primarily Census Bureau data but including files on minority and female entrepreneurs, merchant seamen, and so on.
- Department of Labor—over 100 data systems and 20 million records, many involving people in federally financed work and job training programs.
- Civil Service—over 15 data systems and 100 million records, mostly dealing with government employees or applicants for government jobs.

Chapter 13

Some Rules of the Game

Baseball, basketball, bridge, chess, and the board game Monopoly have rules. Chemistry has formulas and shorthand has outlines to memorize. Traffic laws help to save lives. When people know the rules, they know what to do and what to expect. That is the purpose of rules, formulas, outlines, and laws that govern many things that people do. With organization comes efficiency and the relief from tedious thinking. If rules are remembered and applied, what is sought may be found.

The rules for record keeping or filing are no different. A few basic rules are essential. In this chapter, the reader is introduced to some reasons for these rules. Two basic filing systems are alphabetic and numeric. Each of these has subsystems. Alphabetic filing is ordered from A through Z. Two examples of alphabetic subsystems are subject and geographic. A subsystem that uses both alphabetic and numerical systems is alphanumeric (e.g., the British or Canadian Postal Codes).

ALPHABETIC FILING

The alphabetic method is familiar because telephone directories, dictionaries, and library cataloging systems (electronic or card) use this method. Almost 90 percent of all administrative files are arranged alphabetically. *Administrative files* include correspondence, reports, databases, mailing lists and data files, meeting notices and agendas, minutes of meetings, policies and procedures,

Photo 13.1. Computer Graphics

When records, including computer-generated graphics and desktop-published materials, are stored, they are readily retrievable only if labeled and recorded on a file directory. Both filing (or storing) and retrieving are part of the total records management system.

and presentation documents such as articles, editorials, and keynote speeches.

A *unit* may be a single letter or a group of letters that form a word. Lois Barr is a two-unit name, with four units (letters) in each name. Proper names, including those that appear in the names of businesses, are inverted; they are filed by last name first. Lois Barr is filed after Lowell Bar because of the "nothing before something" rule. Bar (nothing) comes before Barr (the second "r" in Barr is the "something"): (1) Bar, Lowell; followed by (2) Barr, Lois.

Hyphenated names are considered as one word. Church-Gehring is filed under "C" for Church, not "G" for Gehring. If a person called himself Robert Church Gehring, then Church would be the middle name, not part of the last name and the filing order of units would be: Gehring, Robert Church.

Britons were well known for using this hyphenated approach to last names. When young people from two families of equal social and economic status married, the woman's family usually do not want to see their name lost to posterity. Thus, the children of a woman with the family name of Church who had married into the Gehring family would be called by both names—hyphenated; thus, Robert Church-Gehring. Today, many women also want to keep their own family name but are willing to take on the husband's family name—only if the two are hyphenated. One should not offend people by filing hyphenated names under, for example, Gehring, if Church is connected to Gehring. It is not the filer's business to establish family values.

Business names such as IBM (which stands for International Business Machines) are used with neither spaces nor periods after the initials and are indexed as one unit: IBM, not I then B then M (or, worse, inverted as in M followed by I and then B). Many abbreviated or letter names have come to be more famous than their full names. If IBM wants to go by IBM instead of the mouthful of syllables, International Business Machines, filers should abide by this commonly accepted practice. Likewise, names such as AT&T (American Telephone & Telegraph Company) or Texaco (an abbreviation of Texas Company), should be filed accordingly. Many companies and organizations use and are known today by their abbreviated name. For example, the Minnesota Mining & Manufacturing Company is better known as simply 3M, the American Federation of Labor and Congress of Industrial Organizations is better known as AFL-CIO, and the Archer-Daniels-Midland Company is known as ADM.

Subject Filing

This method arranges records first into related groups and then alphabetically within each group. The Yellow Pages of the telephone directory and encyclopedia references show examples of this subsystem.

Because people think differently, the subject method is often difficult to decipher. One might file a document under one subject while someone else would file it under another topic. *Cross-referencing* is a trick that uses double, triple, or more filing. The original document should be filed in one place and a copy (or reference to the original) in two or more additional places. An example is "Lawyers" in the Yellow Pages. The notation under this subject might read "see Attorneys." To avoid confusion, filers should establish an index (like that found in the Yellow Pages) of cross-referenced subjects.

Geographic Filing

Geographic filing, like subject filing, depends on alphabetical arrangement. With this method, a subject is filed first by geographic location (which could rightfully be called "subjects") and then alphabetically. Some examples of local, county, and state organizations, which are likely to use geographic filing, include the following: real estate agencies, utility companies, school districts, political groups, and some government bureaus. A city directory (e.g., *polk* directory) illustrates how subjects are arranged geographically by communities, neighborhoods, and streets within neighborhoods.

National and international organizations that use the geographical method include export/import firms, shipping and transportation firms, vehicle rentals, publishers, and federal and state governments that interact with multinational organizations. So many types and sizes of firms now have international dealings that geographic filing is becoming more common.

The major rule for geographic filing is to sequence records from largest to smallest. Look for countries first, followed by provinces or states, counties or shires, cities, and street numbers and street names within cities. For example: Canada, Manitoba, Winnipeg, Post Office Box 2350; or United States, Alabama, Tallapoosa, Alexander City, 153 South Cedar Street.

NUMERIC FILING

Some examples of records that easily lend themselves to numeric filing include any prenumbered documents, such as purchase and sales orders, invoices, checks, and account numbers. These are called *operational records* (administrative records were defined earlier). When consumers write checks in payment of monthly bills, they might think that *everything* has an account number. (To reduce the possibility of filing and credit-entry errors, people should include the account number on every check in payment of every bill.)

When consumers place inbound calls to reach account service reps, the first thing they are usually asked for is not their last name, but the number of their account or their Social Security number. One can visualize what is happening at the other end of the line and can rightfully imagine an operator with headphones in place and hands poised over a computer keyboard. If a caller cannot report a specific account or other number, the operator will generally ask for a customer's last name. This is an indication of cross-reference filing, using both numeric and alphabetic systems.

One's own individual account numbers provides examples. A small local utility company might have no more than five to seven digits; they probably file by the primary numeric method. Credit card companies, with tens, perhaps hundreds of thousands of customers, use long, hyphenated numbers. They file by primary, secondary, or tertiary means.

Primary, Secondary, and Tertiary Numbers

The primary method starts with the first number and continues sequentially through to the end. For example, the zip code number 01435 is filed before 10435.

With the secondary method, the middle set of numbers becomes the first order of filing. The Social Security number 505-*32*-1214 is filed before 302-*33*-1214.

Tertiary numbers indicates the third set of numbers is considered first in filing. The credit account number of 22-0692-*104* is filed before 12-0583-*105*, for instance.

Numeric Codes Communicate

The choice and placement of digits can communicate their meaning (if one knows the code). For example, the zip code designates U.S. regions: the zero covers the northeast region of the United

States; nine includes the west plus Alaska and Hawaii. The next two digits stand for the state and the last two digits for the postal station within states and cities.

After it became illegal to ask applicants to report their race on application forms (e.g., for prospective employment and credit approval), some organizations began to use numeric codes. A quick glance at the account or employee number of a candidate could identify the characteristics of a person whether he or she is a customer, job applicant, or employee.

The following are some examples that define demographic characteristics (see also demographics in Section IV):

- First digit is used to designate gender: 1 = male, 2 = female; the second digit stands for race: 1 = Caucasian, 2 = black, 3 = Latin, 4 = Asian, etc.
- For credit ratings, this code communicates: 1 = employed, 2 = part-time job, 3 = unemployed.
- A variety of demographics: occupation, income level, gender, age range, education, the neighborhood of residence, and whether people own or rent their homes.

The database can then be programmed to sort and compile data by any digit or series of digits. Data are then compared with other sets of data. For employees, the statistics might report attendance, promptness, high versus low productivity, and so on. For credit customers, the report might document high versus low risk potential, salary earned, or duration of time at one's current address or employment locale.

Alphanumeric Filing

Alphanumeric filing combines features from both the alphabetic and the numeric systems; for example, "R" could stand for residence and "B" for business utility customers. When databases include millions of records, they become cumbersome to manage, even with the subnumeric classifications of secondary and tertiary methods. Mixing letters and numbers may categorize records by demographics or by marketing and product classifications. Two countries that currently use the alphanumeric method for their postal deliveries are Canada and Great Britain. Tradition, economies of scale, personal preference, cost, and/or efficiency often dictate what type of filing or record system will be used by a company.

Chapter 14

Records Management Supports
the Need for Information

Organizations need information, they cannot survive without it. Records are an organization's lifeblood. Information from records flow through the firm's networks like blood through the body's veins. At the same time that information provides advantages, it can also create a host of disadvantages, from legal ramifications and criminal activities to cultural and human relations problems. One significant benefit, however, is the many new career opportunities and different types of jobs that are emerging in the information business. People as consumers, producers, citizens, and decision makers also need information.

RECORDS IN SUPPORT OF THE NEEDS
OF ORGANIZATIONS

Records systems within industries (see Section III for the standard industrial classifications–SICs) are often designed to meet unique situations. Construction and manufacturing firms need to keep production records, deadlines proposed and whether met or delayed, and lists of suppliers and their reputation for quality and timely deliveries.

Research firms and individuals employed by such firms, including universities, need to record findings and organize records. They also need to contact one another around the world to compare their studies and the results of research and development.

Banks and other financial institutions file most records in the computer. The need to protect customers' privacy is paramount;

nothing is more private than financial records, not even intimacy among couples. Banks and other financial exchanges move funds around the world electronically. Other types of firms also rely heavily on computer records to conduct business globally and locally. For example, transportation firms and travel agencies use computerized networks to make reservations, track flights, and record the movement of both goods and people.

Hotel PBX (private branch exchange) and voice messaging systems improve guest services. Interactive, high-definition television along with multiuse phones (see Section IV) have changed what and how room services can be delivered. Teleconferencing, videoconferencing, and audio telephone bridges impact hotel revenues as more businesses use them to reduce travel and hotel costs. The impact of telecommunications on records management, though, has reduced the number of employees needed.

Insurance companies coordinate manual and electronic files. They color code the manual file folders so they can easily spot them on the shelves. Colors represent certain types of insurance policies; for example, life, auto, medical, etc. The numeric system addresses the policy number and the alphabetic system uses the last name of the customer. When customers call, the operator can access their records (manual or database) by name when the caller does not know his or her policy number. When detailed or legal information is needed that is not available on the computer, the insurance agent or operator can easily access the customer's file folder by the color code.

When Julie Jones' boss goes out to shoot water buffalo and other big game in Africa, he keeps in touch with her and his real estate business by fax and phone. He also owns a buffalo ranch and, as a land developer, searches for land to develop in the United States. A self-proclaimed absent-minded entrepreneur, he often gets lost. Not yet equipped with a GPS (see introduction), he calls Julie on his cellular phone to describe landmarks. With maps (geographic records) readily available, she eventually tells him his location.

Some players in the natural gas industry use the Link System. Link does for natural gas companies what the airlines' computerized reservation systems do for the travel industry. By dialing in, utility companies can figure out how much gas is available, when it can be delivered, and how much it will cost.

Pharmaceutical companies rely on bulletin board input to help monitor patients' reactions to new drugs. The U.S. Department of Agriculture uses the Internet daily to get timely information out to the farmers who feed the world.

"With the Internet," said the director of the Washington office of the Center for Civic Networking, "we are talking about improving delivery of government services, revitalizing the quality of public debate, reducing poverty, and changing welfare as we know it."

RECORDS IN SUPPORT OF PERSONAL NEEDS

Businesses and consumers use devices to satisfy their information and records management needs: phones, cellular phones, answering machines, voice messaging, interactive TV, pagers, computers, laser and other printers, modems, and software for calculating, word processing, spread sheets, and telecommunications. In addition to these devices, they also use hard copies, file folders and other filing supplies, and "organizers"—small notebooks with prearranged sections for projects, journals, expenses, calorie counting, calendars, and so on.

Software programs that can be used on laptop or notebook-size computers come in many varieties, including the topics named above for the manual organizer. Add cellular phone or paging capabilities, calculator, calendar, personal and bill-paying schedules, notepad, stock quotations, budget and expense records and a record system can be taken wherever one goes; perhaps, like Julie's global gallivanting boss, on African safari.

Lois Bertha, plagued by arthritis and a rapid heartbeat and doctors who insisted she had few viable medicinal options, contacted a database. The World Research Foundation of Sherman Oaks, California (818-907-5483), offers a library search of books and periodicals containing alternative medical therapies, plus a computer search of more than 5,000 medical journals, including pharmaceutical and surgical information. Each search costs about $50.

Armchair tourists may plug in earphones to hear a recording that describes the art, artifacts, and historical significance of places the world over. They can tune in to shows described in TV programming schedules (data collections) on Discovery and PBS channels. Or they can special-order catalogs travelogs on interactive TV.

Microsoft's original Flight Simulator was one of the first and most successful computer games (compared to the arcade-type games such as PacMan). Meanwhile, new arcade games come with impressive graphics and sound effects to challenge and please the young. The wild proliferation of computer games include tank battles and fighter combat games, which are sometimes more sophisticated than business recordkeeping software. The Falcon 3.0 (by Spectrum Holobyte) for example is based on the real F-16 Fighting Falcon and is popular among businesspeople who sneak time on their office machines to play it.

Sometimes people have a need to avoid receiving information! At the Oval Office at 1600 Pennsylvania Avenue, the wrong fax number appeared on a mailing list of people who were supposed to receive a 42-page White House promotional piece. A private family had a fax machine in their basement that suddenly started spitting out PR pages. "Stop sending fax!" was the message they tried to get through to the White House.

RECORDS AND THE LAW

Are the technical skills and mental databases of employees the "intellectual properties" of the organizations that employ them? In today's information era, the information contained in people's minds is valuable. People leave one firm for another, taking with them all they know and can do but also the things they learned and heard from their employers' database collections. When IBM downsized their staff from 475,000 to 225,000 employees, a lot of good as well as private information left IBM too. IBM lost a great wealth of valuable information and expertise when these employees were downsized. Many other firms have experienced similar losses in the process of downsizing personnel.

The Nobel committee may not be ready to recognize the literary or artistic claims of postings on computer bulletin boards, but in many countries, electronic memos, computer programs, and other original material floating around already have the same legal protection as literature and music compositions. Copyright protection doesn't require a judgment on the quality of a work or its purpose. It need only be original in some way. Much of the material on computer bulletin boards qualifies for copyright protection in the 95 countries that are signatories to the Bern Convention for the Protection of Literary and Artistic Works, including the United States, Japan, and the nations of Western Europe.

Discrimination on the basis of race, color, creed, age, gender, disabilities, and so on, is illegal in the United States, Canada, and several European nations. Even though a firm may use a coding system to describe demographics, as long as they do not use these data to discriminate against people, they are not committing illegal acts. In some cases, there may be a fine line between discriminating on the basis of, say, absenteeism and poor productivity by an employee and whether that employee is a member of a protected group. To avoid losing legal cases, if and when sued, organizations need to keep careful records and safeguard the statistical and analytical interpretation of these records. In particular, written records are essential to document absenteeism, incompetence, and/or consistently poor performance.

Because of the potential misuse of computer records, people may worry about the privacy of their personal records, and organizations may worry about the security and confidentiality of the records kept. With proper safeguards, effective measures of internal control, and honest, trustworthy records personnel, the misuse of computer records or confidential information can be greatly reduced.

Privacy and the Law

Laws associated with human and civil rights are designed in part to protect the privacy of individuals and businesses. About five times a day somebody somewhere is entering private information about most average consumers into some database.

Employers may have life-or-death control over employees because of the data they keep on file. A Texas clerical worker claims to be the victim of a psychological test demanded of her by her employer. The results were interpreted by a psychologist, who now knows "all sorts of private things about me!" Supposedly, such tests are said to be used to effectively match person and job; instead, some untrustworthy individuals may use the data to control and manipulate others.

Government databases contain plenty of private data. Private information includes how much one earns, the amount of income tax owed or paid, the number and names of a person's dependents, how one voted in recent national elections, whether one has any driving violations, whether one has traveled in a foreign country, as well as whether one has a criminal record or a recorded medical history.

Several companies and individuals have developed encryption devices and software programs that scramble whatever is going over telephone lines, but the FBI and other law enforcement agencies, arguing that such tools will hamper their ability to track criminal activities, have lobbied against them. "We didn't want to create a safe haven through the use of technology, whereby dangerous criminals and terrorists can utilize the communication networks," explained an FBI spokesman. "It's a double-edged sword."

Managing the Security and Confidentiality of Records

Secret information must not be shared verbally, such as through indiscriminate gossip with unauthorized people. The confidentiality of records must also be protected. Papers on the desk should be covered and documents saved on the screen whenever unauthorized people seem able to read what is being worked on. Confidential manual files should be kept in cabinets that can be locked, and the location of the keys should be kept safe. Passwords should be used for secret computer documents, and the passwords regularly changed. Places where passwords are recorded must be kept secure.

Computer crimes are as prolific as any other kind of white-collar crimes that periodically occur at work. Frustrated, angry people vandalize records, input disks with viruses into systems to destroy vital records, and falsify records to damage a firm or to benefit themselves. People who can get access to confidential records and who are aware of demographic codes might change the digits that prove detrimental to themselves. Criminals establish bogus accounts to direct funds from the firm to themselves via intermediary accounts. People work in collusion to defraud and steal from their employers, former employers, and other unsuspecting sources. They steal and sell vital information to business competitors and to foreign countries who would do the company or country harm.

The "Cave to Satellite" reading in Section III shows examples of how members of the Super Underworld use telecommunications. They also get access to records for nefarious purposes.

According to sources who have access to U.S. Customs records, weaknesses in Customs' cargo tracking (records) system may have opened a door for smugglers of drugs and other contraband. This problem could cost taxpayers millions of tariff dollars. Among the problems: false inspectors' names showing up on cargo entry records, passing containers without inspection, and seals placed on containers bound for distant destinations that are breached in transit. These fraudulent activities allow contraband to be removed or contents stolen between the docks and inspection points.

This laxness in records management is alarming because more than 90 percent of the cargo that enters Los Angeles harbor is shipped from Asia, which is also a primary source of heroin for the United States. The Los Angeles/Long Beach harbor complex is the nation's busiest. Because Mexico has no major seaports on its Pacific Coast, many containers bound for Mexico come through Los Angeles and are transported overland.

Customs depends on a computer network that links its intelligence files with manifests for incoming cargo to help inspectors identify suspicious shipments. False information in either half of the system undermines its integrity. For example, through fraudulent means a computerized record system designed to halt contraband at the border was converted into a tool for smugglers.

HUMAN AND PUBLIC RELATIONS IN MANAGING RECORDS

Internal (LAN) bulletin boards can be a useful management tool. Texas Instruments, Inc., in Dallas maintains a bulletin board on which employees can anonymously air complaints. To minimize gossiping or slander, some firms penalize employees for transmitting misleading information. Routed through a company ethics office, employee suggestions and complaints include everything from tips on possible security breaches at the company's defense operations to allegations of harassment and drug abuse.

A valid question arises in relation to networking, whether it concerns the receiving or giving of information or just talking. If an anonymous concern about an employee or manager turns out to be false and injurious to that person's reputation, how can the anonymous person be held accountable? Much information is exchanged on internal bulletin boards and on employee e-mail, but unfortunately not all of it is true.

People have many needs and sensitivities. The ability to apply good communication principles and human relations concepts (see also Section II) to the management of records is of keen importance in getting along with co-workers. People work together or exchange work tasks in establishing, maintaining, guarding, transmitting, transferring, and destroying records. It is necessary to be careful, yet to try to avoid offending others in the process. Employees need to know whom to trust and to report those about whom they have concrete evidence of wrongdoing.

It is vital to identify who, among outsiders, are privy to which databases and documents and who are not. Courtesy and sensitivity should be used when rejecting the requests of the unauthorized.

VIRTUAL REALITY

Imagine all the world's data since the dawn of time at your fingertips: most every known book and article ever published; every known movie ever filmed; every famous person living or dead with whom to communicate. "Anytime, anywhere" information is the concept, the foundation from which the idea of virtual reality grew.

Put on a helmet and other gear and walk into this wonderworld tool designed to revolutionize the way we live, work, inform and entertain ourselves. Besides data, graphics, visuals, voice, and other sound effects, add sensations to stir all our senses in three dimension. Doing a report on Benjamin Franklin's discovery of electricity? Ask Ben to sit down with you and tell you in his own words. Want to know what it felt like to do a solo flight across the ocean,

Photo 14.1. The Light Fantastic

Hair-thin fibers of ultrapure glass are now transmitting voice, data, and video communications in many parts of the globe in the form of digital signals emitted by semiconductors or lasers the size of a teaspoon. Courtesy of AT&T Archives.

research Charles Lindbergh or Amelia Earhart (who flew long before the invention of the GPS). Or one could ask their biographers.

Think of *one device*. Forget separate devices, such as TVs, computers, phone, VCR, modem, and fax. The future promises great advances in both electronic communications and virtual reality technology.

CAREERS AND COMPETENCIES

Performers, artists, writers, photographers, printers, graphic technicians, researchers, statisticians, poll takers and other data gatherers, librarians, records managers, consultants, and entrepreneurs are all needed to make virtual reality an accepted reality and to make interactive TV accurate and affordable. Telecommunication, telemarketing and computer operators, file and data entry clerks, secretaries and receptionists, switchboard operators and electronic maintenance personnel will also be needed. In preparation for the technological realities, a lot of new careers will be created. While advances in technology make some careers obsolete, many other career fields and opportunities will be forthcoming

The merging of separate discipline knowledge bases, skills and talents will be needed. People with the ability to think differently, to pursue and attain technological dreams and decide how to turn them into reality, and who are challenged by creative problems will be needed. Refer to the following examples of new career opportunities resulting from innovations in modern technology.

Photo 14.2. Still-Image Phone

AT&T's Picasso Still-Image Phone allows people to simultaneously send full-color, high-quality images and talk over a single, ordinary telephone line. Images and graphics are part of the total record system when stored, labeled for retrieval, and listed on a print or electronic directory. When transmitted from one station to another, across town, or around the world, however, such transmissions become part of the overall telecommunication system. Courtesy of AT&T Archives.

- In San Francisco, the Information Store provides information gathering and research services for the business community, with particular emphasis in the areas of competitive intelligence and special interest monitoring and publishing. A worldwide network of information sources supplement the in-house staff of professional specialists in the areas of document retrieval, custom research, and planning.
- In Denver, Information and Communication Specialists, Inc., offers indexing and abstracting information on all subjects, such as, database and thesaurus construction for any field or discipline; bibliographic compilation for any topic; technical and creative speech writing, editing, and photojournalism.
- In Fort Lauderdale, Inquiry, Inc., offers on-line information retrieval primarily for corporate planners, management consultants, marketing executives, and advertising and public relations people.
- In Portage la Prairie, Manitoba, Canada, Betty L. Thauberger provides consultative services in technical information management, including information acquisition, cataloging, and storage and retrieval.

People who cannot or do not want to learn how to access information for themselves frequently pay others to obtain it for them. Because of this, many others have found employment and entrepreneurial career opportunities.

The Unraveling of Yesterday's Dreams

People who grew up in the 1940s and 1950s were constantly treated to the marvels of technology. At school, they got vaccinated against polio, a former deadly disease. Television, dishwashers and other automatic washers, highly advanced defense weaponry, aircraft, ships, nuclear-powered submarines, and missiles arrived on the scene. People worried that factory automation and the huge mainframe computers in government and business would replace the need for their jobs. Simultaneously, they expected to do better than their parents: get more education and better job training; get jobs with more status, satisfaction, and higher salaries; buy more and get more. Those dreams oftentimes unraveled.

Trends for the Twenty-First Century

Many factors in modern society (such as crime, teenage pregnancy, drug use, gangs, violence, standardized test scores, etc.), except technology seemed to be getting worse. Firms have been laying off employees and cutting back on wages. Crowded, polluted, crime-ridden cities have become undesirable places in which to live. Divorce, which is at an all-time high, is reaching epidemic levels. The number of single parent families is increasing, and the absentee father syndrome is prevalent. Television has become the surrogate parent in many homes in modern society. Many families are being called dysfunctional–few remained intact. Findings from a major report focusing on people aged 18 to 30 suggested that "people who have not graduated from a four-year college have discovered that they are in real financial trouble."

By the onset of the twenty-first century, conditions may change again. Information based jobs are increasing so rapidly that *qualified* people are hard to find. In the medical industry alone, there are so many geriatric nurses, therapists (physical and occupational), and technicians needed to provide quality medical service and serve patient's needs, and to process insurance forms and keep medical records that many metropolitan newspapers' classified help-wanted sections devote a full page or more of their Sunday editions to listing vacancies in health care (including office and information-type support areas). Due to an increasing population of senior citizens, longer life spans, greater demand for quality health care, changing demographics, and an increase in health maintenance organizations (HMOs) and managed health care systems, the future demand for health care workers appears to be quite promising.

Competencies Needed

The people who are going to get jobs and succeed at them include the following:

- People with knowledge of and correct skills in using the language, in transmitting messages and interpreting messages.
- People with technical, mathematical and scientific knowledge who can make applications to practical, theoretical, and futuristic innovations.

- People who understand the interdependency of technology, the fine arts, geography, history, economics, and global awareness.
- People who know how to get along with and cooperate with others, who can demonstrate effective human and public relations at work, at home, and in their civic organizations.
- People who can readily see how psychology, sociology, fine arts, economics, and human needs undergird marketing.
- People who can search and research, write and summarize, as well as store and retrieve information.

Information science and records management studies provide excellent opportunities to develop the type of competencies listed above. Developing long-term memory so what one learns today can be applied later, when needed, is a great way to become competent, no matter what the field and no matter what the skills. Also, being able to synthesize and integrate information acquired from a variety of fields will be a vital foundation in many new information-age career fields.

As technology advances, some critics say that the "info-rich" get richer and the "info-poor" get poorer. Becoming aware of news and the world through broadcast and print matter is one way to keep people up to date. People can no longer get a single degree, enroll in a single class, or attend a single inservice or company training session as a means of keeping current with technology. People change careers (not just jobs within fields but entire disciplines) on average about eight to ten times during the 40 to 50 years of work life. People can no longer plan their whole life or career without considering the impact that technology will have on them. Planning for change and learning to adapt can help.

What Do You Think?
Review and Opinions

1. How is the topic of records management related to the topics of telecommunications and telemarketing? Discuss the importance of record systems and give examples. Are manual records still kept, and if so, why?

2. Describe the major filing systems and their subsystems and give examples of each including why, how, and where these are used. List some basic rules and tell why they are important.

3. Discuss some legal issues related to records management and confidentiality and give examples of how you can protect your organization from fraud, crime, and other unethical practices. In what ways have record systems changed during your lifetime, or during your tenure at your place of business?

4. Records management supports the needs of business and also of individuals. Discuss some of the needs involved and share examples of devices, systems, and procedures, including changes that are occurring and the possible impact on careers and telecommunication competencies.

5. Discuss the advantages and disadvantages of the paperless office. What changes do you foresee the future will bring in the area of records management?

From Cave to Satellite

Some measurable changes that have occurred during the past 100 years include:

- The speed and frequency of energy usage has increased a thousandfold.
- Data collection and information storage has increased by 10,000-fold.
- The rate, frequency, and number of communication messages sent by print or electronic media has increased by 100,000-fold.
- The power of massive military weaponry (conventional, chemical, and nuclear) has increased by a millionfold.

If it is hard to imagine how so many things got invented, start with the needle, a simple device. The idea came from nature, as so many things do. Early Native Americans discovered that the yucca plant (a cactus and the New Mexico state flower) has a point and could be threaded; hence, sewing and fancy stitching (as art) began. Today, sewing machines are both highly sophisticated and computerized.

Thomas Edison's original phonograph is housed in the Science Museum in London. These early clockwork phonographs, which used a needle running in the grooves of a cylinder, were the forerunners of the record player. One version of the phonograph was modeled after the wringer washing machine and it was the wringer idea that was used in facsimile machines. With the fax, data are converted into an electronic signal for transmission by cable or radio waves.

By the 1960s, it was discovered that fiber-optic cables could be used to carry telecommunication signals in much greater quantities and for longer distances than copper wires. In fiber-optic systems, information is transmitted by means of coded laser beams. Fiber optics is a branch of engineering concerned with the transmission of light along flexible glass fibers. The basic element in fiber optics is a glass thread less than a millimeter thick, along which light travels by bouncing from side to side, however curved the fiber. Its first use as a transmitter device came in 1955 and is used today in medicine to see inside the body—light is transmitted through the fibers and they return a clear image.

Computers use the binary mathematical system. Computers were invented in the late 1800s, but during World War II they were perfected for military use and later for business, consumer, and educational applications.

With the Global Positioning System (GPS), guidance and tracking measurements are highly accurate even from thousands of miles away. The GPS was perfected during the Gulf War for the purpose of military tracking and engagement. It's use helped bring victory to the United Nations' allies and the United States. Perhaps, if, and when, every country gets the GPS, this device, like atomic and nuclear bombs, will defuse its potential as a means of weaponry. As long as greed, lust, pride, and evil remain in the basic nature of human beings, it seems likely that wars and violence will continue.

Meanwhile, the DEA (Drug Enforcement Agency), the CIA (Central Intelligence Agency, sometimes called "the Company"), the U.S. military, and the FBI (Federal Bureau of Investigation) are working to safeguard the lives and liberty of everyday citizens. "Undercover" sting operations are to the FBI and the DEA what espionage is to the CIA and the military. Hundreds of large and small devices have been designed to conduct undercover and counterespionage activities. Secret agents today use high technology devices that appeared fictional years ago when introduced in James Bond films or on television shows such as *Get Smart*, which features agents talking into a miniaturized cellular phone hidden in the heel of a man's shoe.

Other technological innovations include the following items:

- A camera smaller than a pencil eraser can be mounted at a 30-degree angle on the end of a pencil. An operative can stick the end through a crack and twist it to capture on film everything in the pencil's multidirectional system.

- A tiny camera can be hidden in a TV set. When the screen is looked at, the camera, unbeknownst to the subject, films him. Cable TV can be monitored so that a residence can be bugged even when the TV is shut off.
- A "bug" is a tiny microphone that can be hidden almost anywhere: stuck under a desk or a table, in a plant or fireplace, behind a picture, attached to the underside of a vehicle, in a lampshade or a book, etc. Some bugs are external and need to be planted. Others are internal and can be transmitted via computer modems and cable TV lines.
- A bug can be mounted inside a telephone. It not only picks up phone conversations and the identification of the digits dialed but can also record anyone speaking in the room, even though the phone remains on the hook.
- A ham radio operator listened in on telephone calls placed on British Princess Diana's private phone. Transferred onto audiotape (later referred to as "The Squidgy Tapes" by the media because Diana had been nicknamed "Squidgy" by her male admirer), these conversations were rebroadcast using cellular phones so that the so-called "evidence" could be verified by the several people on the line. The doctored tapes were then sold to a tabloid; when published, the sample included conversations not contained in the original recordings. Voice analysis identified Princess Di's voice but other voices had been inserted.
- Photography from space satellites is so detailed that people can barely hide from one another, no matter where they are on earth. Terrorists and small military factions may try to camouflage their vehicles and huts by digging into the earth, but enlargement photos showing the tiniest details can differentiate male from female, young from old.

Artist and ornithologist John James Audubon shot and killed his models and mounted the birds so he could paint every minute detail on canvas. After Audubon died in 1851, his widow sold the New York Historical Society hundreds of his now-famous paintings for less than $4,000, or no more than $10 each. The supply and demand concept is again in evidence; Audubon can paint no more, thus his paintings are very valuable. The nature group, The Audubon Society, is named after a man who purposely went out to shoot birds.

Now, environmentalists would stop the cutting of trees when there are more trees now than there were over 200 years ago, despite all the houses, furniture, and other uses people have made of wood. They would stop the ranchers from using untamed forests and government-owned grazing land on which to raise the cattle that feed people and provide them with leather and other by-products, despite the fact that studies show that animal grazing helps to churn up the land just enough to keep it fertile for growing grasses, instead of hardening, cracking, and growing nothing.

"Info-rich" versus "info-poor" kids further exemplify that old adage: "Those that have, get; those that don't, lose." Kids growing up in households with computers, on-line capabilities for data searches, interactive TV, and books (and paintings, music, crayons and paper) are likely to learn more, and faster than kids who do not. Affluent school districts get more communication devices than poorer districts do. With grants and special attention, there are ways around this educational dilemma.

In the Issaquah, Washington, school district, parent Mike Bookey walked into his son's classroom and looked around, appalled. There were very few computers, telephones, and interactive on-line learning systems. From this one individual's initial efforts grew what became referred to as "The Miracle at Issaquah." Companies such as Microsoft, Apple, and U.S. West led the way in corporate contributions that turned into a multimillion dollar communication learning system.

Students can still go to the library, search the print stacks manually, and then handwrite their reports, but they don't have to. Instead, they can access the Internet and from there, get into databases around the world. One youngster, assigned to report on a World War II topic, identified a journal of daily war entries from an Australian database and fortified the topic with opinions from a database out of Tokyo (which, obviously, contradicted some impressions from American information sources), to produce a short but startling report that also earned an A+.

School, college, and university classrooms are now being equipped with television sets and videocassette recorders, and in some cases, the

VCR is built into the TV. With interactive TV, should people discard computers with modems, telecommunication software to access on-line databases, closed-circuit TV with VCR, record players and cassettes, and install the new system to take care of everything? If so, won't there be access costs, long-distance charges, and so on?

Some educators and equipment vendors suggest that textbooks and other print matter are obsolete. Can't children and adult learners direct their own learning through accessing databases and interactive TV and by creating their own teaching/learning projects using multimedia? Yes, they can do all of these things.

The print media, however, has not lagged behind the information revolution. In an early Cave to Satellite section, an example showed how newspapers like *The New York Times*, *USA Today*, and *The Wall Street Journal* can distribute papers all over the world at the same times, approximately, that they appear on the East Coast. On-line distribution uses a variety of technologies to send the paper from one spot to another instantaneously.

Textbooks also use modern technologies. Authors write at computers, using standardized software. They print hard copies for copy editors to use in checking grammar, punctuation, and so on. The art and graphics staff determine page layout and select and mock-up photocopies. Meanwhile, the author is still researching and rewriting. With the final draft, off go the disks by overnight U.S. federal mail or some private carrier such as FedEx.

A publishing house's hard copy is sometimes subcontracted (like a contractor does with electricians and plumbers) to a printing firm. There, a photocompositor formerly retyped every last word; that took weeks. No longer; now those last-minute disks that the author submits overnight go to the print subcontractor, where matter off the disks are input to computer, to printer, to editors for last-minute review, to bookbinders, and, finally to market.

Print matter, including textbooks as well as magazines, could be outdated but only if old issues are still lying about. By comparison, students who prepare report projects on multimedia (or leave their reports on-line or print them on hard copy), get their information from somewhere. How old are the encyclopedias they read? How current and how accurate are the data retrieved from on-line databases or from interactive TV sources?

To be as accurate as possible, one should check as many sources as possible, including on-line, broadcast, print media and human resources. Quoting something one's brother-in-law's secretary's maid's great aunt said is not exactly the best source, either. One must verify, verify, and get second, third, and tenth opinions. Interactive TV and on-line data bases are not the only places to get data. Most textbooks and a lot of other print matter are carefully researched.

Today's world cities are just that, world cities. People from all over the world travel to, visit, and live in cities around the globe. With trade barriers between nations coming down and telecommunication systems going up, the Earth has become one giant global village. People chatter in a thousand languages and dialects, yet English is growing in usage.

Not only is English used in business and world trade, but it is also becoming more common, apparently due to the media, TV especially. This is spreading American and Western European cultures abroad. Without a common language, people use nonverbal language. They point and gesture, smile or frown, motion to the foreign coins they clutch and point to products to ask their price.

The two biggest problems in the world today that will follow into the twenty-first century are the population explosion and the depletion of natural resources. The more people there are, the more crowded and polluted the conditions, the more demanding are people. This leads to more crime and violence as people fight for their own small share. The future depends on understanding human needs and reaching common sense balances: a balance between protecting people and protecting the environment and irreplaceable natural resources; a balance between technology and culture, between science and the arts, and between getting and giving.

Activities for Section V

ACTIVITY V-1: COLLECT AND SHARE NEWS OF INTERDEPENDENT SYSTEMS

Directions

1. Independently or in teams, continue to collect and annotate news clippings (or photocopies of articles) and record notes from TV viewing and personal contacts. Topics include telecommunications, telemarketing, and records systems in a global economy. When the topic is not apparent, imagine what might be happening. For example, news about telemarketing deals with either or both outbound and inbound calls. Also record what you imagine that the operator is doing simultaneously and in relation to records.

Number of articles from print sources:_____

Titles:_____

_____

_____

_____

_____

_____

_____

_____

_____

_____

Number of news items from database collections or the Internet:_____

Titles:_____

_____

_____

_____

_____

_____

_____

_____

_____

_____

Number of news items from TV:_____

Titles:_____

_____

_____

_____

_____

_____

_____

_____

_____

_____

_____

Number of items from human network/personal interviews:_____
Subjects/topics:_____

_____
_____
_____
_____
_____
_____
_____
_____
_____

2. Independently read and review topics in this section. Compare the end-of-section questions in Section V with those in the first four sections. Be ready to contribute opinions on all these issues with group members.

3. Convene with your group. Maintain the same leadership personnel of leader, recorder, and memo processor unless the instructor informs your otherwise. The recorder takes notes from group discussion and the processor composes a memo to report to the instructor the total number of news items collected and the completion of objective number one.

4. The leader facilitates discussion to ensure that all members of the group contribute informed opinions. See for example the end-of-section questions from Sections I through V. The purpose of this session is to reach closure on objective number one; namely: "Discuss major section topics and draw comparisons with issues presented previously to identify how these topics are related."

5. The leader proofreads the memo and makes recommendations, if any, for revisions. Memo copies are distributed to team members. If you are on a LAN, each member can download and print his or her own copy. Hold the original to submit to the instructor later. Make sure that every group member has a copy before submitting the original copy to the course instructor.

ACTIVITY V-2: UPDATE DATABASES

Background

You work for a firm that gathers data and develops databases, conducts research, and advises clients on collecting data by various electronic means. The databases that you prepare often need to be updated. People regularly make changes in their lives that require making changes in database records. These changes deal with anything from marital status, address, and telephone number, to account balances, voting status, and so on.

Directions

1. Access and preview samples of databases. Some databases use "Database 1–Customers," "Database 2–Employees," and "Database 3–Citizens." Changes will be made first to DTB1 (customers). The next database, for another firm, deals with updating employee records on DTB2. The last database is for a political party, DTB3 (citizens). Other databases may use different symbols.

2. You may work independently or you may decide to work with one or more other people. If you are working on a LAN, three of you may divide the work, each responsible for one of the three databases. After making the necessary changes, rename each database as follows: DTB1, alphabetically by last name of customer; DTB2, by employee account number, using the tertiary numeric method; and DTB3, geographically, by citizen address. (If you do not have access to a computer, ask your instructor for print copies of sample databases. Type 3″ × 5″ cards that reflect the changes. Sort them manually.)

3. Download the work of your partners, proofread, and print. Make revisions, if any are needed, to ensure accuracy. Hold printouts (or the deck of cards) until the end of the section.

ACTIVITY V-3: PARTICIPATE IN CASE DISCUSSIONS

Directions

1. Read the cases that follow and record your own ideas before discussing the case with others.

2. Keep the same leadership personnel unless told otherwise by your instructor or group leader. The leader facilitates discussion, the recorder takes notes, and the processor composes a memo from the recorder's notes. The leader proofreads the memo and makes recommendations, if any, for revision.

3. Copies of the memo are distributed to group members or, if on a LAN, the memo may be downloaded and printed at each station. Keep the original copy to submit to the instructor later. Members are directed to bring this memo copy to the next group meeting.

Case Study 1: Records Crunch and the Stock Market Crash

The stock market, as an exchange place, is where floor traders buy and sell shares of stock. On Monday and Tuesday, October 19 and 20, 1987, over 600 million shares were traded. This is a lot of information to record and track, even with computers. The following news account recalls the feel and flavor of what happened on these two days, perhaps the most eventful days in the history of the New York Stock Exchange (NYSE):

New York, October 20, 1987. At 2:53 p.m., a senior Stock Exchange trader fields a call. A buyer wants 613,000 shares of General Electric stock. The trader shouts to the dozen men and women in the packed room. "Somebody find a seller, and fast!" Several other traders spring into action, punching at the white buttons from their 140-button phone consoles. (The red buttons connect them with floor traders at the NYSE. Green buttons go to the floors of the American or Midwest Stock Exchanges.) In less than a minute, a bearded trader has a seller with 100,000 shares. At 2:55 p.m., another trader hits pay dirt–someone with 513,000 shares to sell. By 3 p.m., seven minutes later, the whole transaction is completed.

On those two days, the NYSE hit a record 600 million shares sold and bought. Worse was the 508-point drop in the Dow Jones averages (averages of stocks traded in industrials, utilities, and transportation stocks—see the SICs, Section III). This record-breaking drop in the price of shares resulted in a *$1 trillion* total loss in stock values for shareholders around the world. Before October 19 was half over, the effect of the plummeting U.S. market was felt on the Tokyo and Hong Kong markets and elsewhere around the globe. The Hong Kong market closed down for a week. In London, all computers went down and nobody could get through to either buy or sell.

Financial and information specialists wondered whether computerized trading was partly to blame for the crash of 1987. *Computerized trading*, using computers and telecommunications, means that buy-and-sell orders are preentered into the computer. If the price of a stock is currently going for $30 and you want to buy 10,000 shares at $25, you give your stockbroker the order. The computer is programmed to automatically buy your 10,000 shares when the price drops to $25. But suppose 999,999 other people submit similar orders to either buy or sell shares of stock. With all those computers automatically clinking on, that's a lot of information moving back and forth. After each buy or sell is completed, somebody has to *prepare individual account records* and distribute them all over the world.

What were employees doing all this time? Nearly half of the 2,000 NYSE employees worked on the weekend of October 24 and 25, following 15-hour days all week. Thousands of other employees reported for weekend work at brokerages around the country. Clerks and brokers from coast to coast worked overtime, processing information and records to determine who bought what, how much, and from whom.

Like the great Stock Market Crash of 1929, hundreds of thousands of everyday people lost money, some lost an entire lifetime of savings. Too many calls were being sent all over the country and world for telephone operators to keep track of everything; too many computer transactions were input and computers broke down. People experienced incredible anxiety, and some became depressed, suicidal, or violent. In Florida, one man broke into his stockbroker's office and shot him dead.

1. If you were a clerk or stockbroker with all that information to process and records to manage, how would you feel about working 15-hour days under stress? Suppose you made a mistake in entering data at the computer that caused somebody to lose a lot of money. How would you feel?

_____

_____

_____

_____

_____

2. How does the news story illustrate the importance of risk in our information economy, whether risk to business owners or risk to consumers and stockholders?

_____

_____

_____

_____

_____

3. In what ways does the news account show that we are living in a world in which what happens to one nation's economy affects the economies of other nations?

_____

_____

_____

_____

_____

4. How could the problems of computers crashing, telephone and fax messages getting lost, and records getting mismanaged have been avoided? In fact, computer trading has changed since the Stock Market Crash of 1987. What changes do you suppose were made?

Case Study 2: The Paperless Warehouse

Waiting for a paperless society is like waiting for the world to end—it hasn't happened yet. But the paperless warehouse is something else—it's here now. The impact of the desktop computer revolution primarily affected corporate managers responsible for front-room operations, such as financing and marketing. Using corporate networks and e-mail systems, deskbound white-collar workers can generate, record, analyze, and manage information.

Another frontier for productivity gains is in the back room, where shipping, receiving, and inventory functions are handled by on-the-move workers and floor managers who don't sit at desks with computers. Instead, they use portable computers, connected by wireless networks for real-time data communications. As many retailers, manufacturers, distributors, and transporters (see the SICs in Section III) are discovering, superior logistics management is an important way to improve overall productivity.

The cornerstone of this new warehouse is the bar code, which first appeared on selected supermarket items in the 1970s. Bar codes, now standard on product packaging and most shipping containers, have proved to be virtually 100 percent reliable as carriers of information. They provide a key solution to the problem of getting data into host computers on an accurate and timely basis, where it's put to use driving the applications that allow managers to effectively control their logistics operations.

Another strategic technology driving the paperless warehouse is the Spectrum One network, a wireless data network developed by Symbol Technologies, Inc., which a decade ago, invented handheld laser bar-code scanners. Warehouse workers, who once wandered vast aisles with carbon-smeared clipboards, now execute tasks with hand-held laser scanning terminals that use the Spectrum One network to feed and exchange data with any type of desktop or mainframe computer.

The results of these on-the-move data transactions are streamlined inventory control, reduced trucking time, fewer lost shipments, and improved replenishment. For example, The Hudson Bay Company (North America's oldest company, founded in Canada in 1670) relies on distribution centers that use the wireless technology to receive and expedite a continuous flow of bar-coded merchandise from its numerous suppliers to 375 stores throughout Canada.

Workers use Symbol LRT 3800s to scan thousands of incoming items every day to verify that vendor bar codes are on the host computer item file before items are shipped to stores. Shipment turnaround has been cut to one day, with nearly perfect accuracy, remarkable record that paper-based logistics managers cannot dream of equaling.

These recent advances in scanner and computer technology bring data systems into entirely new corporate environments–with opportunities for increased productivity higher than with desktop computers alone. Because hand-held scanners can be customized and dedicated to specific tasks, mobile workers require little training. Also, data entry is simplified by the consistency of bar codes, which ensures speed and accuracy.

1. You have no doubt been aware of the bar codes on consumer items as well as how they are scanned at the cash register. But has it ever occurred to you how that data is entered? Who does it? Who makes the decisions? Call or visit a supermarket or other large retail store and ask to interview the manager to find out. Check with other group members as well. Somebody may have had retail experience, working with scanned information and records.

_____

_____

_____

_____

_____

2. The case discusses the paperless and wireless warehouse but suggests that the paperless office is unlikely to happen (in the near future). Do you agree or disagree and why or why not? Think of records and the management of records as well as information and the processing of records.

_____

_____

_____

_____

_____

ACTIVITY V-4: MANAGING HUMAN RELATIONS AND RECORDS MANAGEMENT

Directions

1. Convene with your group. Review Case Study 1 from Activity III-3 and write a script to portray what might have happened in one stockbroker's office. The characters should include at least two people in the office and one or more call-in stockholders. The purpose of this scenario is to demonstrate the simultaneous effective management of records, human and public relations.

2. Use the spaces provided to plan the script.

_____

_____

_____

_____

_____

_____

_____

_____

_____

_____

_____

_____

_____

3. The processor composes the script from the notes and from annotated changes made as a result of the group conference.

4. Script copies are downloaded and printed or photocopied.

5. Each group presents their script to the others. When viewing scenarios, use the checklist form that follows to evaluate performances. Your evaluation forms are to be submitted to the instructor confidentially.

EVALUATION CHECKLIST

Name of Group Performing:_____

Date of Performance:_____

Directions: use the +, ✔, – evaluation method, where + = outstanding, ✔ = average/satisfactory, and – = poor/unsatisfactory. Use one form for each scenario (confidentially) and submit to instructor.

1. The characters acted realistically, as based
   on the case study   _____

2. The brokerage staff demonstrated effective
   human relations when interacting with each other   _____

Describe words and actions that demonstrate this competency:

3. The brokerage staff demonstrated effective public
   relations when interacting with stockholder callers   _____

Describe words and actions that demonstrate this competency:

OTHER COMMENTS:

Signature of Evaluator (confidential):_____

ACTIVITY V-5: PRESENT THE GLOBAL TELECOMMUNICATIONS PROJECT

Directions

1. Convene with your group to make final preparations. Arrange with the instructor the date to present your group's term project to the full class. Schedule equipment as required. Plan to wear business dress.

2. Review the presentation suggestions in Section I.

3. Present the group project.

4. Use the spaces provided for planning and preparation:

_____

_____

_____

_____

_____

_____

_____

_____

_____

_____

_____

_____

_____

_____

_____

_____

_____

ACTIVITY V-6: REACH CONSENSUS ON LEARNING OUTCOMES

Directions

1. Convene with your group. The leader facilitates discussion to identify learning outcomes and to enable the group to reach consensus on how these compare with meeting the section objectives.

2. Use the spaces provided to record your own ideas before attending the group meeting.

LEARNING OUTCOMES   SECTION OBJECTIVES

_____

_____

_____

_____

_____

_____

_____

_____

3. The recorder takes notes and the processor composes a memo from these notes to report to the instructor consensus on learning outcomes in comparison with section objectives. The leader proofreads the memo and makes recommendations, if any, for revision.

4. Use the checklist that follows to evaluate your own acquisition of knowledge and competencies for the course. Submit these to the instructor (confidentially) as a cover for all section materials.

Bibliography for Section V

Alexander, Suzanne, "The Digital Classroom," *The Wall Street Journal*, November 15, 1993.

Bahree, Bhushan, "A Sense of Belonging: Growing network traffic and copyright issues," *The Wall Street Journal*, November 15, 1993.

Bookey, Mike, "Instructional Technology and Global Data Searches," presentation at Casper College, Wyoming, November 19, 1993.

Bovee, Tim, "FBI Stalks a Criminal on the Information Highway," *Laramie Boomerang*, December 31, 1993.

Briscoe, David, "Worldwide Assemblies Possible through New Computer Talk Station," *Laramie Boomerang*, January 5, 1994.

Brokaw, Tom, "Brokaw Report: The Lost Generation," NBC, July 28, 1993. (The need for technology training to get jobs.)

Caruso, Denise, "Ahead of Ourselves," *The Wall Street Journal*, November 15, 1993.

Chung, Connie, and Dan Rather, *CBS Evening News*, CBS, September 19, 1993. (The mind and memory as intellectual property.)

Church, Olive D., "Crushed by the Job Crash? Analyze, Energize," *Executive Development Journal*, Volume 8(3), 1995, pp. 28-32.

Church, Olive D., "Manual and Electronic Data Searches," *Modern Office Procedures for Administrative Support*. Englewood Cliffs, NJ: Prentice Hall, 1989. (Research consultant careers and entrepreneurships.)

Consumer protection agencies, "A Special News Documentary," CNN, July 21, 1993.

Daggett, William, presentation at Gillette, WY, Spring 1993.

Data: Business Week, Company Reports, *Business Week*, August 30, 1993. (Handwriting recognition software.)

Dorfman, John R., Clare Ansberry and Robert Johnson, "The Crash of '87: Coping on the Day After," *The Wall Street Journal*, October 21, 1987.

Dunkin, Amy, "Power in Your Palm," *Business Week*, March 15, 1993, pp. 128-129.

Dunkin, Amy, " 'Smart' Assistants?" *Business Week*, October 4, 1993, pp. 124-125.

Elstrom, Peter, "Did Motorola Make the Wrong Call?" *Business Week*, July 29, 1996, pp. 66-68.

Englebardt, Stanley L., "Get Ready for Virtual Reality," *Reader's Digest*, December 1993.

Gumbel, Bryant, *Today Show*, NBC, November 28 and December 20, 1993. (Repair of the Hubble satellite.)

_____, *Today Show*, NBC, interviewing Paul Carroll, author of *Big Blues: The Unmaking of IBM*, September 15, 1993. (IBM cut back on the number of employees from 475,000 to 225,000.)

Gunther, Marc, "The Man the Phone Companies Forgot," *Fortune*, May 27, 1996, Volume 133(10), pp. 106-112.

Hansen, Joseph D., "An Interview with the CEO of IAG Financial Services on the Global Positioning Service (GPS)," January 1997, Temple, Texas.

Hays, Laurie, "Personal Effects," *The Wall Street Journal*, November 15, 1993. (Amid all the talk about the wonders of computer networks, some nagging social questions arise.)

"How'd They Do That?" CBS, August 20, 1993. (Nielsen ratings, statistical random sample of people in the country.)

"Investigative Reports: Undercover," A&E Cable TV, September 3, 1993. (Cameras smaller than a pencil.)

Jennings, Peter, *ABC World News*, ABC, October 19, 1993. (One out of four employees in South Carolina has a foreign employer.)

Jennings, Peter, *ABC World News*, ABC, September 7, 1993. (Records and the White House.)

Kapama Game Reserve, near the town of Silverton in South Africa, summer, 1993. (Site of safari stop, with fax and phones installed.)

Kuralt, Charles, *CBS Sunday Morning*, CBS, October 24, 1993. (John James Audubon's art of birds.)

Lavoie, Denise, "IRS Battling the Computer–A Double-edged Sword for Tax Cheats," *Laramie Boomerang*, August 7, 1993.

Lert, Peter, "F-16 Simulation Program is more than 'Just a Game,'" *Air Combat*, September/October, 1993.

Lesley, Ron, Information Systems Manager of Technology Information Program at Issaquah High School, Issaquah, Washington, provided brochure from a telecommunications request, January 1994.

Lewyn, Mark, "Wireless, Wild, Wild North," *Business Week*, March 11, 1996, pp. 87-90.

"Network Earth," TBS, September 12, 1993. (Interlocking various electronic media.)

McNeil-Lehrer News Hour, PBS, August 17, 1993. (Records systems.)

"News from the World of Medicine: Health Help," *Reader's Digest*, September, 1993. (Records management.)

Nightly Business Report, PBS, December 2, 1993. (Movies on demand.)

Nightly Business Report, PBS, November 25, 1993. (About 30 percent of people, among those polled, expressed a favorable reaction to the super digital highway, interactive video, etc.)

Pope, Kyle, "To Whom it May Concern: Network Data Used in Industries," *The Wall Street Journal*, November 15, 1993.

Resnik, Rosalind, "Weapons for Work," *Home Office Computing*, June 1993.

Roten, Robert, "Plane Crash Victim Identified," *Laramie Boomerang*, July 10, 1993. (Emergency locator transmitter to tell where a vehicle is located; same device is available for cars.)

_____, "Carbon Power and Light to Offer Direct TV Locally," *The Laramie Daily Boomerang*, October 20, 1993.

Rukeyser, Louis, *Wall Street Week*, PBS, October 15, 1993. (Advice regarding stock purchases, such as mobile telecommunications, Intel, and cellular companies.)

Safer, Morley, *60 Minutes*, December 26, 1993. (Global Positioning System, GPS; by providing latitudinal and longitudinal coordinates, lets you know wherever you are on earth.)

Samuels, Gary, "Look Ma, No Wires," *Forbes*, Volume 157(6), March 25, 1996, pp. 43-44.

Samuelson, Robert J., "National Affairs: How Our American Dream Unraveled," *Newsweek*, March 2, 1992.

"Saturday is Overtime Day for the Stock Market," *The Laramie Daily Boomerang*, October 25, 1987.

Shears, Richard, "Drama in Real Life: Shark Attack!" *Reader's Digest*, December 1993.

Sisco, Burton, Associate Professor of Adult Education, University of Wyoming, Laramie, presentation on statistics related to census data records, January 6, 1994.

Slutsker, Gary, "The Company that Likes to Obsolete Itself," *Forbes*, September 13, 1993.

Souza, Spinelli Francesca, and Jay J.R. Zajas, "Recruiting Executives in Business: An Organizational and Conceptual Perspective," *Executive Development Journal*, Volume 8(3), 1995, pp. 23-27.

Stevens, Rick, *Travels in Europe*, PBS, August 16, 1993. (Hi-tech tourism.)

Therrien, Lois, "Information Processing–Telecommunications: It's a Mad, Mad, Mad, Mad Wireless World," *Business Week*, November 29, 1993.

_____. "Personal Business–Gadgets: Pagers start to deliver more than phone numbers," *Business Week*, November 15, 1993.

Vincent, Dale, U.S. West, interview to discuss telecommunication predictions, included imagining how data can be input and accessed using the "virtual reality" concept, January 1994.

Weiss, Gary, and Chris Welles, "Was Program Trading to Blame and Did the Specialists Do Their Job?" *Business Week*, November 2, 1987.

"Western Ranching: Culture in Crisis," PBS documentary, hosted by actor Lee Horseley, September 12, 1993.

White, Michael, "Falsified Documents, Purged Records Point to Open Door for Smuggling," *Laramie Boomerang*, December 31, 1993.

"The Wireless Warehouse," *Forbes*, August 1993. ("Bar codes prove 100% reliable as carriers of information.")

World News Briefs–Kourou, French Guiana, *Laramie Boomerang*, December 19, 1993. (Thailand placed in orbit their first telecommunications satellite–launched by a French department from South America–that's "cooperation around the globe!")

Zajas, Jay J.R., "Obstacles to Real Strategic Marketing in Health Care: An Experiential Framework," *Journal of Hospital Marketing*, Volume 8(2), 1994, pp. 18-31.

Zajas, Jay J.R., "Faced with a Major Life or Career Change? Give Yourself the Winner's Edge!" *Executive Development Journal*, Volume 8(3), 1995, pp. 4-8.

Zajas, Jay J.R., "Planning Your Total Career and Life Portfolio: A Group Process Experience for Developing Personal and Career Focus," *Librarian Career Development: An International Journal*, Volume 3(1), 1995, pp. 18-25.

Zajas, Jay J.R., "The Psychological and Social Factors of Career Success," *Executive Development Journal*, Volume 8(3), 1995, pp. 2-3.

Zajas, Jay J.R., "Creating a Vision of Excellence as CEO of a Quality Research University: An Interview with CEO Dr. John M. Lilley," *Career Development International*, Volume 2(1), 1997, pp. 59-63.

Zajas, Jay J.R., and Harold Cates, "The Outplacement and Marketing of Executives in a Challenging Workforce," *Executive Development Journal*, Volume 8(3), 1995, pp. 9-13.

Zajas, Jay J.R., and John M. Lilley, "A CEO's Perspective on Leadership, Values, Vision, and Change: Making the Paradigm Shift to Quality," *Career Development International*, Volume 2(2), 1997, pp. 54-58.

Zajas, Jay J.R., and Jann R. Michener Zajas, "Planning Your Total Career and Life Portfolio: A Model for Management Development," *Librarian Career Development: An International Journal*, Volume 2(3), 1994, pp. 7-10.

Glossary

ad hoc videoconference: A one-time or occasional use of video-conferencing facilities for a specific meeting or event, such as one-way video and two-way audio (business television), rather than on a regular basis. Also called special event video conferencing or tele-conferencing.

area code: A three-digit identification code number used to designate the Numbering Plan Area.

band: (1) A portion of the electromagnetic spectrum. (2) Range of frequencies between two defined limits. (3) In a WATS service, the specific geographical area that the subscriber is allowed to telephone.

baud: A degree which measures transmission speed, which is equal to the number of signal changes per second. When a signal change represents one BIT, the baud's rate is equivalent to bits per second (bps). When a signal change represents groups of more than one bit, baud and bps are not always identical.

binary: A numbering system that uses only the digits 1 and 0. Used internally by computers and digital electronic equipment.

bit: The smallest unit of information in a binary system, represented by either 1 ("on") or 0 ("off").

bridge: A device which can connect two LANS of the same topology. *Local bridges* link LANS within the same building, while *remote bridges* connect remote LANS into WANS.

broadband network: A network which divides its bandwidth into subchannels so that multiple applications including voice, data, and video can be sent simultaneously.

broadcast: A feature in a voice processing system that allows a subscriber to automatically send the same voice message to multiple mailboxes with one command.

buffer: A storage area added to a host computer and/or terminal to compensate for the differences in transmitting rates.

bus topology: Connects all nodes to one cable running the length of the network.

byte: A group of eight bits makes a byte, the smallest addressable unit of information in computer memory.

call forwarding: A custom calling service in which a call can be rerouted from one line to another by dialing a special code sequence.

call history: Record of all the *call information* and *call activity* for each account, from the time of the first call.

call information: General information about a call time, length of call, name of person called–as opposed to specific content.

call purpose: The identified reason for making a call; the goal or objective to be accomplished by a call. Also known as a *telemarketing application.* Call purposes defined in this glossary are all marked *CP.*

call trace: A class calling service that allows the subscriber to initiate a trace of the number of the last call received.

call tracking form: Form used to record the number of calls made in a day, how many contacts were made, what products or services were sold, what appointments were made, and any other information needed for the particular telemarketing application.

call waiting: A custom calling service in which a subscriber engaged in a telephone conversation receives a beep indicating that another party is trying to reach the subscriber.

call-in inquiry: A call for information, literature, or to place an order.

cellular mobile telephone service: Provides common carrier switched mobile radio telephone service interconnecting with the public switched telephone network. The Federal Communications Commission's licensing plan includes two cellular carriers in each market or standard metropolitan statistical area (SMSA) area.

channel: A transmission path between two points. Usually the smallest subdivision of a circuit, such as a voice channel or a data channel.

circuit: A transmission path between two or more points. Also called a link or channel.

citizens band (CB) radio: A system of two-way radio communications for short distances available for public use. The 27 MHz band is most commonly used for CB in most countries.

coaxial cable: A type of guided medium made up of tubes, with each cable containing from 4 to 22 coaxial tubes.

cold call: A call made without a prior appointment.

commission: Percentage of the total amount of the sale. TSRs often receive commissions and *bonuses*, in addition to their regular salary or wage, to motivate performance.

common carrier: An organization that provides telecommunications facilities to the public. In the United States, common carriers are regulated by the Federal Communications Commission if interstate and by the state public service or public utilities commission in intrastate.

Communications Act of 1934: This act established the U.S. Federal Communications Commission (FCC) for regulating national and international communications.

Communications Satellite Corporation (COMSAT): A government-regulated private organization, the U.S. member of INTELSAT.

compressed digital video: To reduce the bandwidth required for transmission over a digital circuit, video conferencing signals in digital form are compressed to a fraction of their original state by eliminating redundant information, and are then transmitted.

computer-based message system (CBMS): A form of electronic mail that allows computers and/or terminals to communicate with each other for the purpose of sending and receiving text and data messages—short messages, memos, and other documents. Commonly referred to as electronic mail or *e-mail*. The two types are in-house CBMS and public electronic mail.

computer conferencing: A process which allows participants to exchange messages with each other by using computer keyboards. May be *synchronous,* that is, interactive in real time, or *asynchronous*, that is, messages are stored in a central computer until retrieved by their intended recipients.

conference telephone call: A telephone call involving three or more persons from different locations.

conventional mobile telephone service: Operates like the regular telephone service by interconnecting with the Public Switched Telephone Network. Uses a transmitter/receiver and an antenna to service an entire metropolitan area. Also called improved mobile telephone service (IMTS). The system is being replaced by cellular mobile telephone service.

cross-sell suggestion (*CP*): *Suggestion selling* option used when a prospect/customer initiates a call but does not purchase the call-in interest item. The TSR suggests an alternate item that is unrelated to the original item.

customer account management: The process of servicing and keeping a large, strong *customer base.* There are three types of customer account management: complete account management, major/marginal account management, and credit account management.

customer base: All the current customers a company has.

data: Facts and information in their raw state–collected information not yet analyzed. Also, statistical information presented in the form of numbers or letters.

database: A collection of stored information, any or all of which is available for retrieval by electronic means. Also, a collection of files containing specific information available to individual departments.

dedicated access line: A circuit assigned to a subscriber for the exclusive use between the subscriber's telephone equipment and the central office.

dedicated network server: A computer designed exclusively to serve a LAN.

delay dialing: An option which allows the facsimile unit to send documents at a later time when telephone rates are lowest or to overcome time zone problems.

direct broadcast satellite teletext: The transmission of teletext signals via satellite.

direct mail: Brochures, letters or other material mailed directly from the company to the prospect/customer.

direct method: Use of marketing tools and techniques to generate leads, to heighten the prospect/customer's acceptance level for outbound calls, and to encourage prospects/customers to make inbound calls. See information in "Defining Telemarketing" in Chapter 9. There are two uses of the direct method: *outbound* and *inbound.*

The **outbound direct method** employs a traditional marketing tool, such as a note of introduction in a letter or flyer, to inform the prospect/customer of a proposed call and its primary purpose.

The **inbound direct method** uses a traditional marketing tool, such as *direct mail* or *media advertising*, to encourage prospects/ customers to make a call to place an order for a product/service or to seek information.

distance learning: The electronic transmission of lessons over great distances.

downlink: The transmission of data from a satellite to a receiving antenna on earth using a separate frequency from that used for the uplink.

download: To retrieve an entire computer program or document from another computer.

800 number: Toll free number used often for inbound telemarketing calls.

electronic banking: The general concept of carrying out banking transactions electronically, without direct person-to-person communication.

electronic blackboard: Device on which images drawn or written are immediately translated into signals, transmitted through a telephone network, and displayed on video monitor(s) exactly as written.

electronic key telephone system (EKS): System that uses microprocessors and integrated circuit chips. Includes pushbuttons to electronically access call forwarding, call transfer, and speed calling.

electronic mail: The generic name for "the noninteractive communication of text, data, images, or voice messages between a sender and designated recipient(s) by systems utilizing telecommunication links." Includes all types of noninteractive communication, such as computer-based message systems, voice mail, and facsimile.

electronic mailbox: An on-line storage area in which electronic mail is stored.

Electronic Office Blackboard System (EOBS): An interface network where on-line users can send or receive messages from other users in the system on an internal or external basis.

ethics: Standards of behavior.

equal access: The 1986 Department of Justice ruling which requires that other common carriers besides AT&T be offered the same quality of connection at the same rates. Enables customers to choose the long-distance network for routing their calls.

facsimile (fax): The sending and/or receiving of an exact replica—a facsimile—of the original document from one location to another by using communication lines. The term "fax" can be used as a noun, adjective, or a verb.

fact finding: The process of determining the prospect/customer's needs, wishes, history, and current situation in order to know which product/service is appropriate and how it can best be presented. Step II of the sale.

fax copier: Equipment that functions as either a facsimile unit or a copier.

faxphone: A compact desktop unit that combines a facsimile unit and telephone into one unit.

Federal Communications Commission (FCC): A board of commissioners, appointed by the President of the United States under the Communications Act of 1934, that is charged with regulating interstate and foreign communications originating in the United States by wire and radio.

fiber-optic cable: Also called lightguide cable, a type of guided medium that replaces electricity with light and copper wires with hair-thin strands of glass.

foreign exchange (FX) service: Connects a subscriber's location to a remote central office, which provides the equivalent of local service from the long-distance exchange.

fund raising (*CP*): Outbound call in which TSRs or volunteers make calls to selected prospects and sell them on the idea of giving a donation. Can also be an inbound call encouraged by radio or television pleas.

human resources configuration: The way in which a company organizes its TSRs' activities, such as *inside only, one person; telemate system,* etc.

human resource management: Selecting the appropriate *human resources configuration* for the telemarketing strategy being used.

in-house telemarketing: Telemarketing done by a company itself, rather than by another company hired for that purpose. See *Telemarketing Service Bureau.*

inbound call: Call made by the prospect/customer to place an order, seek information, register a complaint, or conduct some other business. Also known as a *reactive call* because the company representative receiving the call reacts to the caller by taking appropriate action.

integrated voice processing system: A voice processing system integrated with a private branch exchange or a Central Exchange system by using a special communications link between the two systems to allow each to give commands to each other.

interface: A common boundary between two systems or pieces of equipment where they are joined (EOBS).

international number: The number to be dialed that follows the international prefix. Includes the country code and the national number of the party being called.

International Telecommunications Satellite Organization (INTELSAT): An international satellite organization that owns and operates commercial communication satellite systems that are used by countries worldwide for international and domestic communications.

in-WATS: A system which allows calls to be placed to a location from anywhere in the continental United States at no cost to the calling party. Also referred to as an 800-number service. See also *WATS* and *out-WATS*.

key telephone system (KTS): An arrangement of key telephone sets and associated circuitry, located on a subscriber's premises, with the capability of performing other desired functions, such as call hold and call pickup, and interconnecting with on-premise stations without connecting through the central office or a private branch exchange.

land mobile communication service: Radio communication service to and from mobile stations. Includes paging systems, two-way radios, cellular telephone services, and citizens band radio.

local-area network (LAN): A privately-owned network that offers reliable high-speed communication channels for connecting information processing equipment, such as microcomputers, in a limited geographical area. A company's internal bulletin boards are an example of a local area network (LAN).

market research: Making calls for information, rather than providing a service or making sales.

market survey: Project in which many people are called and asked their opinion on a particular product or service to determine a potential market.

marketing: The effort to create a favorable atmosphere for the sale of a product or service. Compare *selling*.

media advertising: Advertising in radio, television, newspapers, etc.

metropolitan area network (MAN): A type of wide-area network that links together LANS at different sites within a city.

microwave communications: Includes radio signals used by terrestrial microwave systems and by earth stations via satellite although the term is often used to refer only to terrestrial microwave radio systems.

modem (MOdulator-DEModulator): (1) A transducer that transforms digital signals into analog signals at the sending end and sends them in their original form to the receiving end. (2) An electronic device that converts computer or terminal electrical digital signals to analog signals so that data can be transmitted over an analog circuit.

multiplexing: A method of providing a transmission circuit with the capability of handling several separate, individual signals simultaneously. Methods include frequency-division multiplexing, time-division multiplexing, and statistical multiplexing.

multipoint network: A network which consists of two or more terminals sharing the same communications link, which is normally a private or leased line.

multiuser system: A mainframe computer that interfaces with attached dumb terminals, sometimes with intelligent terminals and microcomputers.

network: (1) A system of interconnected elements represented by nodes (switches) and by links that interconnect the nodes. (2) A communications system that allows attached devices, such as computers, to communicate with one another.

node: Equipment, such as a computer or printer, that is attached to a network.

non-blocking PBX: A private branch exchange switch that can handle simultaneously conversations among all users by having enough pathways to carry all the traffic.

number identification: Process which allows the number calling the subscriber's telephone to be displayed on the subscriber's telephone screen to view before answering the telephone.

on-line: The state of operation that exists when a telecommunications device is activated within the system and ready to transmit or receive information.

order entry: Inbound call made by a customer to place an order for a product or service.

outbound call: Call made by a TSR to a prospect or customer, to offer a product or service for sale, arrange an appointment, sell an idea, or perform a business service. Also known as a *proactive call* because the company's representative takes the initiative to make the call.

out-WATS: A service which allows a subscriber to make an unlimited number of calls within a given area from a particular telephone station without registering individual call charges. A single access line permits inward or outward services, but not both. See also *WATS* and *in-WATS*.

patent: A grant made by a government to an inventor that assures the inventor of the sole right to make, use and sell an invention for a certain period of time.

peripheral equipment: Equipment that works in conjunction with a communications system or a computer system but is not part of it.

phone fraud: The illegal use of telephones or telephone lines to avoid charges.

physical topology: A network device which determines the way cables run and the way the nodes are physically connected to each other on a LAN.

piracy: The illegal duplication and distribution of commercially copyrighted software.

port: (1) Point of access into a communications switch, a network, or other electronic device. (2) Physical or electrical interface through which one gains access. (3) Interface between a process and a communications or transmission facility.

private branch exchange (PBX): A telephone communications system serving a specific location such as an office or a building. Includes a switch, a specialized minicomputer performing telephone switching within an organization's private network. Provides for switching calls internally and to and from the Public Switched Telephone Network.

protocol: A set of agreed-on rules and conventions governing the formats and procedures used in communications.

Public Utilities Commission (PUC): An agency charged with regulating communications services and other public utility services within a state.

public utility: A legal monopoly consisting of a privately-owned company that provides an essential public service and is subject to government regulation.

radio paging service: Service that transmits a signal, such as a beep or a continuous tone, via radio from any telephone in the Public Switched Telephone Network to a small, portable radio receiver. Some pagers offer voice messaging or visual displays.

record management system: A computerized or manual way to compile a written record of all calls.

remote vandalism: The use of telecommunications to damage or injure computer information.

ring topology: Network configuration in which each station is connected to two other stations; the process is then repeated until a loop is formed. It is also used to connect the NODES in a continuous loop.

ring topology: Connects all NODES in a closed loop.

satellite: Microwave antenna placed in orbit up to 3,000 miles above the earth.

satellite communications: (1) A type of unguided medium in which microwave signals are transmitted between earth stations via a geosynchronous satellite. (2) The use of orbiting satellites to relay transmissions from one earth station to another or to several other earth stations by means of microwaves.

script: Written record of exactly what to say during a telemarketing call: questions to ask, suggestions to make.

selling: Director efforts to sell specific products or services to a specific prospect. Can include a clerk in a store waiting on a customer, salesperson in a showroom, door-to-door or office-to-office salespeople, and telemarketing calls. Compare *marketing*.

service: Task performed by a company for a customer, either once or on a regular basis. Services are intangible but may involve the use of a *product*.

service and order entry call: Any call a company makes or receives that helps a customer. Specifically, a call to help customers who have made a purchase or who want to make a purchase and have called to place an order, for information, or some other kind of help. Often a follow-up call to one a customer has made. One of the five basic types of telemarketing call. See also *teleservice and teleorder*.

software: Computer programs.

speed calling: Function which allows a user to call frequently called numbers by dialing only one or two digits.

star topology: A network layout in which all stations are wired to a central station (hub) that establishes, maintains, and breaks connections among stations. It is also used to connect all stations to a central NODE, which helps to route data to the appropriate place.

station: Equipment, such as a computer or printer, that is attached to a network.

survey call (*CP*): Call to collect data on which to base marketing strategies or product/service offers.

switchboard: Panel for operating electric circuits.

switching system: An electromechanical or electronic system for connecting lines to lines, lines to trunks, or trunks to trunks.

tap: A legal or illegal connection used for eavesdropping on an existing communications channel.

teleaccount representative: A person who sells to and services a select group of customers. Also known as a *Teleaccount Executive*.

telecollection call (*CP*): Planned reminder call made to keep accounts current. The purpose is to work out a payment arrangement. No selling is done on this call.

telecollector: A person who collects money owed on past due accounts by phone.

telecommunications: (1) The science and technology of communication by electronic transmission of impulses, as by telegraphy, cable, telephony, radio, or television. (2) A message transmitted by telecommunication. (3) Any process that permits the passage of information from a sender to one or more receivers in any usable form (printed copy, fixed or moving pictures, visible or audible signals by means of electromagnetic system—electrical transmission by wire, radio, optical transmission, waveguides, etc.).

telecommunity: The world as a single community brought closer together by telecommunications.

telecommuting: The act of working from home by means of a telecommunications connection with the office.

teleconferencing: The use of a telecommunications system for communicating with two or more groups or three or more individuals who are in separate locations. Communication is via audio, audiographics, video, and/or computer.

telegraph: A communication system that transmits and receives electrical impulses over wire. A telegraph system is one in which the transmission and reception stations are directly connected by wires. An electric needle telegraph was first patented in 1837 by Charles Wheatstone of London. However, the American Samuel F.B. Morse invented the Morse code and telegraph system, which was the main communication system in the world for almost a century. The first successful telegraph message was sent by Morse in May of 1844. The message was "What hath God wrought? To God be the glory; great things He has done!" Of this message, Morse said, "It baptized the American telegraph with the name of its author."

Tele-information service: A service that provides customers with regular updates on new products or services, improvements, changes, sales, special opportunities, and so on.

telemarketing service bureau (TSB): A company created and organized to carry out telemarketing for others, which hires and trains workers to make and/or receive a wide variety of calls for different businesses.

telemetry: The science and technology of automatic measurement and transmission of data by wire, radio, or other means from remote sources, as from space vehicles, to a receiving station for recording and analysis.

telepathy: (1) Transference of thoughts between people by scientifically unknown or inexplicable means. (2) The ability to produce or engage in such communication. Also called "thought transference."

telephone: (1) An instrument that directly modulates carrier waves with voice or other acoustic source signals to be transmitted to distant locations and that directly reconverts received waves into audible signals; especially, such an instrument connected to others by wire. (2) A system of such instruments together with connecting and supporting equipment.

telephone sales representative (TSR): A person who uses the phone to sell a product or service. This includes people who make outbound calls and people who receive inbound sales calls.

telephone service representative (TSR): A person who takes customer service and order entry calls or makes calls that are service-oriented.

telephony: The electrical transmission of sound between distant points, especially by radio or telephone.

telephotography: (1) The process of photographing distant objects with a telephoto lens or telescope on a camera. (2) The technique or process of transmitting charts, pictures, and photographs over a distance.

teleport: A communication distribution center that allows its customers to share access to receiving and transmitting voice, data, and video information via satellite, Fiber-optic cable, and microwaves without directly incurring the large expense of their construction.

teleprinter: An input/output terminal device that utilizes a keyboard. The device produces a paper readout.

TelePrompTer: A trademark for a device used in television to show an actor or speaker an enlarged line-by-line reproduction of a script, unseen by the audience.

teleran: A system used in air traffic control in which the image of a ground-based radar unit is televised to aircraft in the vicinity so that a pilot may see his position in relation to other aircraft.

telesales: Efforts to sell products and services, arrange appointments, and sell ideas. One of the four telemarketing career paths.

telesalesperson: A person who sells products/services by phone.

teleservice and teleorder: Making or receiving *service and order entry* calls for customer service, such as taking orders, providing information, answering questions and giving assistance, handling complaints, and so on. This includes two of the four telemarketing career paths:

> **with no selling:** Making or receiving *only* service calls. Also known as *pure teleservice.*

> **with selling:** Service calls that can be expanded to include sales activity.

telescope: An instrument for collecting and examining electromagnetic radiation that is found in any of the following: (1) An arrangement of lenses or mirrors or both that gathers visible light, permitting direct observation or photographic recording of distant objects; or (2) Any of various devices, such as a radio telescope, used to detect and observe distant objects by their emission, transmission, reflection, or other interaction with invisible radiation.

teletext: A pseudointeractive information retrieval system that uses a one-way television link for information transmission.

traffic: Term which describes the flow of information or messages through a network. This information flow may be generated by telephone conversations or may be the result of providing data, audio, and video services.

transducer: Any device that converts energy from one form to another, such as a codex or a modem.

transmission: The process of sending information in the form of electrical signals over a network or facility from one point to another. It also involves dispatching information from one person, device, or place to another, or may refer to the information itself.

transmitter: The part of a telephone that converts sounds into electrical impulses, which are then sent over telephone lines.

trunk: The transmission circuit or link that carries telephone calls between two switching systems, such as central offices, toll switching systems, private branch exchanges, and key telephone systems.

two-way videoconferencing: Provides two or more sites with interactive, two-way video, audio, and graphics capabilities.

universal product code (UPC): A code consisting of lines (bars) and numbers that can be read by an optical scanner. This code is placed on most retail products.

uplink: The transmission of data from a receiving antenna on earth to a satellite using a separate frequency from that used for the downlink.

uplink/downlink: In satellite communications, separate frequencies used for the two directions of transmission are expressed in frequency pairs, such as 6/4 GHz band pair. The higher figure represents the uplink, while the lower represents the downlink.

upload: To send an entire computer program or document to another computer.

videotext: Interactive electronic services that allow a user to access textual or graphics information and services on a personal or a dedicated videotext terminal.

video display terminal (VDT): A data terminal that receives incoming signals and generates outgoing signals; it consists of a monitor and a keyboard. A smart VDT may be programmed and have a limited primary storage capability.

virus: A hidden, and often destructive, computer program that can infect or spread to other computer systems.

voice mail: This function in a voice processing system provides for "nonsimultaneous" conversations that allow a subscriber to send messages to one or more subscribers or groups of subscribers as well as to reply to these messages. Also called voice store-and-forward or interactive messaging.

voice messaging: In an automated office system, allows a user to retrieve, create, reply to, or forward voice messages by following the display prompts and pressing the appropriate keys on the system. Telephone conversations can also be recorded by using this feature.

voice processing: The umbrella terms for the various voice functions, such as telephone answering, caller routing, interactive messaging, information providing, and transaction processing.

voice recognition: The ability of the computer to transform the wavelengths of the human voice into computer text.

wide-area network (WAN): A network which connects computers that are geographically separated, such as across a city, a country, or countries.

wide-area telephone service (WATS): A service that allows customers to make (out-WATS) or receive (in-WATS) long-distance calls and to have them billed on a bulk basis rather than individually.

Index

Page numbers followed by the letter "i" indicate a photo; "t" indicate a table.

Abstracts, 38
  financial, 38
Accounting, language of business, 184
Act of God, 19
Actualization needs, 100i,102-103,
    117
Administrative files, 303-304
Advertising, 266-269
Advertising Age, 103
AGNET, 33,165
Agriculture, 164-165
Airmail service, 127
Alphanumeric
  filing, 310
  pagers, 296
America Online, 37
Ameritech, 8
Answering machines, 43
  use by business, 183
Answering services, 43-44
  use by business, 183
Art, as form of media, 266-267
AT&T, 7
Audioconferencing, 39
Australia, impact of U.S.
    Telecommunications Act
    of 1996, 11
Automobiles, early development
    of, 59
AVA, 1

Baby Bells, 7
Balloons, 189
Bandwidth, 30-31

Banks
  and other financial institutions,
    record management
    in, 311-312
  and telecommunication, 189
Barron's, 3
Battleships, and telecommunication,
    189
Baud, 31
Beepers, need for, 50
Bell Atlantic Corporation, 7
Ben & Jerry's Ice Cream, 14
Boeing 777, 128
Braille, 93
Break-even-point, 252
Bulletin board networks, 33
Bulletin boards, internal, 317-318
Business and Financial services, SIC
    codes, 175,176
Business education, 1-2
  technological enhancement, 2
  telemarketing, 1
Business goals, 183
Business names, filing of, 305
Business owners, 182-183
Business, risks in going into,
    253-254
Business Week, 3
Buyer beware, 241

C-SPAN, 52
Cable
  deregulation of, 8-9
  entering local telephone market, 9
  high speed data transmission, 9

Cable *(continued)*
  market, promotion
    of competition in, 10-11
  wireless service, 9
Call forwarding, 43
  use by business, 183
Calling list, removal from, 239
Calls, inbound, 225,229,235-237,299
Calls, outbound, 225,229,230-231,299
Canals, 58
Caring, recipe for, 111-112
Cash cow phase, 250-251
Cellular phones, 50
Center for Civic Networking, 313
Center for the Study
    of Commercialism, 237
Central America
  competition in, 5
  manufacturing in, 168
Central Intelligence Agency (CIA),
    and telecommunication,
    189-190
Centrex, 30
Chat line, 33
Chicago's Board of Trade, 260
Christian Value Firm, 238
Closed-circuit TV, 39-40
CNN, 52
Coal mines, 165
Cold customers, 233
Collect calls, 45
Commercial airlines, establishment
    of, 127
Commercial sector, 163
Commercials, 225
Communication
  forms of, 89
  reasons for, 91
Communication services, expansion
    of, 6
Communications
  electronic voice, 96
  SIC codes, 175,176
Communications Act of 1934,
    obscenity, 6

Communicator
  space as a, 105
  time as a, 104-105
Community colleges, 184
Competencies, needed for new
    careers, 322-323
Competition, 120-121,181-182
  external business force, 19-22
  pricing, 247
  risk of, 252
Competition Continuum Diagram,
    The, 20
Competitors, 20
Compressed videoconferencing,
    40-41
CompuServe, 37
Computer(s)
  birth of, *xv*
  business use, *xv*
  invention of Apple, 126-127
Computer crimes, 316-317
Computer disk directories, 258
Computer games, 314
Computer Monthly, 3
Computer networks, 29-31
  business use of, 31
Conference call, 43
Conflict resolution, 119
Construction
  scope of, 169
  SIC codes, 163,169
  startups index, 182
Construction industry, records
    in, 311
Consumer index, 182
Cooperation, in human relations,
    119-120
Corpus callosum, 106
Cox Enterprises, 8
Cross-referencing, 305
Cyber-porn, 14
Cyberpunks, 33,301
Cyberspace, 33,301

Data, business use of, 291
Data searches, 36-38
Data transmission, high speed, 9
Database, retrieval, 297
Databases
    commercial, 36-38
    government, 301-302
    government, privacy, 316
Deceptive advertising, 261
Decline, product life cycle, 20
Declining phase, 251
Delta Pi Epsilon nation research
        society, 1
Demographics, definition of, 249-250
Descriptors, 38
Desktop publishing
    videoconferencing, 41
Devices
    encryption, 316
    support record management
        needs, 313-314
Diamond minds, 165
Dictating equipment, 96
Digital highway, 50
Digital Music Express (DMX), 296
Direct Distance Dialing (DDD), 44
Directories, 258,295
Discretionary products, 116
Dispatchers, 171
Dividends, 183
Dog phase, 251
Drug dealing,
        and telecommunication, 192
Dual-brain theory, 106-109

E-mail, *xiii*, 29
    business uses of, 31
    and networking, 34
EasyLink Services, 30
Economic growth, 16
Economic indicators, 182
Economic motivation, 103-104
800 numbers, 225,227,228,235,
        236,257
    callback scam, 238

888 numbers, 223,227,228,235,
        236,257
Electronic communication, 96
Electronic information age, 12,13
Electronic lounge, 33
Electronic mail. *See* E-mail
Encryption devices, 316
Energy sources, 58
Entertainment, 258
Environment, external business
        force, 19
ERIC (Educational Research
        Information Center), 37
Esteem needs, 100i,102,117
Europe
    competition in, 5
    e-mail and networking, 36
Extraction
    agricultural sector, 164-165
    mining sector, 165-166
    scope of, 164
    SIC codes, 163

F2F, 33
Facsimile. *See* Fax
FAQ, 33
Far East, competition in, 5
Fax
    attendant, 28
    response, 28
Fax machine, 28
    first use of, *xiii*
FBI, Internet use, 300-301
FCC (Federal Communications
        Commission), 5,9,10,238
    deregulation of, 11-12
    regulation of multiservice
        telecommunication, 12
Federal Express, establishment of, 128
Feedback, 47
Fiber optics, *xv*
Files, administrative, 303
Filing, 303
    alphabetic, 303
    alphanumeric, 308

Filing *(continued)*
  business names, 305
  geographic, 306
  hyphenated names, 305
  numeric, 306-307,307-308
  by subject, 305
Financial institutions,
      and telecommunication, 189
First impressions, 95
Five Cs, 46,119
Five Ps, 245
Five senses, 93
Flags, signals by, 57
Flaming a newbie, 33
Forbes, 3
Fortune, 3
Fossil fuels, 58,165
Four little dragons, 168
Free market economy, 16
Fuels, birth of, *xv*

Gender
  and culture, technological impact
      on, 114-115
  differentiation, 113
  roles, changing, 113
Generational differences, 116
Genie, 37
Geographic filing, 306
Germany, united, 15
Global economic village, *xvi*
Global market place, *xvi*
Global Positioning System (GPS),
      294-295
Goods, sale of, 163
Goodwill, 122
Government, Internet use, 300-302
Great Britain, e-mail
      and networking, 36
Gross national product (GNP), 182
Growth phase, 250-251
Growth, product life cycle, 20
GTE, 7

Hackers, and telecommunication,
      193
Harriet Jump Jet,
      and telecommunication, 190
Harvard Business Review, 3
Helicopters, and telecommunication,
      189
Hieroglyphics, 57
Hold, 43
Hong Kong, 15
  manufacturing in, 168
*Hoover's Handbook of American
      Business*, 157
*Hoover's Handbook of World
      Business*, 157
Hospitality services, SIC codes, 175,
      177,179
Hotel industry, record management
      in, 312
Hotel PBX system, 312
Human needs
  actualization, 100i,102-103
  esteem, 100i,102
  hierarchy of, 99,100i,101-103
  physiological, 100i,101
  safety, 100i,101
  social, 100i,101-102
Human relations, scope of, 119-121
Hyphenated names, 304-305

IBM, 167
Inbound call, 225,227,235-237,298
Inbox folder, 29
Infinity Broadcasting Company,
      acquisition of, 9-10
Info-poor, 323
Info-rich, 323
Information Store, 321
Insurance industry, record
      management in, 312
Intel, 167
Intellectual properties, 314-315
Interactive services, types of, 50-51
Interactive television, 38
Internal combustion engine, 59

International business, 3
Internet, *xiii*,34,300-302
   market, promotion of competition
      in, 10
   obscene materials on, 6-7
   services, competition in, 9
   telecommunications law of 1996,
      6
Intimate zone, 105-106
Introduction phase, 250
Introduction, product life cycle, 20
IRS, 185
ISDN (Integrated Services Digital
   Network), 12-13

Japan
   e-mail and networking, 36
   impact of U.S.
      Telecommunications Act
      of 1996, 12
   manufacturing in, 168
Job, entry level, 186
Junk mail, 233

L.A. Screening, 257
Labels, 295
LAN (Local Area Network), 29-30,
   51
Landmarks, 265-266
Language, nonverbal, 93-94
Laser, invention of, 127
Left-brain hemisphere, sequential
   107
Legal issues, record management,
   315
Lexus, 37
Link system, 312
Listening, competency, 47
Logo, 184
Long distance carriers, and
   Telecommunications
   Act of 1996, 8

Mail folder, 29
Mailing lists, 233
   removal from, 236
Manufacturing
   impact of telecommunications,
      169
   scope of, 166
   SIC codes, 163,166-169
Market niche, 251
Market share, 252
Marketing, 225
   campaigns, 234-235
   directed to human needs, 244-245
   human needs, 243
Marketing mix, 245
Marketing reps, 239
Maturity phase, 251
Maturity, product life cycle, 20
MCI, 7
Media, 225
   origin of, 265
Men, marketing to, 249
Mergers, radio stations, 9-10
Mexico, manufacturing in, 168
MFS Communications Company, 8
Microsoft, 167
Monitors, 233,239
Morse code, 93,125
Motivation, 103-104
   economic, 103-104
   sexual, 103
Multimedia, 41

Natural gas industry, record
   management in, 312-313
Natural law, as business regulation,
   15
Natural resources, depletion of, 181
NBEA, 1
Net income, 164
New York Stock Exchange, 260
New Zealand, impact of U.S.
   Telecommunications Act
   of 1996, 11
Nexus, 37

900 numbers, 225,227,229-230,235
NordicTrack, 52
North American Defense (NORAD), 189-190
Numbers, primary, secondary and tertiary, 309
Numeric filing, 306-307
Numeric pagers, 296
Nynex Corporation, 7

Obscene materials, on Internet, 6-7
Odor and taste, 95
Older people, marketing to, 249
On the floor, 232-234
On-Line, 3
OPEC, 166
Operational records, 306
Operator, for telephone, 125
Opportunity cost, 182
Outbound call, 225,227,230-231,297

Pager market, promotion of competition in, 10
Pagers, 296-297
need for, 50
Paralanguage (vocal effect), 93, 95-96
Paramedics, and telecommunication, 189
Passwords, 296
confidentiality, 316
Patent innovations, 16
People, one of Five Ps, 248
Personal Communications Services (PCS), 13
Personal Digital Assistants (PAD), 296,297
Personal networking, 33
Personal services, SIC codes, 174, 179
Personal zone, 106
Personnel managers, 240
Petroleum, 165-166

Pharmaceutical industry, record management in, 313
Phone numbers, retain, 8
Photo machines, 256
Physiological needs, and communication, 100i,101
PIN, 44
PIN number, 256
Place, one of Five Ps, 245
Pony Express, 57
Population explosion, 181
Pornographic materials, on Internet, 6-7
Pornography, and telemarketing, 229-230
Portfolio, 1
Postal telegraph, *xiii*,17
Prestige pricing, 247
Price, one of Five Ps, 245-247
Pricing, 247
Primary numbers, 307
Print directories, 258
Print media, 225
origin of, 268
Privacy, record management and, 315-316
Proactive firm, 21
Problem child phase, 251
Prodigy, 37
Product life cycle, 20,250,250i
Product, one of Five Ps, 245
Production plus pricing, 247
Products, 163
intangible, SIC classifications of, 174
tangible, SIC classifications of, 163
Professional services, SIC codes, 174,176
Profit, 164,183
Profit motive, *xv*,89
Promotion, one of Five Ps, 247-248
Protocol, 31
Public relations, 89
scope of, 121-122

Public sector, 163
Public services, SIC codes, 174, 179-180
Public zone, 106

Radar, invention of, 127
Radio, regulation of, 5
Radio stations
  impact of deregulation, 10
  limitations on ownership, 10
  ownership of, 8,9-10
Railroads, 58-59
Raw products, 165
Reactive firm, 21
Record keeping rules, 303
Record(s) management
  banks and other financial
    institutions, 311-312
  business use of, 291
  construction industry, 311
  hotel industry, 312
  insurance industry, 312
  legal issues, 315
  natural gas industry, 312-313
  pharmaceutical industry, 313
  privacy, 315-316
  research firms, 311
  scope of, 295
  systems, 3
Records
  business use of, 291
  confidentiality of, 316-317
  support of organizational needs,
    311-313
Recreation and tourism, SIC codes,
    174,178-179
Regional Bell operation companies
    (RBOCs), 7
Regulation
  business force, 14-16
  business view of external, 14
  by government, 13-14
  natural law, 15
  self-imposed, 14

Remembering, recipe for, 110-111
Research firms, record management
    in, 311
Research, scope of, 295
Resources, unlimited, 181
Retail sales index, 182
Retailers
  SIC codes, 163,171-173
  types of, 171
Right-brain hemisphere, 107-108
RTC model, 19-20

Safety needs, 100i,101
Sails, 58
Satellite television technology, 9
Satellites
  spy, and telecommunication, 191
  transmission via, *xv*
  weather, and telecommunication,
    189
Scarcity, 121
  economic concept, 181
Schedule C, 183
Secondary numbers, 307
Service operator, 236
Services, 174
  sales of, 174
Sexual motivation, 103
Shanghai Securities Exchange,
    The, 260-261
SIC codes
  business use of, 183
  IRS use of, 183
Signaling glass, 57
Singapore, manufacturing in, 168
Sitel, 230, 231
  General Motors campaign, 235
Smart machines, 49
Smoke signals, 57
Social needs, 100i,101-102
Social zone, 106
Software programs, 313
South America
  competition in, 5
  manufacturing in, 168

South Korea, manufacturing
   in, 168
Space, economic resource, 181
Space zones, 105-106
Sprint, 7
Standard Industrial Classifications
   (SIC), scope of, 157,
   162-163
Star phase, 250
STAR TV, 259
Stock Markets, 260
Stockholders, 183
Stocks, 183
Store mix, the, 248-249
Strategic Air Command (SAC),
   and telecommunication, 189
Subject filing, 305
Submarine, and telecommunication,
   189
Super Overworld, 191,192
Super Underworld, 191,192
Supply and demand, 181
Swedish Trade Council, 259-260
Symbol shorthand systems, 93
Synergy, 17

Taiwan, impact of U.S.
   Telecommunications Act
   of 1996, 11
Tallies, 57
Team leader, 232,239
Team quota, 231
Techno-nerds, 33,300
Technological change, 257,261-262
Technology
   accelerating pace, 3
   changing size, 49-50
   as external business force, 16-19
   history of, *xv*
   impact on telecommunication, 17
   overview of, 3
   recent telecommunication
      innovations, 17
   scope of, 16-17

Teenagers, marketing to, 249
Telecommunication(s), *xv*,3
   accelerating pace, 3
   devices, 296-297
   field of, *xiii*
   impact of technology, 17
   market, competition in, 10-11
   multiservice, 12
   recent innovations in, 17
   and records, 295-297
   the RTC model of, 19-20
   scope of, 296
   wheel of, 17-18,18i,19
Telecommunications Act of 1996,
   5-13,50
   anticipated impact of, 13-14
   deregulation impact on, 11-12
   impact on Australia, 11
   impact on Japan, 12
   impact on New Zealand, 11
   impact on Taiwan, 11
   obscenity, 6-7
   and technological innovation, 12
Telecommuting, 50-51
   self-employed, 51-52
Teleconferencing, 39
   scope of, 38
Telecopier, 30
Telegraphy, invention
   of, 125-126
Telemarketing, *xv*,3,227
   in business education, 1
   competencies, 240-241
   evaluators, 234
   extrovert, 239
   fraud in, 237
   introvert, 239
   legal issues, 236-239
   occupations, 239-240
   personnel, 227,298
   record keeping, 297,299
   trainers, 239
   training for, 230,240
   turnover, 234
Tele-nuisance list, 237

Telephone
  business use, *xv*
  competition, 7-8,9
  functions of, 43-44
  invention of, 125
  manners, 46
  market, promotion of competition
    in, 10-11
  multiuse, 255
  single number, 50
Telephone calls, keeping records,
  45-46
Telephone companies
  enter cable market, 9
  and Telecommunications Act
    of 1996, 7
Telephone Service Representatives
  (TSRs), 230-231,232,233,
  234,235,297
  entry level, 239
Television, 258
  business use, *xv*
  high resolution, 12
  invention of, 128-129
Television stations, 8,9-10
Telex, 29,30
Telstar, 129
Tertiary numbers, 307
Thailand, manufacturing
  in, 168
Timed out, 33
Times Mirror cable company, 8
Title V, 6
Toll-free calls, 44-45
Tone, 93
Touch, 93-94
Tourism packages, 260
Trade schools, 184
Trainers, 239
Transportation
  birth of, *xv*
  scope of, 170
  SIC codes, 163,170-171
Travel agencies,
  and telecommunication, 189

Trends, 322
TV channel directories, 258
TWX, 29,30
Typewriter, invention of, 126

U.S. Customs, records of, 317
Unemployment index, 182
Unions, development of, 167
Unit, administrative, 304
Upper class, marketing to the, 249
USA Today, 3,53
Utilities
  necessary for telecommunications,
    173
  scope of, 173
  SIC codes, 163,173-174

V-Chip, authorization of, 6
VCR, 41,257
Video capabilities, *xv*
Videoconferencing
  compressed, 40-41
  desktop publishing, 41
Virtual reality, 318-319
  careers in, 319-320
Vocal effects, 93
Voice mail, 45
  automated, 44
  use by business, 183
Voice mailbox, 28

Wall Street Journal, The, 3,53
WAN (Wide Area Network), 30-31,51
Warm customers, 232,236-237
WASPS (Women Air Service Pilots),
  127
Waterwheel, 58
Western Union, *xiii*,17
Westinghouse Electric, acquisitions,
  9-10
Whistling, second language, 57
Whole brain thinking, 108,109-110

Wholesalers, SIC codes, 163,171
Wireless communication, 298t
Wireless phones, 50
Women, marketing to, 249
Work ethic, 230
World Research Foundation
    of Sherman Oaks, The, 313

XPRESS, 34

Yankelovich Partners, 52
Yel-Low Talk, 229

Order Your Own Copy of
This Important Book for Your Personal Library!

APPLYING TELECOMMUNICATIONS AND TECHNOLOGY FROM A GLOBAL BUSINESS PERSPECTIVE

_____ in hardbound at $49.95 (ISBN: 0-7890-0115-2)

_____ in softbound at $29.95 (ISBN: 0-7890-0199-3)

COST OF BOOKS_____

OUTSIDE USA/CANADA/
MEXICO: ADD 20%_____

POSTAGE & HANDLING_____
(US: $3.00 for first book & $1.25
for each additional book)
Outside US: $4.75 for first book
& $1.75 for each additional book)

SUBTOTAL_____

IN CANADA: ADD 7% GST_____

STATE TAX_____
(NY, OH & MN residents, please
add appropriate local sales tax)

FINAL TOTAL_____
(If paying in Canadian funds,
convert using the current
exchange rate. UNESCO
coupons welcome.)

☐ **BILL ME LATER:** ($5 service charge will be added)
(Bill-me option is good on US/Canada/Mexico orders only;
not good to jobbers, wholesalers, or subscription agencies.)

☐ Check here if billing address is different from
shipping address and attach purchase order and
billing address information.

Signature_____

☐ **PAYMENT ENCLOSED: $**_____

☐ **PLEASE CHARGE TO MY CREDIT CARD.**

☐ Visa   ☐ MasterCard   ☐ AmEx   ☐ Discover
☐ Diner's Club
Account #_____

Exp. Date_____

Signature_____

Prices in US dollars and subject to change without notice.

NAME _____

INSTITUTION _____

ADDRESS _____

CITY _____

STATE/ZIP _____

COUNTRY _____ COUNTY (NY residents only) _____

TEL _____ FAX _____

E-MAIL_____
May we use your e-mail address for confirmations and other types of information? ☐ Yes   ☐ No

Order From Your Local Bookstore or Directly From
The Haworth Press, Inc.
10 Alice Street, Binghamton, New York 13904-1580 • USA
TELEPHONE: 1-800-HAWORTH (1-800-429-6784) / Outside US/Canada: (607) 722-5857
FAX: 1-800-895-0582 / Outside US/Canada: (607) 772-6362
E-mail: getinfo@haworth.com
PLEASE PHOTOCOPY THIS FORM FOR YOUR PERSONAL USE.

BOF96